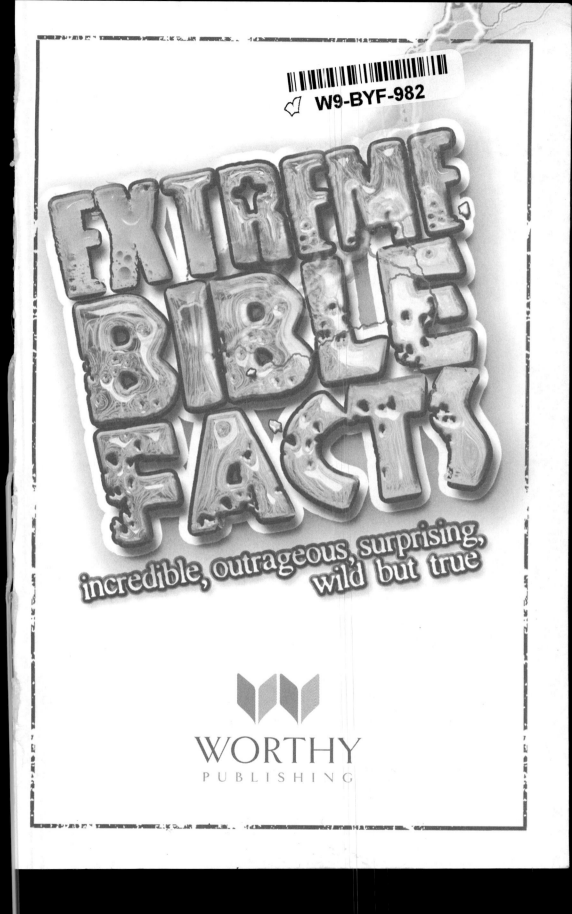

W9-BYF-982

EXTREME BIBLE FACTS

incredible, outrageous, surprising, wild but true

WORTHY
PUBLISHING

CONTENTS

Welcome iv

Contributors v

Miscellaneous Munchies 1

Ballistic Battles 11

What a Way to Go 21

Puzzles and Riddles 33

Fortune-telling and Magic 43

Visions and Dreams 51

From Zero to Hero 63

Dastardly Villains 75

Name That Tune 85

Gross and Gory 97

Unnatural Nature 109

Great Escapes 119

Creepy Places 131

Back to Life 143

Touched by an Angel 153

Hooray for Healing 163

Special Effects 173

Bible Beasts 189

Kooky Kings 205

When Good Guys Go Bad 218

Index to Bible Topics 229

GO to the EXTREME!

What do you think of when you think of *extreme*? Bungee jumping off the Grand Canyon? (Watch out for that wall!) Skateboarding off the rails of a 200-step staircase? Opening your gym locker after a week and a half of grueling gym classes and taking a whiff? A punishment that involves no TV or video games for a whole month? Eating a whole slice of your great-aunt's prize-winning fruitcake? Guess what? We think of those too. We also think of people like Samson, David, Deborah, Hannah, Joshua, and Herod. You won't find their profiles on the latest social network. Instead, you can read their stories within the pages of this book.

Besides being a book of God's awesome promises, the Bible has some amazing stories. Just because we like you, we've captured 200 of the most extreme stories in the Bible and corralled them in this book: stories of evil kings, gruesome deaths, weird storms, angry animals, bad hairstyles, horrible food (and you thought your school cafeteria was bad), music you can tap your feet to, battles that would make even *Braveheart* look like a Sunday school picnic, and special effects better than anything you'll see at the movies. Behind everything is the all-powerful God for whom nothing is impossible.

Each of the stories has a section called *Go to the Extreme*—trivia facts based on the stories and also from our world today. Many of the stories also have a *Joke Alert*. Read those if you dare! But we're pretty sure you'll dare, especially since you have this book in your hands!

Get ready for the wildest, most *extreme* reading ride your eyes and mind will take this year!

—The Editors

Contributors

Katie Arnold

Jeanette Dall

Carol Chaffee Fielding

Mark Jackson

Dave Jorgensen

Afton Rorvik

Tyler Shockey

Linda Taylor

Dave Veerman

Tom Vick

Linda Washington

Joel Worden

MISCELLANEOUS Munchies

Are you the kind of person who likes to eat unusual things? Maybe you like to mix your spaghetti with mashed potatoes. (Yum?) Or, perhaps you like three different types of juice mixed together before you find it drinkable. What is the weirdest thing you've ever eaten? Hold that thought and think about this: What's weird to you might not be weird to someone else, and vice versa. Many individuals in the Bible have eaten some unusual things by anyone's standards. But there were some specific purposes for these items. Many times, people ate—or did without—to honor God. These "miscellaneous munchies" showed their trust in God.

So, grab your favorite munchies and savor the flavor of these stories—stories of God's amazing provision in the lives of his people.

Don't Rise to the Occasion

For seven days the bread you eat must be made without yeast.
Exodus 12:15 (NLT)

Good bread is soft. Light. Tasty. A PBJ sandwich or a fluffernutter tastes best on fresh bread. The bread that comes from those plastic bags at the grocery store—and maybe even from your oven—is made with yeast, which fluffs up the loaf as it sits in a warm place to rise and puffs it up again as it bakes.

Bread that is purposely flat, thick, heavy. Does that sound appetizing? This is the bread the Israelites were told to eat during Passover. Why would God instruct his people to eat something so. . .yucky? Well, back in Bible times there was no such thing as "quick bread." The only way to have fresh bread was to grind the wheat into flour, hand mix it with yeast, oil, and eggs, wait for it to rise, punch it down, wait for it to rise again, then bake it. . . do you get the drift? Making good bread in ancient days took a lot of time.

During the first Passover, the Israelites had to be ready to move at a moment's notice. No time to wait for the bread to rise! By not adding the yeast, they could cut a few hours off the bread-making process. God knew they needed the energy provided by bread, but he also knew they wouldn't have the time to make it in the traditional way, so he instructed them to leave out the yeast.

When Pharaoh told them to leave, they were in a hurry to get out of Egypt—better to leave with flat bread than no bread at all!

GO TO THE EXTREME

• **The** oldest baker's oven in the world was known in Babylon in 4000 BC Bread was baked in hot ashes or on heated stone slabs in Egypt as long ago as 2500 BC Egyptian bakers (c. 2500 BC) discovered that kneading the dough with their feet instead of their hands made the dough rise instead of staying flat and hard, because of the natural yeasts between their toes.

• **Bread** is mentioned about 250 times in the Bible. In the Gospel of John, Jesus calls himself "the bread of life."

• **Bethlehem,** or Beith-lehem, where Jesus was born, means "House of Bread."

2

Cloudy, with a Chance of Manna

That evening quail came and covered the camp, and in the morning there was a layer of dew around the camp. When the dew was gone, thin flakes like frost on the ground appeared on the desert floor. . . . The people of Israel called the bread manna.
Exodus 16:13–14, 31 (NIV)

You might have seen a movie in which burgers, spaghetti, and ice cream fall from the sky. While this was the result of a human invention, the food that fed the Israelites for forty years in the wilderness was God's creation!

Imagine waking up every morning to see a blanket of Frosted Flakes® or Frosted Mini-Wheats® covering your backyard. Time to grab a bowl, a spoon, and some milk, right? And whatever you don't finish just melts away.

God didn't want his people to starve to death in the desert, so he provided them with nourishment, and it even satisfied their sweet tooth in the process. He also provided quail so the people would have meat and eggs. Every morning, for six days in a row, week after week, year after year, God sprinkled the desert with the sweet treat. On day six, the people gathered twice as much so they'd have food on the seventh day—the Sabbath—a day of rest.

By the end of the first year, you can imagine the people trading recipes for Boiled Manna Mush, Manna Muffins, Manna-Stuffed Quail, Manna & Eggs, Manna Surprise. If it happened today, some enterprising cook would write the books, "101 Ways to Cook Manna" or "Manna for Dummies."

So the next time you see frost on the ground, think about how God provided manna for his people. Then thank God for the food he provides for you.

Go to the Extreme

- **Post Toasties**® was the Post® version of corn flakes, popularized by Kellogg's®, and was originally called "Elijah's Manna," but the government wouldn't allow C.W. Post to trademark the biblical name. The cereal was temporarily discontinued in April 2006 but was reintroduced in early 2010.

- **On** March 13, 1977, hundreds of hazelnuts rained down on a parking lot in the city of Bristol, England. Hazelnuts were out of season at that time of year, but the falling nuts were perfectly fresh! To this day no one knows where the hazelnuts came from.

- **The** name *manna* is connected with the exclamation "Man hu," which the Israelites most likely uttered on first seeing the stuff on the ground. This expression is translated, "What is this?"

Joke Alert!

Here's a verse for vegetarians:
"I will never eat meat again as long as I live" (1 Corinthians 8:13, NLT).

Read the story in Exodus 16.

Make Mine a Cricket, Well Done!

You may eat any animal with divided hooves and that chews the cud. . . . You may eat everything in the water that has fins and scales, whether in the seas or streams. . . . You may eat these kinds of all the winged insects that walk on all fours.
Leviticus 11:3, 9, 21 (HCSB)

Have you ever watched one of those TV shows that showcases foods from other cultures? When the people sat munching on large bugs were you grossed out? Maybe you wondered what a praying mantis or chocolate covered ants really taste like.

Or maybe not.

But, did you ever wonder why it's okay to eat some animals and not okay to eat others?

God was very patient with the Israelites, and he took the time to tell them what was okay (clean) to eat and what wasn't okay (unclean). After all, he did create our bodies, so he knows what is best to keep them running smoothly! By providing an extensive list, God ensured that his people would have the best chances of staying healthy.

The list of clean and unclean animals in Leviticus 11 is a long one! You might be glad to know that God says it's not okay to eat things like camels, rats, vultures, owls, termites, or anything with paws (cats and dogs). But God does say it's okay to eat things like locusts, crickets, and grasshoppers! If you've ever swallowed a bug by mistake, the thought of eating a grasshopper on purpose might make you cringe.

But think about this: some of the food we take for granted today would have made the Israelites cringe. Can you picture Moses eating Spaghettios® or Sour Patch® candy?

GO TO THE EXTREME

- **The** cicada is often considered a pest, especially to farmers. Its large, meaty body and pleasant flavor (if skillfully cooked) make it one of the world's favorite edible insects.

- **God's** Word says it's okay for us to eat cows. But if you're eating out in India, don't expect to have a burger or a steak. Cows are considered sacred and they freely roam the streets, parks, and even the beaches . . . holy cow!

- **Grasshoppers** are rich in protein (62.2 percent) which is why the people of Indonesia "hop to it" when the dinner bell rings.

JOKE ALERT!

Here's a warning if you know a not-so-good cook:

"'Man of God, there is death in the pot!' And they could not eat it"
(2 Kings 4:40, NIV).

Read the story in Leviticus 11 and Acts 10.

When's Break-fast?

And there by the Ahava Canal, I gave orders for all of us to fast and humble ourselves before our God. We prayed that he would give us a safe journey and protect us, our children, and our goods as we traveled.

Ezra 8:21 (NLT)

Have you ever hit the snooze button so many times that, when you finally woke up, you had barely enough time to dress and dash out the door? No time for breakfast? Funny how your stomach began to get growly waaaaaay before lunchtime.

Now, if you think missing a meal is rough, think about going without an entire day of meals, and no snacks either! This act of willingly going without food is called fasting. Lots of people in the Bible fasted—from Moses to Ezra to Esther to the prophets to Jesus and his disciples—and people even do it today. In the Bible, three people fasted for forty days: Moses, Elijah, and Jesus. You can read about why they fasted in Exodus 34:28–29, 1 Kings 19:7–9, and Matthew 4:1–11.

You're wondering why someone would choose to go hungry, aren't you? Well, for Christians, fasting is always accompanied by prayer. When there is a big issue that Christians want God to pay special attention to, they fast and pray. It's difficult to do, but it teaches self-control and helps us to appreciate God's gifts—such as burgers, french fries, ice cream, and apple pie—a lot more.

GO TO THE EXTREME

• **The** longest official (certified world record) fast was set in 2003 by a fifty-year-old Chinese doctor named Chen Jianmin. For forty-nine days he drank only water and ate no food.

• **Fasting** can involve more than just food. During the season of Lent (forty days preceding Easter), many people choose to give up something in order to improve self-discipline. People fast from everything from chocolate to television!

• **The** word "breakfast" actually means "breaking of the night's fast." By the time you've finished dinner until the time you wake up in the morning, you probably haven't eaten for eight to ten hours. So unless you can eat in your sleep, you break your overnight fast at breakfast.

JOKE ALERT!

What excuse did Adam give his children for why they no longer lived in Eden?

Answer: *"Your mother ate us out of house and home."*

5

Read about some people who fasted in Ezra 8; Esther 4; Luke 4:1-13.

Flour Power

The flour jar did not become empty, and the oil jug did not run dry, according to the word of the LORD He had spoken through Elijah.
1 Kings 17:16 (HCSB)

If you had been going hungry for a while and were suddenly given an endless supply of your favorite food, what would you do? Would you invite your friends for dinner? Have a party to celebrate? Take a truckload of extras to a local shelter?

The widow from the village of Zarephath knew what it felt like to be hungry. What's worse is that she wasn't the only one starving—her son was also suffering from the effects of a nationwide famine (a severe shortage of food). As she was planning their last meal, Elijah—a prophet—showed up at her door asking for bread and water.

You're thinking if he was a prophet, he should have known she had no food to spare! Why would he ask her to give up her last meal? Because God wanted to bless her and show her that he could meet all of her needs.

She could have told Elijah, "No way! You're nuts! We have no food to give." But instead, she fed Elijah. Because of her kindness, God multiplied the flour and oil in her house. Every time she took some out, God replaced it. She kept making food for herself, her son, and Elijah for many days, and never had to go buy more!

The widow had some serious flour power— her act of kindness produced a miracle.

GO TO THE EXTREME

• **During** the twentieth century, an estimated 70 million people died from famines around the world.

• **No** stranger to hunger, Elijah was one of three people in the Bible who once fasted for forty days (1 Kings 19:7-9).

• **Flatbread** is a simple bread made with flour, water, a little olive oil, and salt and then thoroughly rolled into flattened dough. Find a recipe and have an adult help you make the same kind of bread the widow made for Elijah!

JOKE ALERT!

What you don't want to hear after dinner:
"You will vomit up the morsels that you have eaten" (Proverbs 23:8, ESV).

6

Read the story in 1 Kings 17:8–16.

Savoring a Scroll Sandwich

I opened my mouth, and he fed me the scroll. "Fill your stomach with this," he said. And when I ate it, it tasted as sweet as honey in my mouth.

Ezekiel 3:2–3 (NLT)

Wait ... what?

You read it right. Ezekiel ate a scroll. Not just any scroll, either. This scroll was covered on both sides with funeral songs and words of gloom and doom. The scroll was a list of the sins of the people of Israel and their punishment. You'd think that something so bad would taste bitter, but when Ezekiel ate it, he said it tasted sweet like honey!

It's probably not a good idea to write down everything you've done wrong and make a meal of it. If you did that, you'd have too much fiber in your diet. (Get it? Fiber? From wood pulp which makes paper? Anyway ....)

You don't need to tear pages out of your Bible to make "Scripture Sandwiches" to get the sweet taste of God's message to you. The scroll that Ezekiel ate wasn't an actual piece of paper—it was a vision given to him by God. God used the image of a sweet-tasting scroll to remind him, and us, that when we give up the bad things in our lives to him, our lives will become sweeter. "Chewing on" and "digesting" God's Word strengthens and nourishes your spirit, just like a sandwich and milk strengthens and nourishes your body.

So take a taste of God's Word by reading a little bit from it today.

Sweet!

GO TO THE EXTREME

• **Another** man in the Bible, John the apostle, had a vision and ate a scroll. His tasted sweet too, but unlike Ezekiel's scroll, John's scroll made him sick (Revelation 10:10).

• **Edible** rice paper made from a flour ground from rice kernels and mixed with tapioca powder is a product made in Southeast Asia. It is used to roll vegetables into spring rolls and other dishes.

• **Xylophagia** is the name for a medical disorder in which people eat paper, pencils, tree bark, and other wood-related items.

JOKE ALERT!

Good news for dieters:
"All fat belongs to the LORD"
(Leviticus 3:16, HCSB).

7

Read the story in Ezekiel 2:3—3:3.

Communion Celebration

Jesus took some bread and blessed it. Then he broke it in pieces and gave it to the disciples, saying, "Take it, for this is my body." And he took a cup of wine and . . . said to them, "This is my blood, which confirms the covenant between God and his people. It is poured out as a sacrifice for many."

Mark 14:22–24 (NLT)

This story in the Bible tells of a special meal Jesus had with his disciples—the last one before he died on the cross. That's why it's called the Last Supper. This became the pattern for what your church does now, called Communion or Eucharist.

So what's the story behind Communion? On the night Jesus was betrayed by Judas, he and his disciples were celebrating Passover (a special Jewish holiday celebrating the time when the Israelites were freed from slavery in Egypt—that story is in the book of Exodus). Jesus knew he was heading for death on the cross (after all, that's the whole reason why he came!) and he wanted to give his disciples, and us, a way of remembering his sacrifice.

Jesus took the bread and broke it (so it was probably the hard, crisp flatbread we read about before). The broken bread reminds us that his body was broken on the cross. Jesus passed around a cup of wine—a bitter taste with a deep red color, reminding us of the bloody crucifixion sacrifice for our sins. Bread and wine were traditional parts of the Passover meal, which is still celebrated by Jews today. In that meal they remember their deliverance from slavery in Egypt. In the Communion meal, we remember our deliverance from sin.

The next time you receive communion, remember what it represents, and celebrate what it means for you.

GO TO THE EXTREME

• **In** Leonardo DaVinci's famous painting, "The Last Supper," Judas is the only disciple shown who has his elbows on the table. DaVinci must have figured since Judas was a traitor, bad table manners must have been one of his many shortcomings.

• **Q:** Can you name the two Christian denominations that don't practice communion?

• **A:** Quakers (Society of Friends) and the Salvation Army.

• **Catholic** schools used to teach their First Communion classes (second grade) using NECCO® Wafers candies in place of the bread.

JOKE ALERT!

A verse for your waiter when he asks how you want your steak cooked:

"Well done, good and faithful servant" (Matthew 25:21, ESV).

8

Locust Salad with Wild Honey Dressing

John's clothes were made of camel's hair, and he had a leather belt around his waist. His food was locusts and wild honey.
        Matthew 3:4 (NIV)

We're back to the bugs again. And, yes, locusts are on the list of "bugs-that-are-okay-to-eat" because they are winged insects that have jointed legs, etc. (see "Make Mine a Cricket, Well Done"). But now we're talking about a guy who lives in the desert, wears strange clothing, and has a really weird diet!

If you had lived during the time John the Baptist was preaching, what do you think your reaction would have been when you saw him coming? Imagine sitting on the edge of an oasis, building sandcastles, and this prophet of God comes walking across the dunes. He was definitely a survivalist kind of guy. He wore camel-hair clothes held up by a leather belt, and may have had plenty of bee stings from going after the sweet, energy-rich honey. And in the desert, the best source of protein was during locust season. Maybe when he smiled he had bits of bug between his teeth!

Because John was the first real prophet to show up in Israel in over four hundred years and because he dressed in strange clothes and ate honey and locusts, people were drawn to him out of curiosity. He lived differently from the religious leaders of the day, and his message was unlike any preached by the Pharisees. Those who went to see him usually ended up hearing his message and repenting of their sins!

Luckily, you don't have to eat bugs to get people to be curious about your faith. Just be sure to be ready to answer when someone does ask. And leave the camel-hair coat at home.

GO TO THE EXTREME

- **Of** all the animals on the planet, 80 percent of them walk on six legs (which means they're bugs). More than a thousand species of insects are eaten by 80 percent of the world's population every day.

- **BugOut** NYC is a fast-food takeout restaurant in New York City that opened in April 2011. Every item on its menu includes edible bugs.

- **The** locust is sometimes referred to as "the shrimp of the land," as it is very closely related to the bottom-dwelling sea creature that most people enjoy with cocktail sauce.

JOKE ALERT!

Vanity license plate for John the Baptist: 4 RUN R

9

Read the story in Matthew 3.

The Miracle of the Multiplying Munchies

Jesus took the five loaves and two fish, looked up toward heaven, and blessed them. Then, breaking the loaves into pieces, he kept giving the bread to the disciples so they could distribute it to the people. He also divided the fish for everyone to share.
Mark 6:41 (NLT)

GO TO THE EXTREME

- **The** miracle of feeding five thousand men and their families is the only miracle (prior to the resurrection) that is mentioned in all four Gospels—Matthew, Mark, Luke, and John.

- **The** amount of fish and bread consumed by all those people would equal approximately 12,000 pounds of food. If each of the disciples served sixty people per minute, they could serve 3,600 people per hour, taking a little more than four hours to serve everyone.

- **Twelve** thousand pounds of food could feed a family of four for four months, an elephant for a month and a half, and a blue whale for one day.

Think about this: you ask your mom if you can go hear Jesus preach in the wilderness. She packs you a nice picnic basket full of bread and fish, and just as your stomach starts to growl, someone asks you to share. With everyone. All five thousand men and their families.

Jesus is surrounded by people who have followed him to hear him speak. He's had a long day. He's tired and probably hungry himself. But even under these circumstances, Jesus had compassion (a feeling of deep sympathy) for everyone. It's late in the day and he understands that everyone needs dinner. He doesn't just want to send everyone home, but how do you feed so many people in the middle of nowhere?

Run to the local market? Nope, that's nine miles away in the nearest town (and the only way to get there was on foot). Call for a pizza delivery? Uh, wrong century. Send someone to buy bread? Again, it's too far away and, as one disciple pointed out, they'd have to work for months to pay for that much bread!

Have a little boy share his lunch with everyone? Yeah! Wait . . . what? You're joking, right?

Jesus had already fed the people's hearts and minds through his teaching. Now he has an opportunity to miraculously feed over five thousand people. Jesus blesses the food and, suddenly, there's enough food to feed everyone!

And there are *twelve* baskets of leftovers! Now that's a miracle of multiplying munchies!

JOKE ALERT!

Laconic Limerick:
There once was a boy with a lunch
who thought to himself, "I've a hunch,"
if I give to this Man,
all that I can
with my little, he'll make a bunch!

Read the story in Matthew 14:13-21; Mark 6:30-44; Luke 9:10-17; John 6:1-14.

BALLISTIC Battles

Throughout human history, wars have been fought and casualties suffered. If you've ever played a videogame or watched a movie about war, you've seen some of the strategies involved in maneuvering soldiers and using weapons at the right time.

Fighting in a real battle was never easy. There were many, many battles in the Bible. Some were fought by the people of Israel as they conquered Canaan, others by individuals. In a battle there is usually a winner and a loser. Anyone who fought on the side against God was always the loser. Sometimes the loser was God's own rebellious people.

An Uncle to the Rescue

When Abram heard that his relative had been taken captive, he called out the 318 trained men born in his household and went in pursuit as far as Dan.
Genesis 14:14 (NIV)

In a battle of four kings (the armies of Shinar, Ellasar, Elam, Goiim) against five (Sodom, Gomorrah, Admah, Zeboiim, Bela [Zoar]), the four kings were on the winning side. The main king was Kedolaomer, a king who had cruelly ruled over the five kings for twelve years. The winners took everything from the kings of Sodom and Gomorrah—their food, their clothes, and a man named Lot. *One of these things is not like the other*, you might be thinking. But Lot is the whole point of the story, because of his uncle: Abram.

GO TO THE EXTREME

- **The** Battle of Stalingrad during World War II is considered one of the biggest battles ever fought. It took place from August 1942 to February 1943. Almost two million people died during the battle.

- **A** tar pit, also known as an asphalt lake, is an area where a sticky black underground liquid leaks to the surface. Animals can get stuck in these, which makes them great places to excavate the bones of prehistoric animals.

- **Abram** refused to accept any gifts from the king of Sodom— he even promised God that he wouldn't take anything from them. Could you promise God that you wouldn't receive a present from someone else?

When Abram, who would later be known as Abraham, was told of the battle, he didn't waste any time. Instead, he took the men named in the verse above and went to rescue his nephew and the people taken away by the kings. Keep in mind that Abram was well over 75 years old! Also, they fought in a land with tar pits. Anyone could get stuck in them. In a battle that took place at night, Abram the general led his men to victory.

Abram gave a tenth of the spoils to a priest-king named Melchizedek who spoke a blessing to Abram. This was a reminder that God was the real general who won the battle for Abram.

JOKE ALERT!

Why did Abram chase after the kings?
Answer:
Because they had taken a "Lot."

❶❷

Read the story in Genesis 14.

The Fall of a Wall

After the seventh time, the priests blew the trumpets, and Joshua said to the people, "Shout! For the LORD has given you the city."

Joshua 6:16 (HCSB)

How's this for a battle strategy: For six days, march around a city once a day, not making a sound. On the seventh day, march around the city seven times, then shout. Sound like a winner? Most people would say no way. But this was the strategy that won the battle of Jericho.

Jericho was a walled city that looked invincible. When Joshua sent two spies to look over the land, they discovered a city with thick, double walls. Houses were built into the walls—that's just how thick the inner wall was. Conquering this city would take a miracle, especially with the strategy above. But that was just what God had in mind when he came up with that strategy.

This battle was not just a battle over a Canaanite city. It was a test for God's people. The people of Israel passed the test when they followed God's instructions. The priests carried the ark, as the fighting men marched around the city once a day. But on the seventh day, Joshua gave the command above. RUMBLE! BOOM! CRASH! The walls fell down.

Israel had won the battle without having to fight at all.

GO TO THE EXTREME

- **The** city wall of Jericho had an average height of about 13 feet in some sections.

- **The** Berlin Wall, built in 1961, separated East from West Germany. When Germany decided to unify in 1989, the wall was knocked down over the next two years.

- **The** Great Wall of China is 5,500.3 miles long. Although the wall began in the fifth century BC, much of the wall seen today was built during the Ming dynasty, starting in the fourteenth century.

JOKE ALERT!

Famous last words of the people of Jericho before the walls came tumblin' down: "My mother plays better trumpet than that!"

1 3

Read the story in Joshua 6.

Ai Anguish

> Then the LORD said to Joshua, "Stretch out the javelin that is in your hand toward Ai, for I will give it into your hand." And Joshua stretched out the javelin that was in his hand toward the city.
>
> Joshua 8:18 (ESV)

In order to understand the victory at the city of Ai, you have to know why Joshua and his army were defeated at first. When the city of Jericho was destroyed, God told Joshua that no one was to take anything from the city to keep for himself. Gold and silver were to be given to God for the tabernacle. But little did anyone know, someone from Israel took something from Jericho and kept it for himself. Joshua and his army found this out the hard way when they went into battle against the men of Ai. Thinking they could easily win this battle with God on their side, Joshua sent only about 3,000 men.

They lost. Badly.

So when Joshua and the other leaders sought the Lord, God explained that someone had stolen something from Jericho. After the people were presented to Joshua based on their tribes and families, God revealed the thief: Achan. Achan couldn't resist taking a robe, some silver, and a gold bar. After the loot was discovered, Achan and his family were stoned to death.

Then the battle of Ai could take place once more. Joshua sent 30,000 men to hide behind the city. But later, he took a decoy group of 5,000 men to Ai and pretended to retreat before them. The men of Ai chased Joshua and the 5,000 men. But when Joshua held up his javelin, the 30,000 men ran to the city and burned it to the ground.

The fact that they won proved that God was with them once again.

GO TO THE EXTREME

- **This** shows that God has excellent military strategy. In this case, it looks like the Israelites used a deceptive flank maneuver. This means they would send in a decoy, but have many more troops to attack all of the "weak parts" of the opposing army.

- *Blitzkrieg* is a German word that means "lightning war." This is a method in which an army overwhelms another through the use of tanks, aircraft, infantry, and artillery. In World War II, the German invasion of Poland in 1939 was described as a blitzkrieg.

- **In** the Battle of Thermopylae in 480 BC, King Leonidas led 300 Spartans, 700 Thespians, and 400 Thebans to guard a narrow pass against an invading army of Persians that vastly outnumbered them.

JOKE ALERT!

Laconic Limerick:
Ai was theirs for the takin',
but the army of God had forsaken.
So though favored, they lost
and counted the cost.
The cause of it all—he was Achan.

Read the story in Joshua 7—8.

Cut Down to Size

David replied to the Philistine, "You come to me with sword, spear, and javelin, but I come to you in the name of the LORD of Heaven's Armies—the God of the armies of Israel, whom you have defied. Today the LORD will conquer you."

1 Samuel 17:45–46 (NLT)

If you've ever faced a problem you consider gigantic, consider David's story. David actually faced a giant problem: a man named Goliath who was a giant headache for the army of Israel.

In the time of David, two armies sometimes each sent out a champion to fight each other. In that way, they determined the winning army. Goliath was the champion of the Philistines—the enemies of Israel. The men of Israel were terrified of him. Check out his stats: over 9 feet tall, with armor weighing 125 pounds, and a spear with an iron head weighing 15 pounds. No one thought he could defeat Goliath.

Every day Goliath would shout insults against the army of Israel and against God. One day David came to visit his brothers who were in the army. When he heard the insults shouted against God, he decided to fight Goliath. Check out David's stats: a much shorter, young shepherd with no armor and no weapons other than a slingshot. With stats like this anyone would assume that David would die that day. Goliath certainly did. But David had a secret weapon: God. Taking only five smooth stones, David ran toward Goliath and took aim. The only one who died that day was Goliath.

JOKE ALERT!

Why was Goliath so surprised when David hurled the small, smooth stone at him?

Answer: *Because such a thing had never entered his head before.*

GO TO THE EXTREME

- **Back** in ancient Israel times, it was said that the people who used projective weapons such as the sling were more accurate than the people who used a bow and arrow!

- **Some** theories say that Goliath was so sure that he would win that he took off his helmet because it would "get in his way." This cocky decision cost him his life.

- **The** tallest living man is Sultan Kösen, who lives in Ankara, Turkey. He is 8 feet 3 inches tall.

1 5

Read the story in 1 Samuel 17.

Sharing the Spoils

David said, "My brothers, you must not do this with what the LORD has given us. He protected us and handed over to us the raiders who came against us. Who can agree to your proposal? The share of the one who goes into battle is to be the same as the share of the one who remains with the supplies. They will share equally."

1 Samuel 30:23–24 (HCSB)

For many years David, the anointed king of Israel, ran from Saul, the reigning king of Israel. So David was forced to hide in the territory of the Philistines—the enemies of Israel. But David proved that he was not a traitor to Israel, even as he sometimes helped the Philistines in small battles against other nations.

David, his family, and his 600 men and their families lived in a city called Ziklag. Achish, the king of Gath, a city of the Philistines, had given Ziklag to David and his men.

GO TO THE EXTREME

• **The** spoils of war from many battles in the last 300 years have centered around art: paintings and statues. For example, Napoleon took four bronze horses from St Mark's Basilica in Venice.

• **The** Koh-i-Noor diamond, once the world's largest diamond, has been a spoil of war at many points in history.

• **Would** you have shared something you earned to people you think didn't earn it at all?

While David and his men were away, the Amalekites, another group of enemies, attacked the city of Ziklag and took away all of the women, children, and possessions. They then burned the city.

Imagine returning home to find your city burned. David's men blamed David for the tragedy. But David prayed and asked God for advice. God assured David that this was a battle he would win. David and his men, as tired as they were, went after the Amalekites. Before they could get far, however, 200 exhausted men decided to stay behind.

Along the way, they found the Egyptian slave of one of the Amalekites. When David gave him food, the Egyptian slave led them to the camp of the Amalekites. David and his men then fought and defeated the Amalekites. But when it came time to divide the spoils—the money and possessions of the losing army—400 of David's men refused to share with the other 200 men. But David refused to listen to them. Everyone was given an equal share.

JOKE ALERT!

Top enemies of Israel not mentioned in Scripture:

Moabetterites   *Cellulites*

Startafites   *Fraidahites*

What-a-bites   *Menintites*

Parasites

Read the story in 1 Samuel 30.

An Army of One

> *That night the angel of the LORD went out and struck down 185,000 in the camp of the Assyrians. And when people arose early in the morning, behold, these were all dead bodies.*
> 2 Kings 19:35 (ESV)

Bullies come in all shapes and sizes. The bully of Isaiah's day was a king named Sennacherib. Around the time of King Hezekiah of Judah, Sennacherib was the king of Assyria. The powerful Assyrians were known for their cruelty and the fact that they were undefeated. Sennacherib's army conquered many of the cities of Judah and seemed unstoppable. To make things worse, Sennacherib sent his officers to threaten the people of Judah and demand that they surrender.

If that wasn't bad enough, Sennacherib sent a letter to Hezekiah, reminding Hezekiah that Assyria had conquered other nations. He also insulted the God of Israel.

What's a godly king to do?

Pray.

That's what Hezekiah did. He went straight to the temple to talk to God. The prophet Isaiah had a word from God. God himself would fight against the Assyrian army. All he needed was an army of one: an angel. Take a look at the Scripture verse above. Sennacherib was the one who ran the next day. God had defeated the biggest bully around. When Sennacherib returned home, he was killed by his own sons.

JOKE ALERT!

Here's something you *won't* find in the Bible:

After this terrible defeat, Sennacherib became the butt of many jokes. People would often say, "Are you Sennacheribbing me?" or "You can't be Assyrious!"

GO TO THE EXTREME

- **China** has the largest army in the world—over two million people.

- **Alexander** the Great was the well-known conqueror of his day. He was never defeated in battle. He died in 323 BC.

- **Julius** Caesar was another well-known leader who was killed by someone close to him (Brutus and others). Brutus was a dear friend, but he betrayed Caesar thinking it was for the best for the people.

17

Read the story in 2 Kings 18—19.

The Fall of Jerusalem

So in the ninth year of Zedekiah's reign, on the tenth day of the tenth month, Nebuchadnezzar king of Babylon marched against Jerusalem with his whole army. He encamped outside the city and built siege works all around it.
2 Kings 25:1 (NIV)

The destruction of a city is always a terrible thing. In our day, we've seen cities badly damaged or completely destroyed by hurricanes and earthquakes. In the prophet Jeremiah's day, many cities were destroyed by conquering nations. The conquerors of the time were Babylonians led by King Nebuchadnezzar.

Picture it: a vast army surrounding the city of Jerusalem. No one can get in or out. A siege was a common tactic of enemies in ancient times who set out to conquer a walled city. All they had to do was wait until the people in the city grew hungry enough to surrender. And that's what happened in Jerusalem. They ran out of food. Worse still, the Babylonian army finally broke through the city wall.

You may be wondering how God could allow something this awful to happen to the city where the great temple of Solomon stood. But God had a plan. In fact, God allowed these enemies to conquer the people of Judah, because of their sin.

While Jeremiah wept, the beautiful temple was destroyed and the city set on fire. The king, Zedekiah, was blinded by the enemy army and led away in chains along with many of the people of Judah.

GO TO THE EXTREME

• **Another** famous siege was at the Battle of the Alamo in Texas, in 1836. About 1,500 Mexican soldiers advanced on the Alamo, where around 250 American soldiers were garrisoned. The siege lasted for 13 days before the Mexican army attacked and defeated the Alamo.

• **The** siege of Harlech Castle during the War of the Roses (fifteenth century) lasted seven years.

• **The** very first recorded siege was the Battle of Megiddo. It was actually a battle between the Canaanites and the Egyptians, dating back as far as 1482 BC.

JOKE ALERT!

A verse NOT to use as a church motto:

"Listen, you foolish and senseless people, with eyes that do not see and ears that do not hear"
(Jeremiah 5:21, NLT).

1 8

Read the story in 2 Kings 25.

The Last Battle

Then I saw the beast and the kings of the world and their armies gathered together to fight against the one sitting on the horse and his army.
Revelation 19:19 (NLT)

Many books and movies have battles that can be described as the ultimate battle between good and evil. Some of those battles were inspired by the events in the book of Revelation. There really will be a final battle that will take place at some future time—the last days—between the forces of good and the forces of evil.

The apostle John had a vision of heaven and of a time in the future when Jesus will return to earth. At that time, Jesus returns to lead the army of heaven against the forces of evil led by Satan, the antichrist, and the fallen angels. This is known as the battle of Armageddon (Revelation 16:16).

Jesus is described as a rider on a white horse, whose name is Faithful and True. With Jesus as the general leading the army, the battle was already won before it began. The enemies of heaven were thrown into the lake of fire. Jesus' thousand year reign would now begin.

GO TO THE EXTREME

• **C.** S. Lewis wrote a book called *The Last Battle*, the final book in the Narnia series. It is based on the battle of Armageddon.

• **Other** imagery of Jesus in this passage states that out of his mouth will come a sharp sword to strike down the nations. It's not a real sword, but it really shows that Jesus is here to win!

• **In** 1998, a disaster movie called *Armageddon* was a huge hit.

19

Read the story in Revelation 19.

WHAT A WAY to Go!

There's an old saying, "Truth is stranger than fiction." That means sometimes real life is way more weird than anything you might read in a book. Within the pages of the Bible are stories that fit this old saying. In this section, you'll read about the weird ways people have died. In every case, the death was a result of disobedience to one of God's commands. All of these stories were reminders to the people of Israel and to us that you can't try to pull one over on God. He always sees and hears everything. Also, he's always fair in his judgment.

So pull up a chair and get comfortable, because you'll be squirming in your seat very soon.

An Awful A-Salt

But Lot's wife looked back as she was following behind him, and she turned into a pillar of salt.
Genesis 19:26 (NLT)

Do you like salt? Salt wakes up the flavor of just about anything you eat—french fries, burgers, you name it. Now imagine *turning into* salt. Hard to believe? It happened to the wife of a man named Lot. Lot was the nephew of Abraham—one of the great patriarchs (founding fathers) of Israel.

Because the people of Sodom and Gomorrah kept doing wrong things, God decided to send two angels to destroy both cities. Lot lived in Sodom. But Abraham prayed for Lot and his family. In answer to Abraham's prayer, God sent the angels to warn Lot and his family to get out of town. When Lot, his wife, and their daughters hesitated, the angels grabbed their hands and dragged them out of the city! But Lot still wanted to bargain. Instead of heading for the hills as the angels told them, he begged to flee to the nearest town. The angels allowed them to go there, but warned them not to look back at Sodom.

Lot and his family ran for their lives. But at the last minute, Lot's wife couldn't resist one final look back. Instantly, she became a pillar of salt. Poof. What a way to go! It just goes to show that when an angel tells you not to look back, *don't*.

GO TO THE EXTREME

- **The** average adult's body contains enough salt for three salt shakers.

- **The** phrase "head for the hills" might have come from this story. Lot and his family were told to run for the hills to escape the destruction of Sodom. To "head for the hills" means to run from danger.

- **A** 20-meter (65-foot) high salt pillar was found in a cave in Mount Sedom, near the Dead Sea.

JOKE ALERT!

Laconic Limerick:
Lot's wife had one tiny fault,
though God had told her to halt,
despite what he said,
she still turned her head,
and instantly turned to salt.

Read the story in Genesis 19.

Strange Fire

Aaron's sons Nadab and Abihu each took his own firepan, put fire in it, placed incense on it, and presented unauthorized fire before the LORD, which He had not commanded them [to do].
Leviticus 10:1 (HCSB)

You've probably read about unexpected fires that destroyed homes or cars. But you've probably never read about a fire that suddenly destroyed two people without damaging anything else. Keep reading....

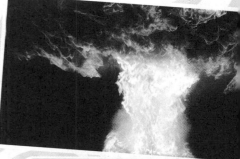

Nadab and Abihu were the sons of Aaron, the high priest. As priests Nadab and Abihu had the job of offering sacrifices on the tabernacle altar to the Lord. Fire to burn the sacrifices came from God (Leviticus 9:24). Rules for sacrifices and using incense were written in the Law of Moses (Leviticus 16:12-13.) These rules showed the people of Israel that God is holy. Priests had to be very careful to obey the commands of God. If they disobeyed even one, they could die. Nadab and Abihu disobeyed a rule. As soon as they came to the altar, fire from God suddenly consumed them. While the Bible doesn't say exactly what Nadab and Abihu had done to offer "unauthorized fire," there is a possibility that they might have been drunk when they stood before the altar.

Because Aaron and his other sons still served in the tabernacle, they were not allowed to join the rest of his family to mourn the loss of Nadab and Abihu. Moses also reminded them that God was not wrong to put Nadab and Abihu to death. A holy God had to be obeyed.

GO TO THE EXTREME

- **Centralia,** Pennsylvania is practically a ghost town, because of a mine fire that has been burning underneath the town since 1962.

- **The** incense the priests used was made from frankincense and other spices. It was only to be used by the priests for worshiping God. Anyone else who used it was banished or executed. (See Exodus 30:34-38.)

- **The** tabernacle was a special tent where God was worshiped before the first temple was built.

JOKE ALERT!

Speaking of "unauthorized fire," where is smoking mentioned in the Bible?

Answer: *"Rebekah lifted up her eyes, and when she saw Isaac, she lighted off the camel"* (Genesis 24:64. KJV).

Read the story in Leviticus 10:1-8.

A Hole in One

But when Sisera fell asleep from exhaustion, Jael quietly crept up to him with a hammer and tent peg in her hand.
Judges 4:21 (NLT)

If **you've ever had** a splinter in your finger, you know how much that stings. Now imagine if that splinter were a nail . . . Ewww. Are you squirming yet? When a nail met the head of a general named Sisera, bad things happened.

A long time before Israel had kings, they had judges—leaders to help them conquer the enemies that mistreated them for twenty years. At the time of this story, Deborah was a judge. The Canaanites made trouble for the people of Israel. The commander of the army of the Canaanites was the extremely powerful Sisera. His army had 900 iron chariots, which probably had the Israelites shaking in their sandals. But they had two secret weapons: God and a woman named Jael.

GO TO THE EXTREME

• **In** Bible times, tents were put up and taken down by the women of a family.

• **Death** by impaling—piercing the body with a stake—was a form of execution many countries used in the past.

• **The** tent peg Jael used was probably made of wood.

While God helped Barak's army to defeat Sisera's army, Sisera escaped and made his way to the tent of the wife of a man named Heber. Heber had been an ally of the king of Canaan. Heber's wife, Jael, pretended to be friendly to Sisera, even giving him milk to drink. Just when Sisera fell asleep, Jael grabbed a tent peg and a hammer. And that was the end of Sisera.

JOKE ALERT!

Soon after this event, the rumor spread that Sisera was hammered in his tent, and Jael became known as "Peg."

2 4

Read the story in Judges 4.

A Promise of Punishment

When he mentioned the ark of God, Eli fell backward off his chair by the side of the gate. His neck was broken and he died, for he was an old man, and he was heavy. He had led Israel forty years.
1 Samuel 4:18 (NIV)

Ever had to tell someone bad news? The prophet Samuel was just a kid when he was told by God to deliver bad news to Eli, the high priest. He had to tell Eli that God planned to punish Eli's family. Why were they to be punished? Hophni and Phinehas, Eli's sons, were priests, but also crooks. They disobeyed God by taking a portion of the meat sacrificed on the altar *before* God's portion was offered. Even though Eli knew about their behavior, he did nothing to stop them. So God said that he would punish Eli and his sons.

The Ark of the Covenant, a special chest kept in the tabernacle, was captured by the Philistines—the enemies of Israel. When it was taken, Eli's sons were put to death. Eli was standing on a chair at the city gate when he heard the news. When Eli heard about the ark being taken, he fell over backward, broke his neck, and died. The promise of punishment had been fulfilled.

GO TO THE EXTREME

- **A** broken neck is called a *cervical fracture*. Many people have suffered a broken neck, but have not died.

- **The** Ark of the Covenant was a huge part of the story of the 1981 film, *Raiders of the Lost Ark*.

JOKE ALERT!

These names could have been in the Old Testament:

Abel Bodied

Noah More

Esau You

Jethro Theball

Achan Back

Jezebel Ringer

2 5

Read the story in 1 Samuel 2:22–36; 3:13–18; 4:11–18.

The Touch of Death

The anger of the LORD was kindled against Uzzah, and God struck him down there because of his error, and he died there beside the ark of God.
2 Samuel 6:7 (ESV)

Some fighters claim to have a touch of death—one touch that can kill a person. For an Israelite named Uzzah, one touch for him meant death. Here's how . . .

Whenever the army of Israel went into battle, the priests went before them carrying the Ark of the Covenant. This wooden chest was so special it had to be carried on poles. Only the priests could touch it and the other items used in the tabernacle (Numbers 4:5–6, 15). Anyone else who touched the ark would die.

The Philistines stole the ark, but tried to return it to Israel after God sent a plague that killed many Philistines or made them very sick. But the ark made it only as far as the threshing floor of an Israelite man. When 70 men were killed for looking into the ark, the ark was moved to the home of a man named Abinadab, where it remained for over sixty years.

When David became king and defeated the Philistines, David wanted the ark returned to Jerusalem. David traveled with over thirty thousand men to bring back the ark. As the ark traveled on the cart, one of the oxen pulling the cart slipped. Thinking that the ark would fall off the cart, a helpful man named Uzzah reached out to grab the ark. For touching the ark, he died on the spot.

David was upset with the Lord for Uzzah's death, and decided to leave the ark at the home of Obed-Edom for three months. But once more God showed that his commandments were to be obeyed.

GO TO THE EXTREME

• **Some** animals have a no-touch rule. The poison arrow frog has enough poison in its skin to kill the person or animal that touches it.

• **Lots** of plants are poisonous to the touch as well—like poison ivy, poison oak, poison sumac, and poison hemlock (the word "poison" in the name is sort of a clue!). Touch these and you'll probably get a very itchy rash—or worse reaction. And it goes without saying not to *eat* them!

• **The** Ark of the Covenant was quite beautiful and probably *did* look something like what you may have seen in some movies. But did you know that the cover was made of pure gold?

2 6

Read the story in 2 Samuel 6:1–11.

JOKE ALERT!

Those who look for Noah's ark and the Ark of the Covenant are engaged in **"ark-eology."**

Hair Today, Gone Tomorrow

Now Absalom happened to meet David's men. He was riding his mule, and as the mule went under the thick branches of a large oak, Absalom's hair got caught in the tree. He was left hanging in midair, while the mule he was riding kept on going.
2 Samuel 18:9 (NIV)

Perhaps like many people, you have good hair days and bad hair days. But did you ever think that hair could lead to someone's doom? For David's son, Absalom, long hair led to more than just a bad hair day. It led to his death.

When David sinned with Bathsheba (see 2 Samuel 11), God promised David that trouble would never leave his family. That promise came true, especially with David's son Absalom. David disapproved when Absalom killed his half brother Amnon for assaulting their sister. When Absalom ran away, David didn't see him for three years. Sounds like the subject of a bad talk show.

One day Absalom schemed to take over David's throne, forcing David to flee the city. David's army later went into battle against Absalom's men and defeated them. But when Absalom tried to escape on a mule, his long hair was caught in the branches of an oak tree. The mule kept on going, leaving Absalom dangling from the tree. The armor-bearers of Joab, David's Army General, ran up and killed the helpless Absalom.

Go to the Extreme

- **Xie** Qiuping of China holds the record for the longest hair. As of 2004, her tresses measured 18 feet 5.54 inches. She has an assistant who carries her hair whenever she wants to go anywhere!

- **How** long is your hair? Did you know that there are over 100,000 strands on the average person's head?

- **Afraid** your hair isn't long or thick enough? Don't be nervous. You would have to lose about 50 percent of your hair before it would be noticeable to others.

27

Read the story in 2 Samuel 18.

You're Fired!

Elijah responded to the captain of the 50, "If I am a man of God, may fire come down from heaven and consume you and your 50 [men]." Then fire came down from heaven and consumed him and his 50 [men].

2 Kings 1:10 (HCSB)

Prophets in the Bible were God's spokespeople. When the prophet said something would happen, it usually came true if that prophet spoke for God. Now that's power. Elijah was one of the most well-known Old Testament prophets. One time when he spoke, many people died on the spot. Wondering how? Listen . . .

When King Ahaziah, the son of Ahab, suffered an injury, he decided to seek help from an idol. God sent an angel to Elijah with a message Elijah was to deliver to Ahaziah: Ahaziah would die. Not liking that answer, Ahaziah sent a captain and fifty men after Elijah. Bad decision. Take a look at the verse above. Boom. Fire came down from heaven and killed the captain and his men. Well, that didn't stop the king from sending more men. Same words from Elijah; same result. But Ahaziah was slow to learn. He sent more men. But this time, the captain of the guards begged for his life. (Wouldn't you?) God had mercy on that captain and his men. But guess what? What God said came to pass. Ahaziah died.

GO TO THE EXTREME

- **While** fire doesn't flash down from heaven these days, there is such a thing as a flash fire. According to Wikipedia, a flash fire has "a rapidly moving flame front" and is caused by "ignition of a mixture of air and a dispersed flammable substance."

- **Back** in the early nineteenth century, people believed that falling meteorites (chondrites) were a sign of God's wrath, like fire from heaven.

- **Combustion** needs three elements: oxygen, fuel, and heat. This is what scientists call the fire triangle.

JOKE ALERT!

Where is tennis mentioned in the Bible?

Answer: *"Before Isaiah had gone out of the middle court . . ."* (2 Kings 20:4, ESV).

Read the story in 2 Kings 1.

Get the Point?

*Then Jehu drew his bow and shot Joram between the shoulders.
The arrow pierced his heart and he slumped down in his chariot.*
2 Kings 9:24 (NIV)

Ever shoot an arrow? It's not easy to hit the target. A good archer can hit a target at great distances. It takes special skill, however, to hit a *moving* target. Just ask Jehu.

Being a king in the divided kingdom of Israel was a dangerous job, especially if you were a bad king. Because of the evil things that King Ahab of Israel had done, the prophet Elijah had predicted that all of Ahab's male descendants would die. Ahab himself was killed in battle. His son Joram later was wounded in a battle and trying to recover in the city of Jezreel. Meanwhile Jehu was anointed king of Israel by the prophet Elisha. Jehu decided to go to war against Joram.

After learning that Jehu and his army were on the way, Joram tried to escape in his chariot. But Jehu grabbed a bow and shot Joram with an arrow. One arrow was all it took to kill Joram.

Go to the Extreme

- **The** most well-known archers in folktales are Robin Hood and William Tell.

- **An** arrow can fly 300 fps (feet per second).

- **The** first bows and arrows were found in parts of Africa, dating as far back as 50,000 BC.

2 9

Read the story in 2 Kings 9.

A Queen's Downfall

And as Jehu entered the gate, [Jezebel] said, "Is it peace, you Zimri, murderer of your master?". . . He said, "Throw her down." So they threw her down.

2 Kings 9:31–33 (ESV)

The fairy tale, "Snow White and the Seven Dwarfs," is known for its evil queen. Perhaps that queen and others like her were patterned after Jezebel. Jezebel, the wife of King Ahab, is considered the wickedest queen who ever lived. Because she schemed to have a man killed just to take his vineyard, the prophet Elijah predicted that Jezebel would die horribly. Wild dogs would eat her remains at the city gate (see 1 Kings 21:20–24).

The prophecy came true many years later. Jehu, who had been anointed king of Israel, vowed to get rid of Ahab's son and his wife Jezebel. Jezebel had just given herself a makeover (hair, makeup, etc.) when Jehu arrived in Jezreel. Just as Jezebel began to heckle him, Jehu ordered those standing near Jezebel to throw her out of the window! And they did! As Elijah predicted so many years earlier, Jezebel died horribly.

GO TO THE EXTREME

- **Even** wild dogs can reform. The breed of dogs known as Canaan dogs came from wild dogs in Israel. They're used to herd sheep.

- **As** this story shows, makeup is not a modern invention. Women have used beauty products for thousands of years.

- **Jezebel** wasn't the only person to be thrown out of the window. In Prague in the year 1618, three men were thrown out of a building and fell about 70 feet. However, they survived by landing in a large pile of manure!

JOKE ALERT!

Laconic Limerick:
Jezebel the queen was a hog,
she lived in a morality fog.
But when stripped of her power
and thrown from the tower,
she made a nice meal for a dog.

Read the story in 2 Kings 9.

Lying like a Rug

> Peter said, "How could the two of you even think of conspiring to test the Spirit of the Lord like this? The young men who buried your husband are just outside the door, and they will carry you out, too."
>
> Acts 5:9 (NLT)

Has a lie ever gotten you into trouble? There was a time in the first century when a lie caused two people to lose their lives. After the Holy Spirit came at Pentecost, many Christians generously shared their possessions with each other. Ananias and Sapphira sold a field, kept part of the money, and gave the rest to the apostles—the closest disciples of Jesus. Was that wrong? No. But it was wrong when Ananias lied about the amount of money he gave to the apostles. He said he gave *all* of the money from the sale. This was the lie that ended his life. When Peter declared that Ananias lied to the Holy Spirit, Ananias died on the spot.

Sapphira had the chance to make things right. But when asked about the money, she chose to lie instead, just as her husband did. Once more, Peter declared that a lie had been told to God. He also said that the same people who carried out her husband would soon carry her out. Sapphira died that minute. Everyone who heard the story was terrified! (Wouldn't you be?)

Go to the Extreme

• **One** time in the Bible a lie actually saved lives. Wondering how? Read Exodus 1:15–20.

• **If** you were to sell something, how much of the money would you donate to God? Why?

• **The** most expensive home in the world (as of 2010) is a house in Mumbai, India that costs about $1 billion. It is 570 feet tall and belongs to Mukesh Ambani.

JOKE ALERT!

Laconic Limerick:

On that strange and eventful day
Ananias and wife came to say,
*   "Lord, we are giving it all!"*
Then down dead they did fall
*   What a terrible lie-price to pay!*

Read the story in Acts 5:1-11.

Three Strikes and He's Out

At once an angel of the Lord struck him because he did not give the glory to God, and he became infected with worms and died.
Acts 12:23 (HCSB)

Herod Agrippa, the ruler of Judea, had a number of strikes against him in God's book. Strike 1: He persecuted many Christians. Strike 2: He had James the apostle and brother of John killed. Strike 3: He had Peter thrown into prison in order to await trial. You know what happens when you get three strikes. You're out.

Having already angered God, Herod didn't seem to know when to quit. One day, when he was at a feast, he decided to make a speech. When the people called him a god, Herod accepted the praise that only the one true God deserved. God, the ultimate umpire, called Herod out of the game. His death was like a horror movie—gross and memorable. But it proved one thing: you can't stop God.

GO TO THE EXTREME

• **Thankfully,** it's rare for people to get infected with worms. If there is a case, there are many different medicines and procedures to safely get rid of them. Phew!

• **The** tapeworm, a large intestinal parasite, can reach up to 30-foot lengths in humans and over 120-foot lengths in whales.

• **Other** parasites (things that live off of other living things) include lice, ticks, leeches, fleas, and hookworms. All of them are pretty gross.

JOKE ALERT!

Overheard outside the palace:
"Hey Herod—what's eating you anyway?"

3 2

Read the story in Acts 12:19–23.

PUZZLEs & Riddles

When you hear the words, "Have you heard the one about . . .?" or "Why did the chicken cross the road?" you know that a riddle is coming. Puzzles and riddles are fun to solve. Believe it or not the Bible has plenty of puzzles and riddles. Throughout the Old Testament, many prophets solved puzzles or spoke in riddles. Many times, Jesus hid the truth about God's kingdom in a riddle he asked.

God used riddles to encourage his people to seek him for more information. Solving a riddle is a great way to use the brain God gave each of us. So put on that thinking cap and see if you can solve these puzzles and riddles.

A Honey of a Riddle

"All right," they agreed, "let's hear your riddle." So he said: "Out of the one who eats came something to eat; out of the strong came something sweet."
Judges 14:13–14 (NLT)

Before reading further, see if you can solve the riddle in the Bible passage above. (We'll wait.) Got your answer? Keep reading. . . .

Samson was the real-life Hercules of the Bible. He had super strength, which he proved by breaking the jaws of a lion with just his hands. (Don't try that at home.) But what amazed him was the fact that later he saw that some industrious bees had made honey in the carcass of the lion.

At his wedding feast, Samson decided to ask a riddle about the lion. In those days, asking riddles were a popular pastime at weddings and other feasts. If the thirty guests couldn't answer the riddle by the end of the seven-day feast, they had to give Samson "thirty fine linen robes and thirty sets of festive clothing" (Judges 14:12, NLT). If they guessed correctly, Samson had to give them the same amount of clothing.

Well, the guests cheated by forcing Samson's bride to demand the answer. Samson was so angry, he killed thirty men, took their clothes, and gave them to the wedding feast guests. It just goes to show you: we should never cheat the strongest man in the world.

Go to the Extreme

- **Lions** have a bite pressure of 600 pounds. Imagine how much more strength Samson would have needed to break the lion's jaw!

- **Love** riddles? Then try reading *The Exeter Book.* Compiled between the years 960–990, this old book is filled with over ninety riddles written in Old English. Many of these riddles are still unsolved today.

- **Probably** the most famous riddle in the world is in the story of the Sphinx who guarded the entrance to Thebes. To get in, you had to answer the riddle or be killed. The riddle was: "Which creature in the morning goes on four legs, at midday on two, and in the evening on three; and the more legs it has, the weaker it is?" What do you think is the answer?*

 JOKE ALERT!

Here's something you *won't* find in the Bible:

The descendants of Samson became expert luggage makers and were known as the Samsonites.

3 4

Read the story in Judges 14.

*Answer: Man

The King Is Coming

For a child will be born for us, a son will be given to us, and the government will be on His shoulders. He will be named Wonderful Counselor, Mighty God, Eternal Father, Prince of Peace.

Isaiah 9:6 (HCSB)

Take a look at the verse above. Recognize the words? If you've ever sung in a "Do-It-Yourself Messiah," you've sung these words from Isaiah. Old Testament prophets like Isaiah, Micah, Zechariah, and others wrote prophecies—true predictions from God—about the coming Messiah. He would be born in Bethlehem (Micah 5:2) and come riding into Jerusalem on a donkey like a triumphant king (Zechariah 9:9). While this prophecy in Isaiah and others like it might not sound much like a riddle, many people of Israel puzzled over them for centuries. God gave these hints about the coming Savior so that his people could watch for him. They would know the Messiah when all of the statements made about him came true.

Every prophecy came true through Jesus' coming, many centuries after Isaiah proclaimed the words above. The child "born for us" was man and God, the promised Savior who would bring peace. This "Wonderful Counselor"—another way of saying "king"—would someday rule over all.

Go to the Extreme

- **Jesus** fulfilled as many as 365 prophecies in his lifetime that were written hundreds of years before he was born. It's more than just a simple coincidence!

- **George** Frideric Handel wrote his oratorio, *Messiah*, in 1741. He used Isaiah 9:6 in the libretto (the text of the musical).

- **Professor** Peter W. Stoner has made the statement that the chances of just eight of these prophecies coming true by sheer chance is 1 in 10^{17} (100,000,000,000,000,000). That would be the equivalent to covering the whole state of Texas with silver dollars two feet deep, and then asking a blind man to walk across the state and find a specific coin.

Read the story in Isaiah 9:6.

A Puzzling Dream

These are the visions I saw while lying in bed: . . . before me stood a tree in the middle of the land. Its height was enormous. The tree grew large and strong and its top touched the sky; it was visible to the ends of the earth.
Daniel 4:10–11 (NIV)

In Bible times, kings had advisors to help them rule over their people. These advisors also helped the kings understand the things that puzzled them. During a time when the people of Israel were exiled in Babylon, Daniel was one of the advisors to Nebuchadnezzar, the king of the Babylonians. Since Daniel correctly interpreted one of the king's dreams before, Nebuchadnezzar knew that Daniel could figure out the riddle of his latest dream. But Daniel had skills because of God.

GO TO THE EXTREME

• **Nebuchadnezzar** was known for commissioning the building of the Hanging Gardens of Babylon—one of the seven wonders of the ancient world.

• **Studies** show that the more deep sleep you get (called REM sleep) the better it is for your brain to remember and process the things you learned during that day.

• **From** representing the passage of time to revealing how stable your personality is, trees can mean many different things if seen in a dream.

Nebuchadnezzar was a powerful king—one of the most powerful in the world. Because his army had conquered other nations, including Israel, he became proud and refused to offer God praise. Daniel had bad news for Nebuchadnezzar: God planned to humble the proud king. The tree that was cut down in Nebuchadnezzar's dream represented Nebuchadnezzar.

Imagine having to tell a king that he was about to be totally humiliated in front of everyone. Some people were put to death for giving a king bad news. But Daniel told the truth to King Nebuchadnezzar. And God made the dream come true. Once the proud king was humbled, he finally praised God.

(Read the rest of the story in "Were You Born in a Barn?" in Kooky Kings, page 214.)

Read the story in Daniel 4:4–27.

The Handwriting on the Wall

Immediately the fingers of a human hand appeared and wrote on the plaster of the wall of the king's palace, opposite the lampstand. And the king saw the hand as it wrote.
Daniel 5:5 (ESV)

The popular phrase *the handwriting on the wall* actually comes from this story. Imagine sitting at dinner one night and suddenly seeing a hand appear (no arms, head, body, or legs—just a hand) and begin writing on your wall. What would you do (besides scream or run to find the nearest digital camera or cell phone)?

After the time of Nebuchadnezzar, Belshazzar became king of Babylon. Belshazzar invited a thousand people to a huge feast. During the feast, he decided to bring out the sacred items stolen from the temple in Jerusalem and use them in the feast. That was bad enough. Even worse—Belshazzar praised the false gods he believed in, rather than Israel's true God.

God decided to get his attention in an unusual way. A hand suddenly appeared and its fingers began writing a puzzling message on the wall. The message read: *MENE, MENE, TEKEL, PARSIN.* These words are Aramaic words for weights and measures. But Daniel had an interpretation: *"Mene:* God has numbered the days of your reign and brought it to an end. *Tekel:* You have been weighed on the scales and found wanting. *Peres:* Your kingdom is divided and given to the Medes and Persians" (Daniel 5:26–28, NIV).

Too bad for Belshazzar.

He lost his kingdom and his life that night.

GO TO THE EXTREME

- **Jesus** spoke in Aramaic.

- **The** most famous sign made of letters is the Hollywood sign of Hollywood Hills, California, in the Santa Monica Mountains. These letters are 45 feet tall and 350 feet long. This sign was built in 1923.

JOKE ALERT!

Here's something you *won't* find in the Bible:

Just before the writing appeared on the wall, the emcee introduced the king and said, "Let's give him a hand!"

Read the story in Daniel 5:13–31.

Child's Play

To what can I compare this generation? It is like children playing a game in the public square. They complain to their friends, "We played wedding songs, and you didn't dance, so we played funeral songs, and you didn't mourn."
Matthew 11:16–17 (NLT)

Did you ever tell a joke that someone didn't understand (like some of the JOKE ALERTS in this book)? Perhaps he or she gave you a puzzled look or simply said, "I don't get it." Jesus probably received hundreds of puzzled looks from listeners who had a hard time understanding his messages. Many times, he used a riddle to compare one thing to another.

In the Scripture passage above, Jesus compared the people of Israel to kids playing a game or singing a song used during a game. He did that because of the way they criticized John the Baptist. Some complained about John's lifestyle. Others said that he was demon possessed. But Jesus knew that the people weren't just criticizing John. They also criticized Jesus.

Jesus didn't want his people to be "childish." He wanted them to believe in him and the kingdom of God. Those who are followers of God would be wise to learn the difference between being a child of God and being childish.

GO TO THE EXTREME

- **Lullabies** are among the oldest children's songs in history. A Turkish writer mentioned lullabies in a book written in 1072.

- **Jesus** used children in quite a few of his teachings. Check out Matthew 19:13–15 for an example.

- **Children** in ancient Israel played games like early versions of checkers and chess and games with toy weapons and dolls.

JOKE ALERT!

Top perks on being one of the disciples:

- *Knowing the secret disciple handshake*
- *Getting backstage passes to Jesus' sermons*
- *Having a tax collector (Matthew) on their side for a change*
- *Having all the loaves and fishes they can eat*
- *Hearing free parable interpretations*

Read the story in Matthew 11.

Riddle Me This

Jesus . . . said to them, "Why are you reasoning these things in your hearts? Which is easier: to say to the paralytic, 'Your sins are forgiven,' or to say. 'Get up, pick up your stretcher, and walk'?"

Mark 2:8–9 (HCSB)

If you were to witness someone being miraculous y healed, what would be the first thing you would say? "Wow, cool!" or "How dare that happen?" The Pharisees would have said the second statement. They often criticized Jesus for what he did and said. When the four friends of a paralyzed man tore through a roof to bring their friend before Jesus, Jesus told the man that his sins were forgiven. The Pharisees and other leaders were outraged that Jesus would dare to say that. Only God could forgive sins. So Jesus

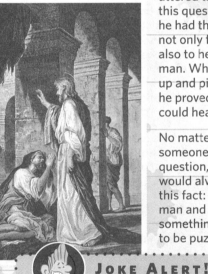

uttered the riddle above. He didn't expect them to answer this question. Instead, he wanted to prove that, as God, he had the authority to not only forgive sins, but also to heal the paralyzed man. When the man got up and picked up his mat, he proved that Jesus could heal and forgive.

No matter what answer someone gave to Jesus' question, the answer would always point to this fact: Jesus is both man and God. That's something you don't have to be puzzled about!

GO TO THE EXTREME

- **The** apostle John writes in John 21:25 that the miracles of Jesus were so plentiful that no amount of books could hold the list of all the events.

- **Many** roofs in New Testament times were flat and made out of wood beams. Clay and branches were packed on top. A stone roller was used to press down the layers of the roof.

JOKE ALERT!

The Pharisees could have used this acronym, calling their group **LAWS**:

Let's

All

Worry

Someone

Read the story in Mark 2:1–12.

A Hard Question

Then Jesus asked them, "Which is lawful on the Sabbath: to do good or to do evil, to save life or to kill?" But they remained silent.
Mark 3:4 (NIV)

Has anyone ever asked you a question you couldn't answer? (And we don't mean question #12 on your math test.) Jesus often answered those who criticized him with a question they couldn't answer. One Sabbath day at a synagogue just as Jesus was about to heal a man with a shriveled hand—a hand the man could not straighten—the leaders of Israel were all set to accuse him of wrongdoing. According to the Law of Moses, no one was supposed to work on the Sabbath. Since they didn't like Jesus, they chose to believe that healing was "work." But Jesus asked the question above then healed the man anyway.

The shriveled hearts of the leaders of Israel made Jesus sad. These leaders cared more about rule keeping than they did about God's people. They couldn't see that God always cared about people more than rules. The compassion of Jesus would always be a puzzle to them.

GO TO THE EXTREME

• **A** tough question was presented by German mathematician Bernhard Riemann in 1859. This math problem, the Riemann hypothesis, has stumped mathematicians since then.

• **Two** of the most asked questions in the world are "Is there a God?" and "What is the meaning of life?"

JOKE ALERT!

Jesus' disciples could have used an acronym and called themselves **HITS**:

Having an
Inside
Track to the
Savior

Or **GUYS**:

Gaining
Understanding
You
See

4 0

Read the story in Mark 3:4-5.

A Puzzling Parable

He said to them, "Do you not understand this parable? How then will you understand all the parables?"
Mark 4:13 (ESV)

Jesus is well known for the stories he told. These stories—parables—explained truths about God and his kingdom. Many involved agricultural stories. Jesus' parable of the sower is one of the most puzzling among his parables. Check it out:

"Listen! A sower went out to sow. And as he sowed, some seed fell along the path, and the birds came and devoured it. Other seed fell on rocky ground, where it did not have much soil, and immediately it sprang up, since it had no depth of soil. And when the sun rose, it was scorched, and since it had no root, it withered away. Other seed fell among thorns, and the thorns grew up and choked it, and it yielded no grain. And other seeds fell into good soil and produced grain, growing up and increasing and yielding thirtyfold and sixtyfold and a hundredfold." And he said, "He who has ears to hear, let him hear." (Mark 4:3-9, ESV)

Do you get it? If not, you're in good company. Jesus' disciples didn't understand it either. But instead of scratching their heads and going, "Huh?" they asked Jesus to tell them what it meant. The sower is the person who spreads the Word of God, while the different soils represent the people who hear the message of the gospel. The seed that fell on the path means the person doesn't believe the message. The rocky soil means the person believes for a little while, but then stops believing. The seed among thorns means the person gives up believing, because of problems and fears. The last soil—the good soil—is the person who believes and begins to produce fruit: good deeds. What kind of soil are you?

GO TO THE EXTREME

- **Wheat,** barley, figs, chick-peas, cucumbers, dates, olives, flax, pomegranates—these are just a few of the many crops that the people of ancient Israel would grow and harvest.

- **"Old** MacDonald Had a Farm" is one of the most well-known nursery rhymes about agriculture.

- **Even** though the birds ate the seeds, they could still be planted somewhere else. How? The seeds can travel and be deposited through the waste of the birds!

JOKE ALERT!

Jesus did not tell these parables:

- *The Parable of the Wise Sheep*
- *The Parable of the Ketchup Seed*
- *The Parable of the Lost Wool Sweater*
- *The Parable of the Man Who Built His House on a Sand Trap*
- *The Parable of the Rich Man Who Got Stuck Going through the Eye of a Needle*

41

Read the story in Mark 4:1-20.

FORTUNE-TELLING and Magic

You've probably read stories about people with magical powers. Some of the most popular stories in literature today are about a certain kid with magical ability. Maybe you once wondered whether or not magic *was* real. (It's okay to admit it, if you did.)

God has unlimited power to do amazing things. The Holy Spirit gave angels and God's people (Moses, the prophets, Jesus' disciples) the ability to do the amazing things God called them to do. They knew that God was the one with the power to work through them. But when some angels rebelled and left heaven, they still had some power. These fallen angels, now called demons, were able to work through those who mistakenly trusted in them. That's why many people in ancient times believed that "magic" was at work when fortune-tellers predicted events or staffs turned into snakes.

These stories are all about the beliefs about magic and fortune-telling and the God who is more powerful than anyone or anything.

It's All Done with Mirrors?

Moses and Aaron did as the LORD commanded. In the sight of Pharaoh and in the sight of his servants he lifted up the staff and struck the water in the Nile, and all the water in the Nile turned into blood. . . . But the magicians of Egypt did the same by their secret arts.
Exodus 7:20, 22 (ESV)

Ever see a magician? Maybe you saw one at a party doing tricks. The pharaoh of Egypt had magicians. But they didn't pull rabbits out of hats or turn scarves into doves. These magicians turned water into blood.

Whoa! What's all that about? you might be thinking. During the time of Moses, the people of Israel were slaves in Egypt. They had been slaves for over 400 years. God sent Moses to tell Pharaoh to release his people from slavery. But God also said that Pharaoh would refuse. So when Pharaoh did, Moses wasn't shocked. God gave Moses and his brother Aaron the ability to perform wonders. The first was when Moses threw down his staff and it turned into a snake. But guess what? When Pharaoh's magicians threw their staffs down, they also turned into snakes! The Bible says they used "their secret arts" (Exodus 7:11). This meant that they used demonic power. But to show that God's power was greater, Moses' snake ate the magicians' snakes!

Later, Moses used God's power to turn the water of the Nile to blood. But as the Scripture passage above says, the magicians were able to do that, too. When God later sent a plague of gnats that the magicians could not duplicate, even they realized that God was all-powerful.

Go to the Extreme

• **Magic** was a big part of ancient Egyptian culture. They used it for protection, healing, the dead, agriculture, and even fate.

• **Egyptian** priests even had ivory wands, potions, and lists of spells for every occasion.

Joke Alert!

Some researchers assert that this gathering of Moses with Pharaoh's magicians was the first recorded "staff" meeting in history.

Note: the magicians must have had spare staffs since Moses' snake ate all the magicians' staffs-turned-into-snakes.

44

Read the story in Exodus 7.

Don't Do It

Do not practice fortune-telling or witchcraft.
Leviticus 19:26 (NLT)

Our world is filled with signs that tell you what *not* to do. *Don't walk. Don't litter. Don't smoke.* When the people of Israel wandered in the wilderness on their way to the Promised Land of Canaan, God gave Moses laws for them to follow. One of the laws, given in the verse above, might have seemed strange. But if you read the previous story, maybe it won't.

God wanted his people—the people of Israel—to be different from other nations. He wanted them to be holy, just as he was holy, and also to love and obey him. Many people in other nations believed in other "gods." For example, the people of Egypt worshiped many gods. But there was only one true God. God wanted to protect his people from actions that could harm them.

Fortune-tellers made predictions about the future. But any power they claimed to have came from evil spirits. Many of them lied. Only God really knows the truth about the future. He spoke through prophets, rather than fortune-tellers. So, when it came to fortune-telling or witchcraft, he has only one rule: don't.

JOKE ALERT!

One Canaanite to another:

"Where's the doctor?"

"Which doctor?"

"Yes, that one."

GO TO THE EXTREME

• **The** Salem, Massachusetts witch trials of 1692–1693 are the most well-known witch hunts in U.S. history. Twenty-six people were convicted of witchcraft in 1692.

• **Between** 1480 and 1750, approximately 40,000 to 100,000 people were executed for witchcraft in North America and Europe.

• **Witchcraft** in the Old Testament meant (mostly) women who used spoken curses to injure others. Witchcraft in the New Testament meant murderers who used poisons to kill people.

4 5

Read the story in Leviticus 19:26.

A Medium-Sized Problem

Saul then said to his servants, "Find me a woman who is a medium, so I can go and consult her." His servants replied, "There is a woman at Endor who is a medium."
1 Samuel 28:7 (HCSB)

Who gives you advice? Your parents? Your best friend? In Bible times, a prophet or a priest gave a king advice because God spoke through them. When the Philistines, the enemies of Israel, wanted to fight against Israel, Saul, the king of Israel, desperately wanted advice. But the prophet Samuel was dead. God refused to answer Saul, because Saul had been disobedient. So Saul sought advice in all the wrong places.

A medium was someone who believed he or she could communicate with the dead. But in the book of Leviticus, God said, "Do not turn to mediums or necromancers; do not seek them out, and so make yourselves unclean by them" (1 Samuel 19:31, ESV). Earlier, Saul had ordered those who practiced witchcraft or fortune-telling to be banished or put to death. But since he wanted advice, he decided to get it any way he could: by disguising himself and going to a woman who claimed to be a medium. His goal was to talk to the prophet Samuel.

Mediums didn't act for God. But when Saul asked the woman at Endor to speak to Samuel, the woman was shocked that she actually saw and heard the spirit of Samuel. Even *she* was surprised (which should tell us something!). Bible scholars aren't sure whether God allowed Samuel to speak or if this was an evil spirit. Either way, Saul got bad news: his army would lose the battle and he and his sons would die.

GO TO THE EXTREME

• **The** famous escape artist Harry Houdini did more than just get out of sticky situations! He was a skeptic who wanted to expose the fraudulent thinking of supernatural phenomena.

• **In** the Old Testament, the Hebrew term *yidde'oni* literally meant "gainer of information from ghosts."

JOKE ALERT!

Saul sought advice from one of the very few fortune-tellers/witches in the area because he wanted his "medium rare."

4 6

Elymas Eliminated

Elymas the sorcerer (for that is what his name means) opposed them and tried to turn the proconsul from the faith.
                    Acts 13:8 (NIV)

In New Testament times, Saul (also known as Paul) and Barnabas traveled as missionaries spreading the gospel wherever God sent them. Traveling around, they met all kinds of people. One day when they were sent to the island of Cyprus, they encountered two men: Bar-Jesus, a false prophet, and a man named Elymas. While the Bible doesn't describe Elymas's actions, his name means "sorcerer" or "magician." He probably had a reputation for fortune-telling. Elymas tried to stop Barnabas and Saul from telling Sergius Paulus, a Roman official, about Jesus.

Instead of being impressed or afraid of Elymas, Saul boldly spoke the truth from the Holy Spirit. He told Elymas that he would become blind. And that's what happened right away. After seeing a newly blinded Elymas, Sergius Paulus believed in God.

Barnabas and Saul showed who had the real power: God.

GO TO THE EXTREME

• **The** word *sorcerer* comes from the Greek root *pharm*, which relates to words we use today such as *pharmacy*.

• **The** *Sorcerer's Apprentice* is a 1797 poem written by Johann Wolfgang von Goethe.

4 7 . . . .

Read the story in Acts 13:4-12.

Peril at Philippi

One day as we were going down to the place of prayer, we met a demon-possessed slave girl. She was a fortune-teller who earned a lot of money for her masters. She followed Paul and the rest of us, shouting, "These men are servants of the Most High God, and they have come to tell you how to be saved."
Acts 16:16–17 (NLT)

Many Hollywood movies have featured demon possession. Some people might think of it as entertainment and, therefore, not real. But in Bible times, missionaries like Paul and Silas were faced with the reality of this sad truth. While in Philippi, a Roman city in Macedonia, they met a slave girl who was demon possessed. The girl's owners made a huge profit by her predictions.

GO TO THE EXTREME

• **Many** people still think they can learn the future from fortune-tellers and horoscopes.

• **In** 1950, Mattel Toy Company manufactured the Magic 8 Ball—a fortune-telling toy—based on one patented by Albert C. Carter in 1944.

• **When** the movie *The Exorcist* first came out, both psychologists and ministers were barraged by phone calls from worried people who believed that their friends or family were possessed!

For some reason, this girl kept following Paul and Silas around, proclaiming that they were "servants of the Most High God." Paul had had enough and ordered the evil spirit to come out of the girl, using the authority that Jesus gave his followers. Of course the girl's owners didn't thank Paul and Silas at all. Instead, they complained to the city leaders and lied about Paul and Silas. For their actions, Paul and Silas were beaten and thrown in prison.

JOKE ALERT!

Where is drag racing mentioned in the Bible?

Answer: *Paul was "beaten with rods" three times and dragged in the streets (2 Corinthians 11:25, KJV).*

Read the story in Acts 16:16–40.

A Bad Imitation

Some of the itinerant Jewish exorcists attempted to pronounce the name of the Lord Jesus over those who had evil spirits, saying, "I command you by the Jesus whom Paul preaches!" Seven sons of Sceva, a Jewish chief priest, were doing this.
Acts 19:13–14 (HCSB)

Ever try to imitate someone you thought was cool? That's what seven sons of a priest did, when they heard of the apostle Paul's actions. The Holy Spirit gave Paul the power to heal the sick and those possessed by demons. Using the name of Jesus, Paul could drive out a demon. This meant that Paul had a God-given power over that evil spirit. The spirit had to do what Paul told it to do. Even if Paul touched an article of clothing and a sick person then touched that piece of clothing, he or she would become well. (This won't work with your gym socks.)

The seven sons of Sceva the priest decided to drive out demons like Paul did. Unlike Paul, they didn't believe in Jesus. Therefore, their words had no power. When they tried to drive out an evil spirit, the evil spirit spoke through the person it possessed. "Jesus I know, and Paul I recognize—but who are you?" (Acts 19:15, HCSB). And then the demon-possessed man beat the seven men so badly that they had to run away!

GO TO THE EXTREME

• **Martin** Luther, the leader of the Protestants, used exorcism as a means of helping other people. However, others rejected the idea, saying it was too superstitious.

• **Anyone** who could perform exorcisms in Jesus' name was in high demand. This was because the culture back in ancient times attributed many diseases to demon possession.

JOKE ALERT!

New Testament names not to name your children:

Judas *(Matthew 10)*

Caiaphas *(Matthew 26)*

Sapphira *(Acts 5)*

Herod *(Acts 12)*

Sceva *(Acts 19)*

Demas *(2 Timothy 4:10)*

Diotrephes *(3 John 1)*

49

Read the story in Acts 19:11–20.

VISIONS and Dreams

When you go into a deep sleep, you probably have a dream or a series of them. Scientists say that dreams are your way of dealing with things that happened during the day. But many people in the Bible had special dreams from God. Some happened when the person was awake. These dreams were known as visions: special messages from God or glimpses of what he planned to do. Many prophets and kings had visions and dreams. Some of these dreams and visions were surprising, puzzling, and extremely scary. But whenever a dream was hard to understand, God would give someone—usually a prophet—the ability to interpret the dream.

In this section you'll read the stories of some of the most amazing visions and dreams in the Bible. Some of these visions turned out to be nightmares for the dreamers. Others have yet to come to pass.

EZEKIEL'S VISION BY THE RIVER CHEBAR.

יהוה

When I looked behold an hand was sent unto me, and lo a roll of a book was therein.

Ezekiel. Ch. 2. Ver. 9

I Dream of a Nation

[God] brought [Abram] outside and said, "Look toward the heaven, and number the stars, if you are able to number them." Then he said to him, "So shall your offspring be."
Genesis 15:5 (ESV)

Think about how many people are in the United States alone. Imagine having a family as large as the population of this country! God promised to make an entire nation out of one man's family. That man was Abram. The only catch was that Abram was well over 75 years old and his wife was only about ten years younger . . . and, they had no children!

If you were Abram, what would you do? Would you laugh? Say, "No way!" Rather than do either, Abram chose to believe God's promise to make a nation out of his family line. The people of this nation would be as numerous as the stars above. That's a lot of people!

Abram wanted proof that God would do as he said. To show that what he said would come true, God told Abram to sacrifice some animals. When Abram obeyed, he fell into a deep, deep sleep, and saw a smoking pot and a torch pass over the sacrifices he had made. The pot and torch were symbols of God's presence. By passing along the sacrificed animals, God showed that he agreed to fulfill the promise made to Abram. Abram later became known as Abraham, a name that means "father of many."

GO TO THE EXTREME

- **Scientists** estimate that the universe may have as many as 300 sextillion stars. That's a 3 with 23 zeros behind it—yowzers!

- **Nearly** 60 percent of the world's population claims Abram (later called Abraham) as their religious forefather.

- **In** recent times, the oldest woman to give birth was 70 years old.

JOKE ALERT!

Speaking of people, who is the first man mentioned in the Bible?

Answer: *Chap. 1.*

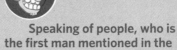

Read the story in Genesis 15.

Stairway to Heaven

As he slept, he dreamed of a stairway that reached from the earth up to heaven. And he saw the angels of God going up and down the stairway.

Genesis 28:12 (NLT)

Most pillows are made of soft, fluffy stuff. That's probably because when we sleep, we like to be comfortable, and fluffy stuff usually helps that goal. Imagine if your pillow was instead made of rocks! That's what Jacob was sleeping on when he had his mind-boggling dream about a strange stairway.

In Jacob's dream a huge stairway reached down from heaven. (Some Bible translations use *ladder* in place of *stairway*.) Angels went up and down the stairway. At the top was God, who repeated a promise he had made to Jacob's father, Isaac, and grandfather, Abraham: "Your descendants will be as numerous as the dust of the earth!" (Genesis 28:14, NLT).

One of the amazing things about the stairway was that it came down from heaven. This was a sign that the God of the universe was coming down to earth. This was important, because Jacob knew there was no way that people could reach up to God. He had to come down to us.

GO TO THE EXTREME

- **The** world's longest ladder is said to be the one our Coast Guard uses for rescues. It is 320 feet long.

- **Eiderdown** (feathers from the nest of a duck called an Eider) is supposedly the world's softest pillow stuffing. A pillow made of it can cost as much as $2800!

- **Some** ancient Chinese pillows were made of porcelain. There would definitely be no jumping on those beds!

JOKE ALERT!

Mr. Cool?

Jacob said, "I am a smooth man"
(Genesis 27:11, ESV).

5 3

Read the story in Genesis 28.

Dream On!

Then he had another dream, and he told it to his brothers. "Listen," he said, "I had another dream, and this time the sun and moon and eleven stars were bowing down to me."
Genesis 37:9 (NIV)

Imagine you had a brother with whom you had a hard time getting along. Now imagine that one night your brother had a fancy dream he was dying to share with the family. He gathers your family together and then tells you, "Hey guys, guess what? I had a dream that I was the boss of all of you. You were all bowing down to me and doing exactly what I said." What would be your response?

Joseph was the favorite son of Jacob. He was favored, because he was the son of Rachel, Jacob's favorite wife. Jacob gave him a special embroidered coat as a sign of his status. As you can imagine, his brothers weren't real happy with him.

GO TO THE EXTREME

• **Famed** psychologist Sigmund Freud said that dreams are wishes we would like to see happen.

• **One** of the most famous speeches in the U.S. is a speech called "I Have a Dream," by Dr. Martin Luther King. It was about his dream of equality for all people.

• **The** story of *Frankenstein* came from a dream the author, Mary Wollstonecraft Shelley, had—what a nightmare!

Then one night, Joseph had a dream about some sheaves of grain: the whole family was out in a field tying up grain into sheaves when all of a sudden Joseph's sheaf stood tall and straight, and all his other family members' sheaves bowed down to his. Then he had another dream. This time, the very sun, moon, and stars were bowing down to him! He told his family both dreams. Joseph's dreams eventually came true, but not until many hard years passed. During those years, Joseph became a slave, thanks to his annoyed brothers who sold him into slavery!

JOKE ALERT!

Recently discovered New Year's resolutions of Joseph, son of Jacob:

1. *Get pants of many colors to go with the coat.*
2. *Get rid of the T-shirt that says, "I'm Dad's favorite."*
3. *Don't fall for the old "we've got a really neat pit to show you" trick.*
4. *Write a Broadway musical about my colorful coat.*

54

Read the story in Genesis 37.

Dreaming 'Til the Cows Come Home

After two whole years, Pharaoh dreamed that he was standing by the Nile, and behold, there came up out of the Nile seven cows attractive and plump, and they fed in the reed grass.
Genesis 41:1–2 (ESV)

Say you're home in your room one night, and the phone rings. Your mom calls up the stairs and says, "Honey, it's the President. He wants to tell you about some wild dream he just had!" Wouldn't you freak out?

Joseph had correctly interpreted the dreams of two fellow prisoners—the cupbearer (butler) and baker of the pharaoh—Egypt's version of a president. The cupbearer recommended Joseph to the pharaoh as someone who could interpret dreams. Imagine the pressure Joseph must have felt when the pharaoh summoned him before his throne and demanded that Joseph explain the following dreams.

The first was about seven fat cows walking out of the Nile River, followed by seven thin cows, which ate the fat cows. Weird, huh? But the weird thing was that even though they ate the fat cows, the thin cows stayed scrawny. Then the pharaoh dreamed of a corn stalk growing seven healthy, yummy-looking ears of corn. But then suddenly, seven withered ears sprang out and ate the healthy ears!

Joseph told the Pharaoh that his dream was God's way of telling him that there would be seven years of plentiful harvests with lots to eat, followed by seven years of famine.

God placed Joseph in just the right place and gave him the ability to interpret dreams. In one day, Joseph went from being a nobody to being second in command over all of Egypt.

GO TO THE EXTREME

- **Did** you know that both male and female cows can have horns?

- **A** good ear of corn has from 400–600 kernels on it.

- **The** Nile is the longest river in the world, at over 4,000 miles long.

JOKE ALERT!

Speaking of dreams, one night Pharaoh had a nightmare—he dreamed he was making a speech to his subjects . . . And he woke up . . . and he was!

5 5

Read the story in Genesis 41.

I Dream of Egypt

That night God spoke to Israel in a vision: "Jacob, Jacob!" He said. And Jacob replied, "Here I am." God said, "I am God, the God of your father. Do not be afraid to go down to Egypt, for I will make you a great nation there."

Genesis 46:2–3 (HCSB)

If you read "Dream On!" a few pages ago, you know that Joseph had some controversial dreams about his family. Well, those dreams came true. But first his family had to get to Egypt. . . .

If you read the previous story, you know that this area was in the middle of a famine. There was no food to be had anywhere—except Egypt. One night God appeared to Jacob in a vision, telling him not to be afraid to take his family and move to Egypt. Jacob's son, Joseph, had invited Jacob and their whole family to move to Egypt to be with him. Jacob longed to see his son again. But moving to Egypt would have meant leaving the homeland that God had promised would belong to the family line of Abraham.

Jacob obeyed God and took his family to Egypt. There, he was joyfully reunited with Joseph, and his family received all the grain they needed. Also, the pharaoh gave Jacob's family a special portion of land, which enabled Jacob's family to prosper in Egypt for many years.

GO TO THE EXTREME

- **The** distance between Egypt and where Jacob lived was about 200 miles.

- **Elias** Howe, who invented the sewing machine, did so after having a dream about being captured and poked by spears with holes in the tips.

- **While** in Egypt, Jacob's family grew from about seven people to about 2 million people in the time of Moses!

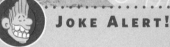

JOKE ALERT!

What excuse did Joseph use to get Benjamin to stay behind?

Answer: *"E-gypt me!"*
(Genesis 44)

5 6

Read the story in Genesis 46.

A Dream of Utopia

This is a vision that Isaiah son of Amoz saw concerning Judah and Jerusalem. . . . They will hammer their swords into plowshares and their spears into pruning hooks.

Isaiah 2:1, 4 (NLT)

Ever heard of a utopia? It's a place where everything is peaceful and perfect. That's kind of what the prophet Isaiah had a vision of, and it was a much different place from Judah at the time of Isaiah.

Isaiah predicted punishment for Judah, the southern kingdom of Israel. Since the people had been rebellious toward God, God promised to allow their enemies to conquer them.

Isaiah had a vision from God about all the wickedness of the people of Judah, but then he also had a vision of the future. In the last days, the Lord's temple would be a place of great refuge and hope for all the nations of the earth. As a result of all people turning to the Lord, Isaiah saw people turning their weapons into things that would be helpful instead of destructive. This was a vision of the hope that Jesus would someday offer to the world. Is that your vision of the future?

JOKE ALERT!

Top misconceptions about the Old Testament:

- *Delilah gave Samson the first Mohawk.*
- *Starbucks Middle East carried manna in four exciting flavors— chocolate latte, banana, mocha, and tangy passion fruit.*
- *Isaiah predicted the first hardware store (Isaiah 2:4).*
- *Jacob's son, Levi, was the father of blue jeans.*

GO TO THE EXTREME

- *Animal Farm* by George Orwell, voted one of the top one hundred books in the English language, is about an animal utopia that gets ruined by pigs that learn to walk on two legs.

- **In** the early 1900s, a dentist moved to the Galapagos Islands to begin a utopia. It was disrupted by a huge wild boar that trampled their gardens!

- **The** word *utopia* was first used by English statesman Sir Thomas More as the name of a fictional island that had none of the problems of More's homeland, England.

5 7

Read the story in Isaiah 1—2.

A Vision of God

In the year that King Uzziah died I saw the Lord sitting upon a throne, high and lifted up; and the train of his robe filled the temple.

Isaiah 6:1 (ESV)

Have you ever had a dream so amazing that when you woke up you thought it must have all happened? Isaiah had one of the most amazing dreams of the Bible: he saw God seated on his throne, with robes flowing and special six-winged angels—seraphim—singing of the holiness of the Lord. He even heard the Lord speak, and it was with a voice so powerful that the foundations of the building shook and the whole place filled up with smoke. It was so astonishing to Isaiah that he thought he was going to die!

Isaiah knew that he was sinful, and once he saw God and was with God, the eye-popping power and purity and goodness of God made Isaiah's sin all the more awful. He thought that a being that amazing would instantly kill a being as wretched as him. But God himself purified Isaiah and sent him out to tell his countrymen about their spiritual blindness. Isaiah's vision of God confirmed his new job: God's prophet.

GO TO THE EXTREME

• **It** would take an earthquake intensity of IX on the Modified Mercalli scale to shake the foundations of a building. A XII is considered total destruction.

• **Prince** Arthur and Catherine of Aragon may have worn the costliest robes ever for their wedding—they were made of pure gold cloth.

• **King** Edward of England had a throne built for himself in 1296 and since then, every king or queen of England has sat in that same chair to be crowned.

Read the story in Isaiah 6.

Name That Image

In my thirtieth year, in the fourth month on the fifth day, while I was among the exiles by the Kebar River, the heavens were opened and I saw visions of God.
Ezekiel 1:1 (NIV)

How do you usually get assignments or chores? Probably a parent or a teacher tells you what you need to do. In Bible times, when God wanted someone to be a prophet, he spoke to that prophet through dreams or gave that person a vision. One day, Ezekiel had a vision of a storm cloud coming quickly at him. And this was no ordinary cloud—it was flashing lightning out of it, and at the heart of it seemed to be a glowing, hot ball of metal.

If that wasn't strange enough, out of the cloud popped four creatures Ezekiel barely had words to describe. They each had four legs like a cow or a deer and four wings, and under their wings they had human hands. They also had four heads—one like a human's, one like a lion's, one like an ox's, and one like an eagle's! On top of that, they were shining like a burning coal and as fast as bolts of lightning.

The four of them flew in four opposite directions, and as they did, a crystal ceiling spread out over top of them, and on top of that was a sapphire throne. Can you guess who was sitting on the throne? God. He had a human-like shape, but he glowed like burning metal. He was shooting out brilliant light and was so dazzlingly glorious that Ezekiel fell to his knees and pressed his face to the ground.

(Wouldn't you?)

GO TO THE EXTREME

- **Lightning** can be 15,000–60,000 degrees Fahrenheit, which is way hotter than even the surface of the sun (a mere 9,000 degrees).

- **A** man in the *Guinness World Record* for the most times struck by lightning has been zapped seven times!

- **A** one-pound sapphire would cost about $3.5 million. Imagine how valuable a throne made out of sapphire would be!

JOKE ALERT!

Do NOT try these at home:

"A woman on the roof dropped a millstone that landed on Abimelech's head and crushed his skull" (Judges 9:53, NLT).

"In his hand was a glowing coal that he had taken from the altar with tongs. He touched my mouth with it" (Isaiah 6:6–7, HCSB).

"I opened my mouth, and he gave me this scroll to eat" (Ezekiel 3:2, ESV).

"Take a sharp sword and use it as a razor to shave your head and beard" (Ezekiel 5:1, NLT).

Read the story in Ezekiel 1.

Daniel's Scary Dream

Earlier, during the first year of King Belshazzar's reign in Babylon, Daniel had a dream and saw visions as he lay in his bed. He wrote down the dream, and this is what he saw.

Daniel 7:1 (NLT)

We know Daniel best for his night of camping out in the lions' den, but he also had some mysterious dreams about the future. In one dream, Daniel saw four beasts coming out of the sea. One looked like a lion, but had eagle's wings. (In mythology, a creature with the head and wings of an eagle and the back part of a lion is called a griffin.) The second was bearlike and was chewing on some ribs. The third had the look of a leopard, but also had bird wings. The fourth was the most terrifying of all: it had iron teeth and ten horns.

These sights freaked Daniel out, but then came a being in the form of a man, with pure white hair and clothes, and who sat on a throne of fire and judged all the people of the earth. This was the Messiah to come, who would save all the people who believed in him and defeat the last and most ferocious of the creatures.

God revealed in this dream and another that these were stories about the end of the world. Although some images badly scared Daniel, God showed that everything would turn out right in the end.

GO TO THE EXTREME

- **The** thorny devil lizard has the most "horns" of any animal.

- **The** Ankole-Watusi cattle are known for having extremely long horns. One Watusi bull, Lurch, holds the record for longest horns—36.3 inches.

- **The** most common animal to be born with two heads is the snake. As if a one-headed snake wasn't scary enough!

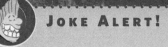

JOKE ALERT!

How did the king find Daniel relaxing?

Answer: *He was "lion" in the den (Daniel 6).*

Read the story in Daniel 7—8.

John's Vision of Heaven

> Then I saw one like a slaughtered lamb standing between the throne and the four living creatures and among the elders. He had seven horns and seven eyes, which are the seven spirits of God sent into all the earth.
> Revelation 5:6 (HCSB)

John had one long vision, one that takes up the whole book of Revelation. With a dream that long, you'd think he had been sleeping for a week!

John's vision of heaven and the end times is also one of the most exciting. John saw some of the same images as Isaiah, Ezekiel, and Daniel, and then some. He saw the same white-haired person dressed in white and radiating light: Jesus! He also saw the creatures with heads of humans, lions, oxen, and eagles. With them, he saw the crystal floor (which he said looked like a sea of glass) and the incredible throne of God.

Maybe the coolest thing he saw though was a multitude of believers all praising God. He saw Jesus gather believers from the whole earth. If you know Jesus, that means you were in that huge throng of people!

In fact, John says there were people beyond number. Sounds a lot like the promise God made to Abram in his dream (the first story in this section), doesn't it? John saw the spiritual sons and daughters of Abram, and they *were* like the number of stars in the sky!

GO TO THE EXTREME

• **The** Crystal Palace was a huge building made entirely of glass and iron. It was built in London in the mid-1800s and was the length of five football fields.

• **The** fabled Rip Van Winkle slept for twenty years—but the story doesn't tell us if he dreamed all that time!

• **People** have tried many, many times to predict when John's dream will come true—when the world will end. But no one can.

61

Read the story in Revelation 1; 4—7.

From ZERO to Hero

A **hero is someone** others admire. And no, we don't mean someone who achieved the highest score on a video game or can spit the farthest. He or she is someone who makes a difference in the lives of others. Who do you admire most? Why? There are many kinds of heroes you might hear or read about: superheroes—fictional people with superhuman abilities; everyday heroes—ordinary people who do special things; heroes of history—trailblazing people in the past who helped change the world.

Many people in the Bible are considered heroes, even though they might not have thought of themselves that way. They weren't born heroic, however. Most of them were fearful about their ability to do *anything* special. But contact with an extraordinary God could turn an ordinary "zero" into a hero of faith.

A Roller Coaster Life

The LORD was with Joseph and showed him steadfast love.
Genesis 39:21 (ESV)

Have you ever ridden on a really *big* roller coaster? First you slowly go up, up, up to the very top. And then you go zooming down—screaming all the way! Just as you catch your breath you're back up on the top, before you go screaming down to the bottom again. That's the way it goes for the entire ride—up and down.

Joseph's whole life was kind of like a roller coaster ride. He was either way up or down in the pits. He was the favorite son of his father Jacob, but that made his ten older brothers hate him. When Joseph had special dreams and told his brothers about them, they sold him as a slave. Joseph went to Egypt and became the manager of a rich man's house.

Lies were told about Joseph and he was thrown into a prison. But after awhile he was put in charge of all the prisoners. Joseph interpreted some prisoners' dreams and they came true, but he still was a prisoner for two years. When Pharaoh had some strange dreams (for more about Pharaoh's dreams, read "Dreaming 'Til the Cows Come Home," in Visions and Dreams, page 55), Joseph was called out of prison to interpret them. Pharaoh was so pleased that he made Joseph second in command of all Egypt. Joseph saved the lives of thousands of people, including his father and brothers, by providing them with food during the famine. Best of all, he forgave his brothers for what they did to him.

In thirteen years Joseph went from being hated and sold into slavery to the second most important person in Egypt. What an amazing up and down ride!

GO TO THE EXTREME

• **Judah,** one of Joseph's brothers, was saved from death during the famine. By saving Judah, God used Joseph to save the whole world! (Check out Jesus' "family tree" in Matthew 1:2, 16.)

• **There** is "fungus amungus." Between 1845 and 1852 about one million people died in the Great Famine in Ireland. The cause was a fungus that killed the potato crop, which was their main source of food.

• **The** story of Joseph is told in the popular musical, *Joseph and the Amazing Technicolor Dreamcoat.*

JOKE ALERT!

Top biblical pets:

Adam and Eve—that cute little furry beast that Adam hasn't named yet

Noah—a pair of partridges in a bare tree

Joseph—peacock (bird of many colors)

Jonah—very small fish

Saul in Damascus—seeing-eye dog

Jesus—lost and found sheep

Read the story in Genesis 37—50.

Be Strong and Brave!

Have I not commanded you? Be strong and courageous. Do not be afraid; do not be discouraged, for the LORD your God will be with you wherever you go.
Joshua 1:9 (NIV)

Your school is putting on a musical and you have a small part. Since you've been at every practice, you know a lot of the other characters' parts too. Two days before the performance, the star gets a really bad case of flu. The director decides that you should take the star's place. Whoa! That's really scary! "I know you can do it," the director tells you. "I'll help you."

Moses died just before the Israelites were ready to enter the promised land of Canaan. God came to Joshua, Moses' helper, and told him to lead the Israelites across the Jordan River and conquer the land. How would you have responded if you were Joshua?

Joshua knew that the Canaanites had a strong army and that the Israelites would have to fight many hard battles to conquer them. Joshua also knew that the Israelites would have to accept him as their leader.

Knowing that Joshua was afraid of the task, God comforted Joshua with the words above. Wow! What a vote of confidence! Giving Joshua these marching orders didn't turn Joshua into a superhero with amazing abilities. But Joshua had something even better—the presence of an amazing God who could do anything.

GO TO THE EXTREME

• **The** Israelites had to cross the Jordan River to get into Canaan. In New Testament times, this was where John the Baptist preached and where Jesus was baptized.

• **Joshua** was only one of two adults who had been a slave in Egypt and lived to enter Canaan.

• **There** are large yucca plants called Joshua trees that grow only in the Mojave Desert. Why they are named that is a mystery. If you want to see these plants you can visit Joshua Tree National Park in California.

Read the story in Joshua 1.

The Best Person for the Job

Deborah said to Barak, "Move on, for this is the day the LORD has handed Sisera over to you. Hasn't the LORD gone before you?"
Judges 4:14 (HCSB)

GO TO THE EXTREME

- **The** Deborah Number, named after Deborah in the book of Judges, is a number used in advanced mathematics, physics, and engineering.

- **Deborah's** name means "honeybee." The Canaanites certainly felt her sting when the Israelites completely destroyed their army!

- **A** woman named Deborah Sampson fought during the American Revolutionary War. She enlisted under the name Robert Shurtleff. She died in 1827.

The small town had always had a man for a mayor. For over a hundred years it had been "Mr. Mayor." But this election was different—there was a woman running for mayor! And believe it or not, she won! Some people were really surprised and they couldn't get used to saying "Mrs. Mayor." But after awhile they had to agree that she was the best person for the job.

The Old Testament judges were leaders who gave advice to the army and to others who needed help. Because of her faith, God chose Deborah to be the only woman judge of the twelve judges who guided Israel. Deborah judged Israel for forty years. She was a prophet, wife, counselor, warrior, poet, and singer in addition to being a judge. Talk about multitasking!

God told Deborah to lead the people into battle. She appointed Barak to lead an army of 10,000 men against the enemy. Barak, however, was afraid to go without her. Deborah agreed to go with Barak and the army. The Israelites won a great battle against the Canaanites—not one of the enemy soldiers was left alive. Deborah and Barak sang a song of praise to God for the great victory he had given them.

Read the story in Judges 4—5.

I Need a Sign

The LORD said to him, "I will be with you."
Judges 6:16 (NLT)

Ever watch base coaches at a baseball game? They touch their noses or ears, but not because they're being attacked by flying insects. They are giving signs to the runners, telling them to run, stay, steal, or slide. These signs help the players to make good decisions.

During a hard time in Israel's history, their enemies, the Midianites, bullied them severely. Gideon threshed his grain in a winepress, because he was afraid the Midianites would steal it. But suddenly an angel of God appeared to him. He had a special task for Gideon from God: go and save his people from the Midianites.

Gideon was ready with some excuses. His family wasn't very important. *He* wasn't all that important either. But as with Moses (see Exodus 4), God didn't take any excuses. He had chosen Gideon to go. Gideon didn't grab a weapon and run off immediately, however. He still wasn't sure, even after offering an animal sacrifice that God accepted. Gideon wanted a sign that God would help him defeat the Midianites. He placed a wool fleece on the threshing floor. He told God that if the overnight dew was only on the fleece and the ground was dry, he would know that he was God's chosen man for the task. And that's what happened. But Gideon still didn't head off to battle. He asked for the fleece to be dry and the ground wet. Once more God did what Gideon asked. Finally, Gideon was ready for battle.

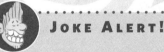

JOKE ALERT!

Using this acronym, Gideon could have challenged his band of men to join his contingent of **JARS:**

Judgment
Against
Religious
Silliness

GO TO THE EXTREME

- **Because** of this story, the phrase "putting out a fleece" became well known. This phrase means "to ask God for a sign."

- **When** collected in large amounts, dew can be used to supply water for areas in the desert where little rain occurs. There are machines that can collect up to 200 liters of dew a night!

- **Gideon** blew a trumpet to call the men to fight. The trumpets were made from animal horns and gave a sharp, shrill sound. Enough to make your hair stand on end!

Read the story in Judges 6.

A Loyal Friend

RUTH GLEANING IN THE FIELD OF BOAZ

Ruth said, "Do not urge me to leave you or to return from following you. For where you go I will go, and where you lodge I will lodge. Your people shall be my people, and your God my God."
Ruth 1:16 (ESV)

What kind of friend are you? Do you stick by a friend no matter what—in good times and bad? That's called being loyal. And a loyal friend is great, especially when we face some rough times. That's the kind of friend Ruth was. In fact, her name means "friend." Here's how she showed loyalty.

After Naomi's husband and two sons had died in Moab, a foreign land, Naomi was left with only her daughters-in-law—Ruth and Orpah. Naomi wanted to go back to Bethlehem in Israel. This would mean leaving her daughters-in-law behind.

Orpah kissed Naomi good-bye. But Ruth refused to leave Naomi. The words above that she said to Naomi weren't just nice words. By going with Naomi, she agreed to give up her family, her country, and the gods her people worshiped. She would become a follower of Israel's God.

Naomi realized that Ruth had made up her mind to go with her. When Naomi and Ruth finally arrived back in Naomi's town, her old friends were surprised to see her. But they were glad that Ruth loved her and would take care of her.

Because of Ruth's loyalty, she gained a husband, Boaz, and a book of the Bible named after her. Best of all, she gained a place in the family line of the Savior.

GO TO THE EXTREME

• **The** Moabites descended from Moab, who was actually a son of Lot, Abraham's nephew. (You can read this rather weird story in Genesis 19:30–38.)

• **The** Moabites worshiped the god Chemosh, whose name most likely meant "destroyer" or "subduer." Doesn't sound like a very nice guy.

• **The** word *ruthless* means "having no pity." This is the opposite of Ruth's actions.

JOKE ALERT!

Laconic Limerick:
*Naomi asked Ruth not to go as
a widow, but Ruth went there so as
together their plan
was to find Ruth a man.
And that's where she met
the man Bo-az!*

Read the story in Ruth 1.

Just Follow Me

Nothing can hinder the LORD from saving, whether by many or by few.
1 Samuel 14:6 (NIV)

Ever play *Follow the Leader?* Maybe you did when you were a little kid. It's fun to imitate the leader's moves and actions—if you have a good leader. But it could be downright dangerous if the leader is a daredevil who likes to walk on railroad tracks or go into a bad part of town. So be sure you have a good leader to follow!

The Philistines were Israel's worst enemy. The Israelite army was afraid of them and ran away, hiding in caves and bushes. Only 600 stayed with King Saul. One day Jonathan, Saul's son, said to his armor-bearer, "Let's go over to the Philistine army camp on the other side of the pass. If the Lord helps us, it won't matter how many of us there are."

Jonathan said, "We'll let the Philistines see us. If they say, 'Wait there,' we'll stay where we are. If they say, 'Come up to us,' we'll climb up because that shows that God has handed them over to us."

So Jonathan and the young man let the Philistines see them. The Philistines said, "Come on up here. We'll teach you a thing or two."

Using his hands and feet, Jonathan climbed up with the young man right behind him. In that first attack Jonathan and the young man killed about 20 men.

A mighty army of two—plus God.

GO TO THE EXTREME

- **There** were no blacksmiths in Israel, because the Philistines were afraid they would make swords or spears for the Israelites. Only King Saul and his son Jonathan had iron weapons.

- **Today,** to be called a "Philistine" is not a compliment! It's a put-down, indicating that the person has an attitude that hates art, beauty, education, and spiritual values. Not someone you want to claim as a friend!

- **John** or Jonathan has been the second most popular name for baby boys over the last hundred years. First is James, then John, followed by Robert, Michael, and William.

JOKE ALERT!

Here's something you *won't* find in the Bible:
Jonathan was carrying all the water for him and his armor-bearer. So the armor-bearer was literally following the "liter."

Read the story in 1 Samuel 14.

The Chosen One

The Lord said to Samuel, "Do not look at his appearance or his stature, because I have rejected him. Man does not see what the Lord sees, for man sees what is visible, but the Lord sees the heart."
1 Samuel 16:7 (HCSB)

Go to the Extreme

- **Anointing** was the use of oil on the head of someone to be honored or consecrated to God.

- **One** of the other uses for olive oil was to put it on dead bodies to help cover the smell of decomposition.

- **One** of the most famous sculptures in the world is a sculpture of David created by Michelangelo between 1501 and 1504. In the sculpture, the hands are disproportionately large compared to the body. Some say it is because David was said to be "strong of hand," so Michelangelo emphasized his hands.

Do you want to crawl under the bleachers when the gym teacher says, "Okay, choose sides for the game." Maybe you're the smallest kid in your class and not exactly a superstar athletically. You're worried you will be the *last one* chosen. Not a good feeling!

God was fed up with King Saul's disobedience and bad attitude and didn't want Saul to be king any longer. He sent the prophet Samuel to anoint a new king. This king would be found among the sons of a man named Jesse in Bethlehem.

Samuel didn't know which of Jesse's sons was the "chosen one." So he asked Jesse to have his sons come before him. The Super Seven older brothers impressed Samuel because they were tall and handsome, strong and aggressive—king material. But *none* of them was God's choice.

Samuel asked Jesse, "Are these all the sons you have?" There was still one more—the youngest one, who was out taking care of the family's sheep. Jesse sent for David and had him brought in. Although good-looking, there was nothing special about him. But he was special to God. So Samuel got the animal horn that was filled with the olive oil used to anoint David as king. Best of all, the Spirit of the Lord came on David with power.

JOKE ALERT!

In the confrontation with Goliath, these weapons were discarded by David in favor of the sling and the small, smooth stones:

Flaming harp ("Lyre, lyre, ball of fire")

Banana peel

The old "look behind you" trick

Bad cheese sandwich and curdled goat's milk

Poisonous sheep

Fruitcake

70

Read the story in 1 Samuel 16.

David's Mighty Men

These are the names of David's mightiest warriors.
2 Samuel 23:8 (NLT)

Kings, presidents, and heads of big corporations never work alone and make all important decisions by themselves. They have cabinets, advisors, and committees to help and counsel them. Even though these "underlings" are very important to the head man, others usually don't know much about them or even know their names.

King David had thirty-seven mighty men working for him—helping him win battles and conquer his enemies. Their names aren't as important as their extraordinary deeds.

Josheb used his spear to kill 800 men—all in one battle. Eleazar fought the Philistines until his arm got tired, but he still held his sword and won a battle. Shammah took his stand in the middle of a field and kept the Philistines from capturing it. These men were called the Three.

One time David was thirsty and the Three fought their way to a well and brought back water for David. David didn't drink the water but poured it on the ground as an offering to God. He said, "These men put their lives in danger by getting this water."

GO TO THE EXTREME

- **The** javelin is a modern-day spear. The javelin throw is a popular Olympic event. Jan Železný of the Czech Republic still holds the world record for javelin throw: 98.48 meters (323 feet, 1 inch), a record set in 1996.

- **The** world's most expensive bottled water is Bling h2o, which costs $40–$60 per bottle.

- **The** U.S. Navy Seals and the British Special Air Service are the most highly trained of the special forces.

JOKE ALERT!

Because of his love for music, David and his mighty men could have called themselves **HARPS**:

Hard-core
Army to
Really
Pound
Saul

Other deeds of the thirty men include the following: killing 300 men with a spear, killing two of Moab's best fighting men, killing a lion in a snowy pit, and killing a mighty Egyptian with the Egyptian's own spear. All thirty-seven are listed in the Bible but the deeds of only a few are mentioned.

These mighty men could do these mighty deeds because God was with them.

Read the story in 2 Samuel 23:8–39.

At Such a Time as This

If you keep quiet at a time like this, deliverance and relief for the Jews will arise from some other place, but you and your relatives will die. Who knows if perhaps you were made queen for just such a time as this?

Esther 4:14 (NLT)

Young girls like to pretend that they are a princess or a queen. They dress up in fancy dresses, lots of jewelry, and a glittery crown. They have lots of fun, but it's just make-believe.

Sometimes real life can seem like make-believe. During a time when the people of Israel lived in exile in Persia, Xerxes became the king of Persia. When Xerxes grew angry with his wife and searched for a new one, a beauty contest was held—but not like the ones shown on television. Many young women were brought before him. But Xerxes chose Esther, a Jewish woman. Esther had been raised by her relative Mordecai, who warned her not to tell anyone that she was Jewish.

Haman, one of the king's officers hated Mordecai and all the Jewish people so much that he wanted to kill them. Mordecai heard about the plot and told Esther to talk to the king about it, but Esther was frightened. No one was allowed to approach the king without first submitting a written request—not even the queen. Disobeying this rule could result in death. Or the king could save the offending person by holding out his scepter. Esther knew she was risking her life, but went anyway.

The king offered to give Esther anything she wanted. She told Xerxes that she was Jewish and asked that Haman's evil plan would not be carried out. Xerxes made a new law saying that the Jews could defend themselves against their enemies.

By her courage, Esther saved her people from death. A new holiday—Purim—was established in honor of the courage of a queen.

GO TO THE EXTREME

• **Persia** is modern-day Iran.

• **There** is a story that King Xerxes captured a Greek diver and sent him to recover treasures from sunken Persian ships. This diver must have been able to hold his breath for a long time!

• **To** this day the Jews celebrate Purim, an annual feast in memory of Esther. The book of Esther is read aloud and many more recent miracles of deliverance are remembered.

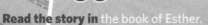

72

Read the story in the book of Esther.

JOKE ALERT!

Here's something you won't find in the Bible:

Haman thought Mordecai was napping that fateful afternoon because he heard Mordecai say that he was going to "see Esther" (siesta).

Son of Encouragement

There was Joseph, the one the apostles nicknamed Barnabas (which means "Son of Encouragement"). He was from the tribe of Levi and came from the island of Cyprus.

Acts 4:36 (NLT)

Ever feel down in the dumps about something? Maybe you flunked a math test or weren't chosen for a part in the school play. Or perhaps you are having a rough time at home. That's the time that you really need a good friend who will listen and encourage you. To encourage someone means to spur someone on—to inspire someone or give him or her hope. Are you an encourager?

All the believers in the early church agreed in heart and mind. They didn't claim that anything they had was their very own—they shared everything. Because of this there were no needy persons among them.

Joseph, a disciple in the early church, was nicknamed Barnabas. The name Barnabas means "Son of Encouragement." He was called that because he had the ability to encourage those who were down. Barnabas was also very generous. He sold a field he owned and gave all the money to the church to be used where needed.

Barnabas joined Paul and they became missionaries traveling to many places spreading the good news about Jesus. They worked together for a year. Missionary work was hard—walking great distances, being disliked by the Jewish leaders, and having no money. Barnabas had to be an encourager to Paul and himself!

Go to the Extreme

- **A** group called The Barnabas Group (TBG), which began in 2000 sends its members to work with ministries around the world.

- **According** to archaeologists, Cyprus used to have dwarf hippos and dwarf elephants. They seem to have disappeared when humans arrived on the island.

- **Also** on Cyprus, archaeologists discovered a grave with an eight-month-old cat buried with its human owner.

Read the story in Acts 4:32-37.

Try This

He began to speak boldly in the synagogue. When Priscilla and Aquila heard him, they invited him to their home and explained to him the way of God more adequately.
Acts 18:26 (NIV)

Have you ever made something and it just didn't turn out quite right? Of course, reading the directions always helps! Maybe one ingredient was missing in the cookies you baked. Or the wheels on the model car wobbled. Then someone came along and said, "Try doing it this way." You followed their suggestion and everything turned out great.

Priscilla and Aquila were husband and wife missionaries. They lived, worked, and traveled with Paul, becoming his good friends and coworkers. Paul lived with them for about a year and a half. Then they started out with Paul on a missionary trip, but stopped in the city of Ephesus.

At that time Apollos came to Ephesus. He was educated, knew the Bible very well, and taught with great power. He taught the truth about Jesus, but didn't know anything about the Holy Spirit. Priscilla and Aquila heard Apollos speaking in the synagogue, so they invited him to their home and gave him a better understanding of the way of God.

GO TO THE EXTREME

• **Paul,** Priscilla, and Aquila were tentmakers. The tents were most likely made from leather and goats' hair and could be of various colors and shapes.

• **Priscilla** is on the short list of possible author names for the Letter to the Hebrews (along with Paul and Apollos).

• **The** kinds of tents used in Bible times were much larger than what we think of today, because people actually lived in them. They often had a front area where people could visit (like a living room), and then a back area separated by fabric walls where the family lived and slept.

JOKE ALERT!

Here's something you won't find in the Bible:

Priscilla and Aquila's vanity plate was N 10SE
("in tents," see Acts 18:1–3).

74

Read the story in Acts 18:24–28.

DASTARDLY Villains

Quick! Name a villain in a book or a movie! Whether you say Voldemort, Cruella de Vil, or Darth Vader, chances are you can easily name at least one villain within a millisecond. The battle between good and evil wouldn't happen without a villain. The fact that there are villains at all is due to the oldest story in the world—the fall of Satan from heaven. This former angel of light became the stamp from which the mold of the villain was made.

The Bible has tons of stories of villains. They remind us that, sadly, all of us were once villains to God. Because of the Savior, we don't have to play that role anymore. But for the individuals on the following pages, the role of villain is what made them infamous.

Blood That Spoke Louder Than Words

The LORD said, "What have you done? Listen! Your brother's blood cries out to me from the ground."
Genesis 4:10 (NIV)

Have you ever wanted to be a detective, to be called in to investigate a crime and figure out who the bad guy is? Holding your magnifying glass you would carefully search for clues. Maybe you would find some fingerprints, a hair, or even traces of blood, which would lead you to consider who the suspect might be.

When Cain killed his brother Abel, he probably never realized that the best detective in the universe would find him out. After Abel's offering to God—the firstborn from his flock—had been accepted and his own (crops) rejected, Cain's anger burned out of control. He invited his brother for a nice walk in the field only to murder him in cold blood. His action made him the first murderer.

At first, Cain thought his plan was so simple. No one else was there. No one else had seen, right? Yet Abel's spilled blood did not go unnoticed. God saw. And as punishment, Cain was sent away from God's presence to become a wanderer for the rest of his life.

GO TO THE EXTREME

• **Hundreds** of years later, Cain's great-great-great-grandson followed in his steps and killed a man (see Genesis 4:23–24).

• **The** earliest example of a murder mystery/detective story is the tale called "The Three Apples" told by Scheherazade in *One Thousand and One Nights* (also known as *Arabian Nights*). In this story, a fisherman discovers a locked chest, sells it, and when it is opened, the dismembered body of a young woman is discovered. A man is sent to solve the crime within three days or be executed himself.

• **Forensics** is one of the best uses of science to help solve crimes.

JOKE ALERT!

Laconic Limerick:

There once were two sons
at the table
who wanted the favorite label.
But missing the mark,
Cain struck in the dark,
knowing he just wasn't Abel.

Read the story in Genesis 4.

A Cloaked Lie

One day, however, no one else was around when he went in to do his work. She came and grabbed him by his cloak.

Genesis 39:11-12 (NLT)

C'mon, it'll be fun!" your friend assures you. "No," you reply, "stealing is wrong."

"What, are you chicken? Besides we could use some more video games." You refuse again, but while you're not looking, your friend slips a video game into your backpack. As you both walk out of the store, the alarm is activated, your bags are searched and you're the one who gets blamed! Some friend!

In Egypt lived a woman who acted like that friend, only far worse. Her husband, Potiphar, had put a Hebrew slave by the name of Joseph in charge of everything he owned. Joseph was considered hot; he was well built and handsome. Unfortunately for him, Potiphar's wife thought so and wanted Joseph to make out with her. But Joseph said no. She tried again and again, but Joseph remained loyal to God and to his master.

Then one day Potiphar's wife found Joseph all alone in the house. She thought this was her chance. When Joseph refused her yet again, she grabbed hold of his cloak in desperation. Joseph slipped out of his cloak and ran out the door. In that instant Potiphar's wife hatched an evil scheme. She showed the cloak to her husband and with a sinister lie told him that Joseph had tried to take advantage of her. Potiphar was furious and Joseph ended up in prison for a crime he didn't commit.

GO TO THE EXTREME

- **In** ancient Egypt, there was no such thing as lawyers who would represent an accused person. Joseph couldn't have gotten a lawyer if he'd wanted to!

- **It's** estimated that about 10,000 people in the United States may be wrongfully convicted of serious crimes each year. Most often the problem is eyewitness misidentification.

- **Sometimes** being honest and doing the right thing is the hardest thing of all.

77

Read the story in Genesis 39.

A Heart of Stone Can't Float

When Pharaoh saw that there was a respite, he hardened his heart and would not listen to them, as the LORD had said.
Exodus 8:15 (ESV)

GO TO THE EXTREME

- **The** deadliest disaster in recent history was the flooding of China in 1931 where up to four million died!

- **The** plagues could be seen as God's way to show the powerlessness of Egypt's gods—for example, they worshiped the god of the Nile (who couldn't keep the river safe), a cow goddess (who couldn't protect livestock), a sun god (who couldn't stop the darkness).

- **Scientists** have tried to explain away all of these events, but the point is that God made sure that each happened directly at Moses' command.

Some of us just have to learn the hard way. Warned not to do this or that, we go ahead anyway and then the trouble begins. And we wish we had listened better.

That was certainly true of one king who ruled Egypt a long time ago. This king was one stubborn dude. When God sent Moses to order him to let the Israelite slaves go, he refused. So God sent a few "minor" catastrophes his way. The river turned to blood, frogs hopped through homes, gnats and flies swarmed as thick as dust. All the domestic animals keeled over dead; nasty, oozing boils covered the people's bodies; the worst hailstorm in Egypt's history crushed crops along with anyone out in the fields. Still the king's heart remained as hard as granite.

After being threatened with a plague of locusts, the king's officials tried to persuade him to back down, but to no avail. His stubbornness meant that everything green was eaten by the insects. Then came darkness so thick it could be felt. Yet the worst was yet to come. In one terrible night the king's heart of stone was finally broken as he woke to find that his own son was dead, along with all firstborn sons of Egypt.

You'd think that would have been enough, but it wasn't. After freeing the Israelites, he decided to chase after them. As a result, he and his entire army wound up dead—washed up along the shore of the Red Sea—while the people of Israel escaped on dry land.

7 8

Read the story in Exodus 5—14.

JOKE ALERT!

Pharaoh's pet peeves:

- *With the river all bloody, his weekend cruise down the Nile was ruined.*

- *He couldn't beat Moses in thumb-wrestling.*

- *Moses and Aaron tracked sand all over the palace.*

- *People who try to sign him up for pyramid schemes.*

A Deadly Date

She said to him, "How can you say, 'I love you,' when your heart is not with me? You have mocked me these three times, and you have not told me where your great strength lies."

Judges 16:15 (ESV)

Did you ever lie awake at night, wondering if that special somebody has a crush on you? Love, or in this case infatuation, can be a powerful thing. It certainly was in the case of Samson. Samson was no ordinary man. God had given him superhuman strength. With his bare hands, he tore to pieces an attacking lion. He caught 300 foxes, tied flaming torches to their tails and let them run wild through the wheat fields of Israel's enemy, the Philistines.

But even a superhero sometimes has a weakness. Superman had kryptonite. Samson's weakness was women. He went from one relationship to another. In the end, it would be his downfall.

One day a woman by the name of Delilah caught his eye. And like a moth attracted to a bug zapper, Samson was attracted by her beauty. He didn't know Delilah's sinister side. Having been offered a whole pile of silver by the Philistine rulers, Delilah set out to discover the secret of Samson's great strength in order to trap him. Samson lied to her three times before she finally wore him down with her constant nagging. One night, with Samson asleep on her lap, Delilah had his hair cut off. His strength left him and he was taken captive by the Philistines. Samson, the mighty one who had killed a thousand men with the jawbone of a donkey, was in the end brought down by a single woman.

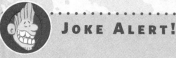

JOKE ALERT!

Samson should have been alerted to the problem right away. After all, the woman's name was **"De-li-lah"** (de-**lie**-lah).

GO TO THE EXTREME

- **One** of the strongest men in recent history was Paul Anderson, a Christian, who could bench press over 400 pounds!

- **The** most well-known work about a barber is *The Barber of Seville,* an opera by Gioachino Rossini (libretto by Cesare Sterbini).

- **If** you offer a bribe to someone (like a public official), you could land in prison for a couple of years.

Read the story in Judges 16.

A Sinister Seductress

There was never anyone like Ahab, who sold himself to do evil in the eyes of the LORD, urged on by Jezebel his wife.

1 Kings 21:25 (NIV)

If you're a girl, are you aware of the kind of spell you might cast over a boy, for better or for worse? If you're a guy, you've got to admit that a girl can have a pretty big influence in your life. She can inspire you to acts of either great bravery or complete foolishness.

Of all the wicked women mentioned in the Bible, probably none influenced her man as negatively as Jezebel did. Born a princess in a pagan nation, she was given in marriage to Ahab, king of Israel. And she at once began to have a negative effect on her husband (who was pretty rotten himself). Ahab had a temple built for her god, Baal, and allowed her to bring in 450 prophets of Baal and 400 prophets of the goddess Asherah. Jezebel enjoyed her position of power and used it for evil, killing off many of God's prophets. Even the great prophet Elijah ran in fear from her. Perhaps her most dastardly act was having a man by the name of Naboth stoned to death simply for refusing to sell his vineyard to her husband, the king.

But like many evil villains, Jezebel's life came to a gruesome end. For that story, read "A Queen's Downfall" in What a Way to Go! (page 30).

GO TO THE EXTREME

• **The** name Jezebel is considered a name that means evil. In fact, in the New Testament, the book of Revelation refers to a future evil person as Jezebel (see Revelation 2:20).

• **Lizzie** Borden became infamous for being accused of murdering her father and stepmother with a hatchet. She was acquitted at her trial, however.

• **Because** she was part of the conspiracy to kill Abraham Lincoln, Mary Surratt became the first woman executed in the United States.

JOKE ALERT!

Biblical "remember whens":

• **Eve**—*"I remember when finding an outfit to wear took no time at all."*

• **Solomon**—*"I remember when married life was simple."*

• **Zacchaeus**—*"I remember coining the term 'shortchanged.'"*

Read the story in 1 Kings 16:29-34; 18—21; 2 Kings 9.

A Bully Finds Forgiveness

Manasseh also murdered many innocent people until Jerusalem was filled from one end to the other with innocent blood.

2 Kings 21:16 (NLT)

Most of us can probably think of at least one bully we know: someone who's just plain mean; someone who picks on others to make themselves look better; someone who preys on the innocent.

A long time ago a twelve-year-old boy became king and grew up to be one of the worst bullies of his time. His name was Manasseh, and he ruled the nation of Judah for fifty-five years. Not only did Manasseh bring his country back into idol worship, but we're also told that he killed so many innocent people that the city of Jerusalem was practically filled with their blood!

Manasseh got some of his own medicine, though, when the Assyrians captured him, put a hook through his nose, and led him in chains to Babylon. Amazingly, he felt sorry for everything he had done and asked God to forgive him. What's even more amazing is that God gave him a second chance, and allowed him to return to his palace in Jerusalem. From then on, Manasseh made an effort to do things God's way. Even the worst bully isn't beyond God's reach!

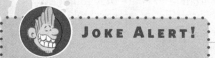

JOKE ALERT!

Here are some Old Testament names that probably shouldn't be used for a child since they name some not-so-nice folks:

Achan *(Joshua 7)*

Sisera *(Judges 4)*

Ichabod *(1 Samuel 4:21)*

Jezebel *(1 Kings 16—21)*

Manasseh *(2 Kings 21)*

Sanballat *(Nehemiah 4)*

Pashhur *(Jeremiah 20)*

Oholah *(Ezekiel 23:4)*

Gomer *(Hosea 1)*

GO TO THE EXTREME

- **Putting** a hook through a prisoner's mouth or nose or gouging out his eyes was common practice among the ancient Assyrians.

- **Bullyingstatistics.org** estimates that each day 160,000 children miss school because of bullying.

- **More** than one in three people have experienced bullying online—called cyberthreats.

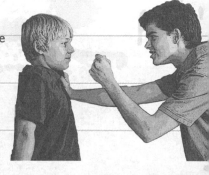

Read the story in 2 Kings 21; 2 Chronicles 33.

A Crazed King

A voice was heard in Ramah, weeping and loud lamentation, Rachel weeping for her children; she refused to be comforted, because they are no more.
Matthew 2:18 (ESV)

GO TO THE EXTREME

- **Herod** was a madman, but he was also an incredible builder. His projects included the port city of Caesarea and the fortress Masada.

- **El** *dia de los reyes magos* (Day of the Three Kings) is celebrated in Spanish-speaking countries on January 6. Children wake up to find gifts placed in their shoes.

- **Some** believe the star of Bethlehem may have been the crossing of paths of two or three planets.

Have you ever been suspicious of somebody? Maybe you wondered if that classmate of yours got the best grades in class because he cheated. Or maybe your new iPod went missing and you were certain somebody stole it.

Of all the kings in history, Herod the Great has got to be number one when it comes to suspicion. His paranoia over who might try to rob him of his crown drove him insane. He murdered some of his own sons and even one of his wives because of it! So just imagine how upset he was when some strangers showed up at his palace, claiming to have seen a star that pointed the way to where the King of the Jews was to be born!

When asked for directions, Herod managed to mask his anxiety long enough to have his scholars point the foreigners to Bethlehem. There they found the child, Jesus, with his mother. After worshiping the boy king, the men were about to go inform Herod when God warned them not to in a dream. They took God's advice and bypassed the palace. Herod was so furious when he found out he had been outwitted that he had his soldiers march down to Bethlehem and kill every boy two years old and under! Jesus and his family managed to escape to Egypt, and stayed there until the maniacal king died.

JOKE ALERT!

Possible reasons why the Magi took over a year to arrive in Bethlehem:

- *Got stuck in the drive-thru at Burger Pharaoh.*

- *Wanted to wait for Jesus to be out of the manger due to Gaspar's allergy to hay.*

- *Couldn't decide whether to bring gold, frankincense, and myrrh—or an iPod, a Wii, and a new laptop.*

Read the story in Matthew 2.

A Gruesome Gift

Prompted by her mother, she answered, "Give me John the Baptist's head here on a platter!"
Matthew 14:8 (HCSB)

What's the worst gift you've ever received? Maybe it was a little kid's toy that you were way too old to be interested in. Whatever that gift may have been, it was probably nowhere near as terrible or as repulsive as the one Herodias was given. Herodias was one mean lady, but that's not surprising when you realize how dysfunctional her family was. Her grandfather, Herod the Great, had murdered her father along with some other relatives. Herodias was first married to her uncle Philip, but later became the wife of Philip's brother, Herod Antipas.

John the Baptist was brave enough to let Herodias know her actions were wrong, yet that led to his imprisonment. Herodias wanted John to be put to death, but Herod was unwilling to go that far. It was only a matter of time, however, before she got what she wished for.

Her daughter danced for Herod and his guests one night and pleased the ruler so much that he promised to give her whatever she wanted. The girl went to her mother for suggestions (bad idea!). Herodias seized the opportunity and had her daughter ask for John's head on a platter. Herod was stuck. He didn't want to have John killed, yet he couldn't go back on his word, especially not in front of his guests. So John was beheaded, and Herodias was given the gruesome gift.

GO TO THE EXTREME

- **The** guillotine (a contraption with a sharp blade that dropped from above and would cut off a person's head) was invented in France and used there for capital punishment until 1977.

- **Throughout** history people have claimed to have found and then lost the head of John the Baptist. A skull is on display in Rome that is reportedly his.

- **Beheading** during John's time was likely done by ax or sword.

JOKE ALERT!

Indications your small-group Bible study/Sunday school class is in trouble:

- *When you ask for favorite verses, quotes come from Benjamin Franklin, the Koran, and the book of Hesitations.*

- *Half the group shows up just in time for refreshments.*

- *Everyone is pretty sure that Jerry and Ray Aboam were brothers (see 1 Kings 11:26—14:31).*

Read the story in Matthew 14:1–12.

The Kiss That Cut Deep

The traitor, Judas, had given them a prearranged signal: "You will know which one to arrest when I greet him with a kiss."
Matthew 26:48 (NLT)

Think for a minute about your friends. What would life be like without them? Having a good group of friends is important. They help us through the rough times, and they add a lot of joy to our lives. Unfortunately, they can also do a lot of harm.

No one knows this better than Jesus. He had a great group of friends. There were twelve in particular who were very close. These men followed him everywhere. They were with him in his moments of joy like when he rode into Jerusalem to shouts of praise. They were with him in his moments of great sadness, like when he heard that John the Baptist had been killed (Matthew 14). The closeness of Jesus' friendship with the twelve must have made it that much harder when one of them betrayed him.

Judas Iscariot: We know him as the one who betrayed Jesus with a kiss. Why? Was it greed? Was it because Jesus didn't meet his expectations of how Messiah ought to behave? Whatever the reason, Judas's story must be one of the saddest in Scripture. He sold Jesus out to the religious leaders for thirty pieces of silver.

Christ had to go to the cross in order to free us from our sins, but how tragic that it was Judas, one of the twelve, who handed him over. One might wonder if that kiss given by a friend didn't hurt Jesus more than the nails driven by an enemy.

GO TO THE EXTREME

- **In** his book, *Peace Child,* Don Richardson tells of how Judas was at first a hero to some of the people in the jungles of Indonesia, who held the act of treachery in high esteem.

- **Judas's** life came to a gory end. We are told that he hanged himself; we are also told that when his body hit the ground, it burst open and his guts spilled out (see Acts 1:18)!

- **Some** of the most infamous betrayers in history include Julius and Ethel Rosenberg, Benedict Arnold, and Ikuko Toguri (Tokyo Rose).

JOKE ALERT!

You may think Judas made a strange disciple, but maybe there were some other rejected disciples:
- *Raul the Goat Herder*
- *Jose the Caesarean Jailer*
- *Marcus the Gravedigger*
- *Scully the Gourmet Ship Cook*
- *Pablo the Most Excellent Tailor*
- *Fred the Fearless Gladiator*
- *Big Vinnie the Grape Stomper*

Read the story in Matthew 26:14—27:10; Luke 22:1-5.

NA**ME** That Tune

You don't have to be a fan of *American Idol* to know that music has an important place in people's lives. Songs and various tunes are important in the Bible as well. The book of Psalms is a book full of songs! But you can find songs sprinkled throughout the Bible. Like many songs throughout the history of the world, songs were used to catalogue victories, defeats, funerals, and life in general. They show the emotions we've all felt: joy, sorrow, hurt, pride, and so on. But most of all, many of the songs in the Bible were worship songs to the one who is always worth singing about: God.

As you read these stories, you might find yourself humming along. Even if you can't name that tune, you can name the truth that each story reveals: An awesome God gives the heart a song you just can't help singing.

Song at the River

Moses and the people of Israel sang this song to the LORD: "I will sing to the LORD, for he has triumphed gloriously; he has hurled both horse and rider into the sea."

Exodus 15:1 (NLT)

Has music ever helped you sort out your feelings when you've been frustrated, angry, hurt, or depressed? How about when you're excited, hopeful, or relieved? Music can be a great way to relieve tension.

Put yourself for a moment in the shoes of one of the Israelites just after they had crossed the Red Sea. One day you're trapped between a great body of water and Pharaoh's revenge-seeking army; the next morning you're on the other side of the sea and your enemies are gone. Wow! How are you supposed to sort that one out in your head?

After witnessing this incredible act of God on their behalf, Moses and the Israelites used music to express the sense of exhilaration, gratitude, and relief they felt. "I will sing to the LORD," they cried out, "for he has triumphed gloriously; he has hurled both horse and rider into the sea" (Exodus 15:1). The people had been awed by God's power in bringing terrible plagues on Egypt, but parting the waters of the sea and drowning Pharaoh's army in it was just mind boggling! "The LORD is a warrior," they cheered, "Yahweh is his name!" (15:3).

GO TO THE EXTREME

• **The** Exodus story is sung before the Passover meal in Jewish tradition.

• **The** Red Sea may get its name from a type of algae that grows in it and whose blooms turn a reddish color after dying.

• **Too** bad Pharaoh wasn't as good a swimmer as Suzie Maroney, an Australian who swam 122 miles from Mexico to Cuba without the aid of flippers!

JOKE ALERT!

In addition to singing, Moses could have increased morale by calling the wilderness expedition **SAND:**

Strategic

Advance to

New

Destination

Or **SPUDS:**

Special

People

Urging

Deliverance from

Slavery

Read the story in Exodus 15.

A Thirst-Quenching Song

Then Israel sang this song: Spring up, well—sing to it! The princes dug the well; the nobles of the people hollowed it out with a scepter and with their staffs.
Numbers 21:17–18 (HCSB)

When was the last time you were thirsty? Not just hankering for a sip of something cold and fizzy, but so thirsty that your tongue stuck to the roof of your mouth like the marshmallow center sticks to a graham cracker in a s'more. At that moment, with no vending machine in site, you would have done anything for a sip of water.

After wandering around in the wilderness for years, the Israelites knew all about being thirsty. Imagine thousands of people trudging day after day through sun-scorched lands. How would they find enough to drink?

God provided in many different ways, like causing water to flow from a rock. In this case, God led the people to a well. We're not told exactly how this well got there, but what we do know is that the people were so happy to have drinking water that they praised the well in song! Seem funny to you? What if you were to go a day or two without anything to drink? You might just find yourself breaking into song about that faucet in your kitchen sink!

GO TO THE EXTREME

- **A** person can only survive from three to five days without water under normal conditions.

- **Up** to three-fourths of your body is made up of water.

- **Seventy-one** percent of the earth's surface is water.

JOKE ALERT!

One Israel noble: "Well, well, well, what have we here?"

Another: "Yes, and when you get to the bottom of it, you're all wet!"

Another: "What a dig!"

8 7

Read the story in Numbers 21:16–18.

Song for a Son

Hannah prayed and said, "My heart exults in the LORD; my strength is exalted in the LORD."
1 Samuel 2:1 (ESV)

Did your parents burst into song when you were born? That's not something you'd remember of course, since you were a baby. But would you expect a parent to start singing just when she's about to give up her son? Hannah did. Here's why.

In Bible times, a woman who could not have a child felt a great deal of humiliation. Hannah, who was married to a man named Elkanah, was not able to have children. But Elkanah had another wife, Peninnah, who could. Peninnah made fun of Hannah, which made things worse.

Every year at the tabernacle, Hannah would pray for a child. She even told God that she would give her son to him if he granted her desire. One day when she was crying and silently praying, Eli the high priest accused her of being drunk. But once Hannah explained why she prayed, Eli gave his approval to her prayer.

God also agreed with Hannah's prayer. A year later, she gave birth to a son and named him Samuel. When he was still a small child, Hannah gave him to Eli to serve God at the tabernacle. The fact that God had answered her prayer gave her a reason to sing.

GO TO THE EXTREME

- **As** of 1999, the modern world record for giving birth belonged to Leontina Albina of San Antonio, Chile, who had sixty-four children.

- **Hannah** describes God as a "rock." Many years later, David would do the same (see "A Song of Gratitude," page 91).

- **This** song is known as the "Magnificat of the Old Testament." Mary's song in "Mary Rejoices" (page 93) is known as the Magnificat of the New Testament.

JOKE ALERT!

What was Hannah's favorite holiday?
Answer: *Labor Day*

Read the story in 1 Samuel 1—2.

Old Time Rock and Roll

Whenever the spirit from God came on Saul, David would take up his lyre and play. Then relief would come to Saul; he would feel better, and the evil spirit would leave him.
1 Samuel 16:23 (NIV)

What kind of music do you listen to when you need to relax? While everyone has his or her own tastes, most would agree that certain music—in the words of a classic rock song by Bob Seger—"soothes the soul."

This was true, also, in the ancient world. We are told that king Saul had a spirit from God that would come upon him and torment him. Some of his servants suggested sending for a good musician. So a young shepherd by the name of David was brought in to play the harp. David was not your average harpist. We are told that he was not only good looking and a talented musician, he was also a fighter. He had already killed lions and bears which had attacked his father's flocks, and he was soon to slay Goliath, the giant whom nobody else was brave enough to face.

As it turned out, all of David's talents came in handy while serving as court musician. His harp playing did indeed soothe the king's spirit. But eventually Saul became jealous of the youth, and David had to make use of his quick reflexes and dive out of the way as Saul attempted twice to skewer him with his spear. (For that story, see "David's Great Escapes" in Great Escapes, page 124.) You might even say that David was the very first rock and *roll* musician!

GO TO THE EXTREME

- **Some** people claim that plants grow better with soothing, classical music.

- **Variations** of the harp have been played since ancient times and may have developed from plucking the string of a warrior's bow.

- **Music** was used to aid recovering soldiers in England following both world wars.

- **Soft** music can also relax nervous and frightened animals, both wild and domestic.

JOKE ALERT!

Although David was handy with a harp, Saul soon chased him out of the palace. When that happened, what did he call his entourage?

Answer: *Banned, on the Run*

Read the story in 1 Samuel 16:23.

Dancing in the Street

David danced before the LORD with all his might, wearing a priestly garment.

2 Samuel 6:14 (NLT)

Dancing can be a great way to celebrate. But in order to do it right, you've got to loosen up and not worry about who may be watching. You have to be willing to make a fool of yourself.

When King David had the ark of God brought into the royal city of Jerusalem, he had good reason to celebrate. After years of running from his enemy, Saul, David had finally become king of all Israel. He had also recently captured the city of Jerusalem and established it as his home. Now he was bringing in the ark—the symbol of God's presence with his people.

As David accompanied the ark, he danced wildly. He wanted to express his joy as well as worship the God who had done so much for him. You would think that such a powerful man—a man who had the respect of a whole nation—would want to carry himself with a bit more dignity as he proudly brought home Israel's greatest treasure. But no, David wasn't in the least bit concerned about what people thought of him. As he jumped and sang and shouted with all his might, he knew just who he was dancing for: his God!

GO TO THE EXTREME

• **The** game *Dance Dance Revolution* came to America from Japan in 1999 and has even been included in some schools' physical education classes.

• **Nobody** knows for sure what became of the Ark of the Covenant after the Babylonians destroyed the temple in Jerusalem in 586 BC. Claims have been made regarding its presence in various locations such as Ethiopia, Southern Africa, Italy, France, the United Kingdom, and even America!

JOKE ALERT!

David was dancing "with all his might," so he may have been doing one of these dances:

- *The Hokey Clokey*
- *The Hinky Kingy*
- *The Funky Fattened Calf*
- *The Electric Leap*
- *The Priestly Pony*
- *The Jericho Walz*
- *The Arkarena*
- *The Jertwistalum*

Read the story in 2 Samuel 6:14–22.

A Song of Gratitude

The LORD is my rock, my fortress, and my deliverer, my God, my mountain where I seek refuge.
2 Samuel 22:2–3 (HCSB)

Does life ever feel like a constant battle for you? You struggle with your parents, with your own feelings, with temptation. You may feel completely helpless and in desperate need of someone who'll step in and save you.

David sure felt that way. If there was ever a man who knew what it was like to live as a fugitive in need of rescue, it was him. Anointed as king over Israel, David spent years running from Saul before he could finally claim the throne. One of his most nerve-racking encounters with Saul happened in the desert of Maon. David and his men were running for their lives on one side of a mountain while Saul and his troops were on the other side. Saul was closing in fast, and it seemed as though all hope was gone. Suddenly a messenger came and informed Saul of an attacking Philistine army. At the last moment, Saul broke the pursuit and turned to go after the Philistines. (See 1 Samuel 23:24–29.) Talk about a close call with death!

It was experiences like this one that inspired David to compose his song to the Lord, recorded in 2 Samuel 22. During the darkest moments of his life, David found God to be the hero he so desperately needed.

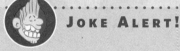

JOKE ALERT!

David wrote his song of deliverance. Here are some other songs to match various occupations:

THE DENTIST'S HYMN:
"Crown Him with Many Crowns"

THE METEOROLOGIST'S HYMN:
"There Shall Be Showers of Blessing"

THE CONTRACTOR'S HYMN:
"The Church's One Foundation"

THE GOLFER'S HYMN:
"There Is a Green Hill Far Away"

THE OPTOMETRIST'S HYMN:
"Open Mine Eyes That I Might See"

THE SALESPERSON'S HYMN:
"Sweet By and By"

GO TO THE EXTREME

- **"The** Battle Hymn of the Republic," a praise hymn written by Julia Ward Howe, debuted in 1862 during the Civil War.

- **David's** battle against Goliath is well known. But did you know that David's nephew Jonathan killed his own giant—one who had twenty-four fingers and toes? (See 1 Chronicles 20:6–7.) Apparently, giant slaying ran in the family!

- **The** world's highest rock face is the Rupal Flank of Nanga Parbat, a mountain in the Himalayans (Pakistan). This rock face is 15,000 feet above ground.

Read the story in 2 Samuel 21:20—23:23.

Song for a Warrior God

The stouthearted were stripped of their spoil; they sank into sleep; all the men of war were unable to use their hands. At your rebuke, O God of Jacob, both rider and horse lay stunned.
Psalm 76:5–6 (ESV)

What gives you goose bumps every time you think of it? If you had been a Jew during the reign of Hezekiah, your biggest fear would likely have been that of the Assyrian army. The Assyrians were deadly. They were known for their aggressive attacks and ruthless treatment of their opponents. Often, their strategy was to first fire a barrage of arrows, then to send in war chariots, and finally the foot soldiers to take care of the rest of the terrified, scattered enemy.

With each victory, Sennacherib, king of Assyria, became more and more overconfident. One day he decided to send his men to mock the Israelites living in Jerusalem and to taunt their God. Big mistake! God saved his people. (For that story, see "An Army of One" in Ballistic Battles, page 17.)

Psalm 76, like many other psalms, is a song explaining how God fought for Israel and crushed the proud. It's a reminder that as long as Israel trusts in God, they have nothing to fear. For God is not only the God who chose them and the one who loves them; he is also the one who fights for them: their Warrior God.

GO TO THE EXTREME

- **If** you've been to a graduation, you've heard "Pomp and Circumstance," composed by Sir Edward Elgar. But "Pomp and Circumstance" is just one of an entire series of military marches.

- **The** Mongol army under Genghis Khan was another force that struck fear in the hearts of anyone in its path. The Mongols were known for wiping out whole populations of civilians as they advanced across Asia.

- **There** are many names given to God in Hebrew. *El Gibbor* refers to God as warrior.

92

Read the story in Psalm 76.

Mary Rejoices

Mary said: "My soul glorifies the Lord and my spirit rejoices in God my Savior, for he has been mindful of the humble state of his servant. From now on all generations will call me blessed."
Luke 1:46–48 (NIV)

What would you expect the mother of a king to be like? This isn't a trick question. Most of us would expect the mother of a king to have been a queen herself or at least someone very important. But the mother-to-be of the Messiah wasn't a queen or someone very important. She was a poor girl from a small town—someone you wouldn't notice.

Life for Mary used to be the same old same old. But when an angel showed up one day, her life would never be the same again. The angel, whose name was Gabriel, had incredible news: Mary would give birth to the Messiah long promised in the Scriptures! This baby would be God's Son! Whoa! This was big news!

But there was just one thing that Mary wanted to know: how could she have a baby when she wasn't married? She was engaged to Joseph, a carpenter. But, as Gabriel explained, nothing was impossible for God.

Mary accepted what the angel had told her, but it took a few days for her to sort it all out in her head. As it all began to sink in, Mary composed a song. She praised God for choosing her out of everyone else. He could have picked a woman from a wealthy family who lived in an important city. But no, he picked her—a poor, young woman who was willing to be the mother of the most important person of all—Jesus.

99

Read the story in Luke 1:46–55.

GO TO THE EXTREME

• **The** prophet Isaiah in the Old Testament predicted that an unmarried woman would give birth to a son (Isaiah 7:14).

• **The** name Mary is a form of Miriam (the name of Moses' sister) and possibly comes from an Egyptian word that means "beloved."

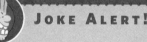

JOKE ALERT!

Possible reasons the inn was full on Christmas Eve:

1. It was offering a Weekend Special—kids and animals sleep for free.
2. It had experienced a surge in popularity since receiving the AAA four-camel rating.
3. It was the last exit before the next oasis.
4. The light was off at the nearest Motel 6.
5. Herod was sponsoring a weekend conference on stargazing.

A Song for the God of Impossibilities

You, my little son, will be called the prophet of the Most High, because you will prepare the way for the Lord. You will tell his people how to find salvation through forgiveness of their sins.
Luke 1:76–77 (NLT)

Certain things in life just seem impossible: flying to Mars; becoming the next famous celebrity; having a day at school where nothing goes wrong.

To a man named Zechariah, having a son to call his own was up there in the realm of impossibilities. He was too old. His wife was barren. It just wasn't going to happen.

But God thrives on impossibilities. He decided he was going to give Zechariah a son, and he sent an angel to tell him the exciting news. Zechariah, however, didn't believe: he said it would never happen. Not even God could intervene. So guess what happened? Zechariah walked away from the angel completely unable to speak. And nine months later he was holding a baby in his arms. God had done the impossible, and Zechariah had learned his lesson.

As soon as he wrote down the baby's name, John, Zechariah's mouth was opened and he could talk again. Full of joy, he sang out to God. He praised God for remembering his promise to the people of Israel, and he prophesied about what his son would do—how he would pave the way for God's Messiah. Sometimes God's miracles just leave us speechless!

GO TO THE EXTREME

• **Approximately** four hundred years passed from the time of the last Old Testament prophets to the time of John the Baptist. This period is known as the 400 years of silence.

• **The** angel Gabriel is known as a messenger: he brought news to Daniel, to Zechariah, and to Mary.

• **In** 2010, the 59-year-old wife of a 94-year-old man from India, Ramjit Raghav, gave birth to a son. This makes Raghav the world's oldest dad.

JOKE ALERT!

Speaking of childbirth, here's what *not* to say to a woman who is experiencing bad labor pains:

The Bible says, "A woman giving birth to a child has pain because her time has come; but when her baby is born she forgets the anguish because of her joy that a child is born into the world" (John 16:21, NIV).

(True, but not very helpful in the midst of labor.)

9 4

Read the story in Luke 1:57–79.

Love Song

*They sang a new song: You are worthy to take the scroll and to open its
seals; because You were slaughtered, and You redeemed [people] for God
by Your blood from every tribe and language and people and nation.*
                    Revelation 5:9 (HCSB)

Do you keep a journal? Do you write about that girl you'd like to talk to or
maybe that guy who broke your heart? Probably most of us have spent
some time wondering about what kind of love story will be written in the
book of our lives. The good news is that a beautiful love story *has* been written
for each of us already!

John caught a glimpse of that story while on the island of Patmos. Among the
visions he saw was one of four creatures and twenty four elders singing to
Jesus who appears as a slaughtered lamb. They praise
him for going to the cross and giving his own life so
that people "from every tribe and language" could be
"redeemed for God."

This song is just one verse in the incredible love
story that God has written for us. Each of us has sold
ourselves to sin, which ultimately leads to death and
separation from our Creator. But God's love for us was
so huge that he paid the absolute highest price to buy
us back—his own blood! Now that's a love story worth
singing about!

GO TO THE EXTREME

- **Christ** is compared
to a lamb elsewhere in
Scripture, the idea being
that he is our sacrifice, the
one who allows us to have
a right relationship with
God.

- **The** word *Revelation*
comes from the word
apocalypse which means
"unveiling" or "revealing."

- **One** of the most well-
known hymns about God's
grace is "Amazing Grace,"
written by John Newton, a
former slave trader.

JOKE ALERT!

Here's a vanity plate for the
apostle John on the
island of Patmos:

NSPYRD ("inspired")

Read the story in Revelation 5:8–9.

The Song of the Redeemed

They were singing a new song before the throne and before the four living creatures and before the elders. No one could learn that song except the 144,000 who had been redeemed from the earth.
Revelation 14:3 (ESV)

All good mysteries have something that really grabs our interest. It keeps us turning the page to find out what happens next; keeps us guessing until everything finally comes together at the end of the movie.

In the book of Revelation, God gives us a peek into how the world as we know it will end, but he doesn't tell us everything. Most of the details are still unknown. We're even told that one of the great songs yet to be sung is still a mystery. It's known as "the song of the redeemed."

Just the sound of this song will be incredible. John, who heard it in a vision, describes it as sounding like water rushing, thunder crashing, and harps playing—all at the same time! What a special experience for those who will get to sing it over and over. What a magnificent mystery it remains until then!

JOKE ALERT!

Pet peeves of the apostle John:

• *Always being listed third after Peter and James*

• *Loving music but can't sing*

• *You think Revelation is tough to read, you should have tried writing it.*

• *People thinking his last name is "Baptist" (and actually, that's the other John)*

• *People who skip to the end of Revelation and miss the other 21 chapters*

• *The elders at Ephesus selling the movie rights*

9 6

Read the story in Revelation 14:1–5.

GROSS and Gory

Are you the type of person who likes to eat with your mouth open to gross everybody out? Do you like looking at the weirdest and ickiest looking creatures? Maybe you even have a collection you're proud of. If gross and gory actions and stories are your thing, you've come to the right place. The Bible has some amazing stories, but also some stories that might turn even the strongest stomach. Have we intrigued you? Good. You don't have to uncover a slimy rock or check out the nearest dumpster. All you have to do is keep reading to discover these weird, wonderful, and ewww-nique stories of the Bible. But don't say we didn't warn you!

All the Blood You Can Drink?

The fish in the Nile died, and the river smelled so bad that the Egyptians could not drink its water. Blood was everywhere in Egypt.
Exodus 7:21 (NIV)

When you were younger baths were the last thing you wanted. In fact, you probably still aren't too wild about having to stop playing to go take one. Well, after all those times running out of the bathroom trying to escape Mom, imagine if this time she was the one running from bath time! It wouldn't be too hard to believe if there was blood coming out of the faucet!

If you think that would be bad, what do you think the Egyptians thought when *all* of their water turned to blood? We're talking lakes, rivers, wells, and even water already in the houses! When the pharaoh of Egypt told Moses that he wouldn't let the Israelites go, God was prepared with his first of ten plagues. God replied by turning all the water in Egypt into blood by a touch of Moses' staff. The Egyptians probably didn't miss bath time either, but with all the water turned to blood they definitely would have been thirsty!

When considering all the plagues of Egypt, turning water to blood isn't the most painful, but it certainly leaves a strong impression. It showed Egypt that water, their life source since they were surrounded by desert, was under God's control. And that God, not idols, was the most powerful of all.

GO TO THE EXTREME

• **Blood** leaves such a penetrating stain that some Native Americans used it for paint.

• **In** 1902, Karl Landsteiner, an Austrian-American pathologist (someone who studies diseases) discovered there are several types of human blood. He called these A, B, AB, O. Ask your parents what your blood type is.

• **If** all the blood vessels in your body were laid end to end, they would reach about 60,000 miles.

JOKE ALERT!

These standby plagues were *not* inflicted on Egypt:

• *Cause all second-born males to be picked last for kickball teams.*

• *Cause an infestation of nose-hair lice.*

• *Turn the Nile River into salsa and hide all the tortilla chips.*

• *Cause the land to be overrun by millions of ravenous, wild toy poodles.*

• *Turn all pyramids into Berry Blue Jell-O® Jigglers.*

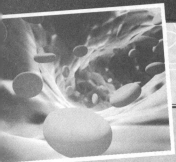

98

Read the story in Exodus 7:14-24.

Skin Deep

The LORD was very angry with [Aaron and Miriam], and he departed. As the cloud moved from above the Tabernacle, there stood Miriam, her skin as white as snow from leprosy.
Numbers 12:9-10 (NLT)

Ever had an itch that you have to keep scratching? Or maybe you're afraid of all the pimples you have or the ones you may get in the future. Skin is a big deal to us. It covers us from head to toe and it affects our looks and our comfort. Causing severe damage to your skin can be a life-changing experience, usually for the worst.

So how do you think Miriam felt when God decided to give her leprosy for disobeying him? She probably wasn't too happy—in fact, she was terrified. In those days, leprosy was a death sentence. People got sent away because leprosy could not be healed. Aaron and Miriam had turned against their brother Moses out of jealousy and selfishness. They thought that they were just as important as Moses, and that God spoke through them as well.

God disagreed, however. He came down in a pillar of cloud and caused Miriam's skin to become white—an unmistakable sign that he had given her the dreaded disease of leprosy. Moses and Aaron pleaded with God but, instead of healing her right away, God told Miriam to stay away from camp for seven days, and then she would be healed. In other words, Miriam got put in "time out."

When God punished Miriam it wasn't out of anger; it was to show her and her brother Aaron that Moses was the leader and would always be the leader.

GO TO THE EXTREME

- **Leprosy** is actually a disease that targets the parts of the nervous system that feel pain, causing skin decay, tissue loss, and numbness. A person with severe leprosy might literally lose a finger or toe and not even know it.

- **Because** of the lack of feeling that leprosy causes, lepers would often have festering wounds as well as other deformities. In ancient times, this led to them being sent away into leper colonies so as not to infect anyone else. Nowadays, medicine can treat leprosy.

- **Each** year there are about 200,000 new cases of leprosy, and many of them are due to the common or garden armadillo. Armadillos carry leprosy—and people often get it from eating armadillo. Ewww!

JOKE ALERT!

A verse *not* to use in a get-well card:

"From the sole of the foot even unto the head there is no soundness in it; but wounds, and bruises, and putrifying sores: they have not been closed, neither bound up, neither mollified with ointment" (Isaiah 1:6, KJV).

99

Read the story in Numbers 12:1–16.

Message Received

As the king rose from his seat, Ehud reached with his left hand, drew the sword from his right thigh and plunged it into the king's belly.
Judges 3:20-21 (NIV)

Movies with swordfights are really cool. But what makes them exciting is the speed. Our jaws drop when a sword seems to move faster than the speed of light. The hand being faster than the eye is the key to great action. When an action hero pulls a sword from nowhere, the movie can only get better.

What's true for action movies also works for Bible stories. The book of Judges is full of the gross and gory, but the story of Ehud is an action movie that comes out of nowhere.

GO TO THE EXTREME

• **The** sharpest swords could literally cut a person in half.

• **The** rest of the grossness of this story (it's right there in the Bible!) is that the king was so fat that Ehud stuck in the sword and the fat closed over the handle. Ehud just left his sword in the guy and ran, escaping through the bathroom!

• **Swords** are very thin but are actually made of several layers of material that are stretched out and folded back on themselves or welded together, depending on the sword-making technique.

When the Israelites stopped listening to God, he allowed an evil king (Eglon) to reign over them. Once they learned their lesson, God sent in his warrior: a man named Ehud. Ehud snuck a sword into the king's chamber, saying he had a message from God to tell the king. Everyone was sent out of the room. Before the king realized what was happening, Ehud—the action hero of this story—pulled his sword as if from nowhere and killed the king! Hidden swords and lightning fast reflexes? Pass the popcorn!

This story is thousands of years old, but it's the kind of action you'd expect from a movie in theatres today. The evil king got God's message alright, and the good guy won!

1 0 0

Read the story in Judges 3:12-26.

A Lion's Share ... of Honey?

[Samson] turned off the path to look at the carcass of the lion. And he found that a swarm of bees had made some honey in the carcass. He scooped some of the honey into his hands and ate it along the way.
Judges 14:8-9 (NLT)

Bee farms are pretty cool places. They aren't actually "farming" bees—although it works out that way—but they're farming honey. The bee farmer dresses in what looks like a white radiation suit, pulls out pieces of honeycomb from several stacks of drawers all while tons of bees swarm around him. It certainly doesn't look very normal.

Now imagine if these bee farmers were walking around scooping honey out of the carcasses of dead lions. Now *that* would be weird.

What would bees be doing around a lion's carcass anyway? It seems like a perfectly logical question, but it's one that Samson didn't even bother asking. Earlier, Samson had been walking along and gotten attacked by a lion! With his bare hands, he killed the lion. Later, walking that same path, he thought he'd check out the carcass. And he found all these bees buzzing around it. They had made some honey right there inside the carcass! Samson helped himself to handfuls of honey. He even brought some back for the folks. Even though Samson gave his parents some of the honey, he never told them where he got it. In this case ignorance might very well be the best option! If he had told them, their reaction would probably have been closer to your own, "Eww, gross!"

You probably won't find any jars of Lion Carcass Honey on your store shelf! We'll leave the honey making to the bees and the gathering to the bee farmers!

GO TO THE EXTREME

- **Bees** make honey through a process called regurgitation, which basically means they throw up their food to make honey!

- **Honeybees** are the only insect that produces food for humans—and they never sleep!

- **To** make one pound of honey, the bees in the colony will fly over 55,000 miles and visit about two million flowers.

JOKE ALERT!

Why did Samson kill the animal?
Answer: Because it was lion (lyin').

101

Read the story in Judges 14:5-9.

Split Decision

The king said, "Divide the living child in two, and give half to the one and half to the other."
1 Kings 3:24–25 (ESV)

When you were really little, you might have cried when one of your playmates had a toy and you wanted it. At that point, your parents probably talked to you about sharing before suggesting that they cut the toy down the middle and give you each half. If you tried, you could probably think of a couple toys that would still be fun if they were cut in half, like Silly Putty® or a box of Legos®. But something like a ball or a bike wouldn't work very well if you only had half!

When Solomon was confronted with two mothers fighting over a child, he was stuck in a similar situation. Each mother had a child, but one of the children had died. There was one child left and both mothers claimed the child was theirs. Solomon didn't know who was telling the truth, so he ordered the child to be cut in half and split between the two of them. He knew that the real mother would rather give up her child than have it die! So the mother who protested dividing the child in half would be the real mother—and that's exactly what happened.

Solomon was known for being a very wise king, and he understood how to solve this problem about who was telling the truth and who was the true mother of the child. It takes a lot of wisdom to be able to tell the truth from a lie!

GO TO THE EXTREME

• **This** story is so popular that it has been named "The Judgment of Solomon." It has been used by television writers and inspired painters, and has become a metaphor for a wise judge in the courtroom.

• **Solomon's** wisdom came as an answer to prayer. God told him he could have anything he wanted, and he asked for wisdom! Did you know that the Bible says that all you have to do is ask for wisdom and God will give it to you? Now *that's* awesome! (Read 1 Kings 3:9 and James 1:5.)

• **Solomon's** wisdom was so legendary that people came from all over the world to talk to him and ask him questions!

JOKE ALERT!

Top pet peeves of King Solomon:

1. *Having people ask, "If you're so smart, why haven't you been on Jeopardy?"*
2. *Finding Christmas cards large enough for the names of everyone in his family*
3. *Signing Christmas cards*
4. *Being a tourist attraction (1 Kings 4:34)*
5. *Not being able to find the tune to "Song of Solomon"*
6. *Having all those mothers-in-law*
7. *Not being able to laugh because he was so "Solomon" (solemn)*

Read the story in 1 Kings 3.

So Hungry I Could Eat . . . You

She answered, "This woman said to me, 'Give up your son so we may eat him today, and tomorrow we'll eat my son.' So we cooked my son and ate him. The next day I said to her, 'Give up your son so we may eat him,' but she had hidden him."
2 Kings 6:28–29 (NIV)

If you went one day without eating lunch you'd probably be really hungry. You might even tell your parents that you were "starving." What if they made you eat something you didn't like? How hungry would you have to be to eat something you didn't like?

If you think eating something you don't like is hard, imagine how much worse it would be if *you* were on the menu! During a famine, people haven't had breakfast, lunch, or dinner in weeks! When the city of Samaria was being taken over by King Ben-Hadad, the king of Aram, he blocked food from coming into the city, and this caused a great famine. Eventually all the food was gone and the people started trying to eat whatever they could. It became so bad that one woman gave up her son to be the next meal!

It's hard to believe that anyone would be hungry enough to eat her own child for lunch. The king couldn't believe it either when the woman told him. After all, some things should never be eaten, no matter how hungry you are.

GO TO THE EXTREME

- **Famine** occurs throughout history and still occurs today. In fact, it's estimated that by the year 2025 Africa will be able to feed only 25 percent of its population.

- **In** 1972, a plane with forty-five people on board crashed in the Andes mountains in South America. Sixteen people survived the crash, but search parties could not locate them. They had no food or heat for over two months and ended up eating the remains of those who had died in the crash in order to survive.

- **Today,** the Korowai of Papua, New Guinea, are one of very few tribes still believed to eat human flesh as a part of their culture.

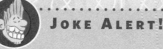

JOKE ALERT!

Some sports that could have been included in the Old Testament Olympics:

- *Lamb hurling*
- *Garment rending*
- *5,000 meter Dead Sea float*
- *Prophet chase (1 Kings 19:1–4)*
- *Downhill "shalom"*

1 0 3

Read the story in 2 Kings 6:24–29.

Good to the Bone

Once, as the Israelites were burying a man, suddenly they saw a marauding band, so they threw the man into Elisha's tomb. When he touched Elisha's bones, the man revived and stood up!
2 Kings 13:21 (HCSB)

You have bones connecting your entire body together. Bones are strong and they let you do all kinds of fun things like running and throwing. But what if they had the power to heal? It would be pretty cool if you could just touch someone in pain and heal him or her instantly!

Elisha helped people so much that even after he was dead, his bones were still on the job. A man was being buried by Israelites when they saw bad guys in the distance. They didn't have time to bury him, so they threw him into Elisha's tomb. When the body touched the bones of Elisha, the man immediately got to his feet and walked out of the tomb alive! Elisha was such a great prophet when he was alive that even after death his bones were still filled with God's power!

Some things as normal as your bones don't seem like anything special, but God thinks they are. He sees every part of you as special and wants to use them for his glory!

GO TO THE EXTREME

• **The** adult human body is made up of 206 bones. We actually are born with 300 bones, but as we grow up, many of the bones fuse together on their own.

• **The** strongest bone is the thighbone (called the femur). It's said to be as strong as concrete—yet it's hollow!

• **Daredevil** and motorcycle stunt driver Evel Knievel holds the Guinness World Record for the most broken bones at one time—35. Guess he must have missed that jump!

JOKE ALERT!

Note: Death can be such a let-down. Can you dig it?

Read the story in 2 Kings 13:21.

Boiling Point

Satan left the LORD's presence, and he struck Job with terrible boils from head to foot. Job scraped his skin with a piece of broken pottery as he sat among the ashes.

Job 2:7-8 (NLT)

In the summertime mosquitoes are everywhere. One or two mosquito bites aren't too bad. But when you have a whole bunch, you know how irritating that is. You scratch and scratch but that only makes it worse. Then maybe your mom puts on some medicine that's sticky and smelly, and it stings too! And all you can do is wait for the itching to stop. Sometimes it's hard to believe God made mosquitoes! What purpose do they serve except to sting us? And we didn't do anything to deserve it!

Satan wanted to torment Job, but he did worse than sending mosquitoes. You see, Job was a really good guy and Satan said that he could cause him to curse God if things got bad enough for Job. So God allowed Satan to torment Job. Satan killed his animals, then his children, and finally he gave Job awful boils all over his body! Job used a piece of broken pottery to scratch at his boils, but even in his pain he never cursed God. He knew that with all the good in life there is always bad as well.

Boils may be worse than mosquitoes, but having had itchy mosquito bites can give us an idea of what Job went through for his faith and trust in God. Sort of makes your mosquito bites a little more bearable, doesn't it?

JOKE ALERT!

Why did Job need his mouth washed out with soap very early?

Answer: "Job cursed the day he was born" (Job 3:3).

GO TO THE EXTREME

- **A** boil is an infection that starts in the skin and then creates pus that needs to be drained. They are very painful.

- **There** are more than 3,000 species of mosquitoes, with 170 different kinds in North America alone!

- **Mosquitoes** are attracted to some people more than others. Scientists think it probably has to do with some of the 300 or more chemicals our skin produces. So if you get lots of bites, consider yourself popular—with mosquitoes!

105

Read the story in Job 2:7-8.

Bare Naked Prophets

The LORD spoke through Isaiah son of Amoz. He said to him, "Take off the sackcloth from your body and the sandals from your feet." And he did so, going around stripped and barefoot.
Isaiah 20:2 (NIV)

Do you ever wonder why, when relatives show up, the first thing your mom pulls out is your baby book? But the worst part is when they get to the pictures of where you're naked! Sometimes they make you sit there with them. If you're lucky, you can escape before undergoing any more embarrassment.

GO TO THE EXTREME

- **When** the Olympics first started in ancient Greece in 776 B.C., all the athletes competed completely naked.

- **Fire** walking is walking barefoot over a bed of hot coals. This has been a part of many cultures going all the way back to around 1200 BC. It was often used as a rite of passage—a way of showing you're all grown up. Ouch!

- **Going** barefoot all the time could cause all manner of health problems like parasites coming in through cuts in your feet, hookworm larvae that can burrow through the skin of a bare foot, or athlete's foot fungus that spreads in the right kinds of moist areas (like in showers and locker rooms). So keep those feet clean!

Unfortunately for Isaiah, he couldn't run away when God told him to take off all his clothes and walk around naked. Not only that, but he had to do it for three years! And if that wasn't bad enough, God proclaimed the deed! Isaiah didn't like it any more than you would, but he obeyed God because he knew it was for a reason. As always, God had a very good reason: he was trying to warn the king of Assyria about the troubles that were coming for Egypt and Ethiopia. God had plenty of experience with kings who wouldn't listen to him, which is why he told his prophets to do weird and crazy things to get people's attention.

If your baby book is the center of attention when family visits, then Isaiah walking around the desert naked and barefoot for three years definitely would get the attention of a king!

JOKE ALERT!

Here's a Bible verse to *not place* over the entrance to a restaurant:

"All tables are full of vomit and filthiness, so that there is no place clean" (Isaiah 28:8, KJV).

Read the story in Isaiah 20:2-4.

The Head of the Party

[Herod] sent and had John beheaded in the prison, and his head was brought on a platter and given to the girl, and she brought it to her mother.
Matthew 14:10–11 (ESV)

On Thanksgiving everyone is so excited to eat all the food that they've been watching or smelling being prepared in the kitchen all day long. Even though there are many different Thanksgiving foods, most people expect to see a turkey. How strange would it be if your mom brought out somebody's head on a platter instead of the turkey? Now that would ruin everyone's appetite!

Well, the guests at Herod's birthday weren't expecting it either. In fact, they probably were just as shocked as you would be when John the Baptist's head was carried through the banquet hall on a tray. Herod had taken and married his brother's wife (which was very scandalous), and John the Baptist had been out preaching to people about repentance and talking about what Herod had done. As you can imagine, this didn't make Herod or his wife very happy at all. In fact, Herod's wife was so angry that she wanted John dead. So on Herod's birthday when Herod promised his daughter anything she wished, she asked for John's head (in other words, she wanted him killed and then his head brought in front of everyone to prove it). Forced to agree to her wishes, Herod had the head brought in on a tray to his daughter who then took it to her mother.

Herod had always respected John the Baptist. He didn't want to kill him, but he also didn't want his daughter to be upset. Thank goodness, today at Thanksgiving all people ask for is turkey!

GO TO THE EXTREME

• **The** average human head weighs 8–12 pounds. The average brain weighs 3.5 pounds, and the average skull weighs 2 pounds.

• **A** chicken can run around right after its head has been cut off, because the last message the brain sent to the nerves was to escape. The nerves do what the last message said, which is why a decapitated chicken runs madly around until its heart stops.

• **A** newborn's skull has gaps—soft spots. Those spots grow together and interlock like a jigsaw puzzle forming a solid skull.

Read the story in Matthew 14:1-12.

UNNATURAL Nature

What happens when you see something or someone act in an unpredictable way? We might immediately say, "Why, that's unnatural." Built into our thinking are rules for behavior and God's creation. You don't have to be an expert on the theories of Sir Isaac Newton or thermodynamics (a science that studies the relationship between heat and energy) to notice what's natural or unnatural. After all, there are many things we expect about nature. Based on the earth's orbit, we expect the sun to move from east to west across the sky. We expect birds to fly, and items that catch on fire to totally burn.

But an unlimited God isn't limited by the laws of science. Many individuals in the Bible learned that God sometimes allowed the unnatural to get people's attention.

"Flame On!"

The angel of the LORD appeared to [Moses] in a blazing fire from the middle of a bush. Moses stared in amazement. Though the bush was engulfed in flames, it didn't burn up.
Exodus 3:2 (NLT)

GO TO THE EXTREME

• **These** days, people can plant a "burning bush" in their yards. Named after the bush Moses saw in the desert, the leaves on this plant turn red in the autumn. This "bush" can grow up to 15 feet tall.

• **According** to firefighters, some things that won't burn in a house fire include jewelry, file cabinets, silverware, and silver coins.

• **Some** cool firefighting phrases: "Flashover"—when certain materials become heated and release flammable gases that burst into flames. The temperature of a room that flashes over is from 1,000 to 1,500 degrees Fahrenheit. "Fully involved"—fire, heat, and smoke are coming from every entrance in a structure.

Except for maybe the "Human Torch" from the *Fantastic Four* comic books and movies, things don't become "engulfed in flames" without burning up. Upon saying "flame on," the Human Torch would burst into flame but never burn up, because fire was his superhuman ability. In reality though, it would be pretty weird if all of a sudden some bushes in your neighborhood lit on fire and never went out!

Although Moses had been raised as a prince in Egypt, he was living far from the palace as a shepherd (Exodus 2—4). It was just another normal day for Moses, while grazing his flocks on the slopes of Mt. Sinai (his backyard!). Suddenly, he saw a bush burst into flame, but it wasn't burning up! That got his attention, and he moved closer. After all, branches and leaves burn to ash when on fire. "Flame On!" wasn't what set this bush on fire; God was doing something surprising to get Moses to listen to God's plan for him.

Moses' encounter with the burning bush turned out to be a very important event in world history. That's when he went from fugitive to leader, outlaw to lawgiver. The nation of Israel was rescued from bondage and returned to the Promised Land all because Moses said yes to God at the burning bush in his backyard!

JOKE ALERT!

Moses' New Year's resolutions:

1. *Steer clear of combustible shrubbery.*
2. *Brush up on palace "knock-knock" jokes to humor Pharaoh.*
3. *Read How to Win Friends and Influence Two Million Israelites.*

Read the story in Exodus 3.

Hopping Mad

The Nile will swarm with frogs; they will come up and go into your palace, into your bedroom and on your bed, into the houses of your officials and your people, and into your ovens and kneading bowls.

Exodus 8:3 (HCSB)

In your house you might have an ant problem and maybe your yard might have a few too many squirrels, but what if you had a frog problem? Now we're not talking about one or two pesky toads jumping around in the basement. There are frogs in your bed when you're sleeping, frogs in your food, and even frogs in your pants! It's a full-out frog invasion!

Egypt wasn't used to frog invasions either. In addition, their weather had never been made up of hail the size of baseballs, swarms of locusts, or all their water replaced with actual blood! God's people had been enslaved in Egypt for many years, and God intended to set them free. He could have just waved his hand and done that, but instead he decided to teach Pharaoh and the Egyptians a little bit about himself and his power. After ten awful plagues, the pharaoh finally had no other choice but to let the Israelites go free.

God's anger was a sign of his commitment to the Israelites, and his works through Moses were a wakeup call for the Egyptians. You know God isn't kidding around when he replaces your alarm clock with a bed full of frogs!

GO TO THE EXTREME

- **A** group of frogs is actually called an "army." Do you think the Egyptians were expecting an "army" of frogs?

- **When** a frog swallows food, he closes his eyes and they actually go down into his head. His eyeballs help to apply pressure that pushes his meal down his throat.

- **Frogs** have strong legs and can jump over 20 times their own length. That would be like you jumping 80 to 100 feet in a single bound! Go measure that out and see how far it is!

JOKE ALERT!

Recently discovered notable Bible quotes:

- Methuselah, after outliving all his friends— *"Happy Birthday to me, Happy Birthday to me . . ."*
- Bezelel when told the deadline for the pieces he was building for the Tabernacle—*"You want it when?"*
- Pharaoh to Moses—*"Talk to the hand!"*

Read the story in Exodus 6—12.

Pressure Points

[Moses] and Aaron summoned the people to come and gather at the rock. "Listen, you rebels!" he shouted. "Must we bring you water from this rock?" Then Moses raised his hand and struck the rock twice with the staff, and water gushed out.
Numbers 20:10–11 (NLT)

You can go outside right now and find plenty of rocks just sitting around. You might even find one with a crack in it where a few drops of water have found a home, but it's not every day you find rocks with water waiting to burst out of them. In fact, for water to shoot out from a solid rock seems pretty impossible. Just think if you had to find water and the only places to look were solid rock!

When Moses went looking for water in the desert, he needed God's help to find it. The Israelites were getting cranky because, even though they had been delivered from Egypt, they were determined to find things to complain about. One of their complaints was the lack of water. This had only been one complaint of many, and at this point Moses was pretty fed up with them. God told him only to touch the rock for water to come out, but Moses was so angry with the Israelites that he hit the rock not once, but twice and hard! Suddenly, water came bursting out of the rock as if from nowhere!

Even though water still came out, Moses was punished for allowing his anger to overcome his obedience and love toward God. When he struck the rock and spoke as he did, it sounded like *he* was in charge—and God was not pleased with that. God needed his leader to obey him and be an example to the people—and Moses' disobedience angered God so much that he told Moses he would not be allowed to enter the Promised Land. That was a high price to pay.

GO TO THE EXTREME

• **There** are layers of breakable rock underground called aquifers that contain large amounts of water.

• **A** desert is an area that can support little plant life because of dry soil and not enough moisture. Thus, Antarctica is technically also a desert.

• **The** Sahara desert is the largest desert in the world. It is as big as the entire United States (not counting Alaska and Hawaii).

JOKE ALERT!

Boys today probably wouldn't go for this:

"Moses brought Aaron's sons, and put coats upon them, and girded them with girdles, and put bonnets upon them" (Leviticus 8:13, KJV).

112

Read the story in Numbers 20.

Flow Stopper

Now the Jordan is at flood stage all during harvest. Yet as soon as the priests who carried the ark reached the Jordan and their feet touched the water's edge, the water from upstream stopped flowing.
Joshua 3:15-16 (NIV)

Imagine a large river with water rushing by your feet as you stand on the bank beside it. If you've ever been next to a river, whether to fish or swim or simply to look at it, you know that it seems like an unstoppable force speeding off to a lake or ocean. You'd also probably find it pretty hard to believe if it just stopped moving right in front of your eyes. What if it did just that? And what if it went from a rushing river to dry land in the blink of an eye? It would be pretty shocking.

The Bible doesn't tell us what Joshua and the Israelites thought when God stopped the Jordan River from moving, but they must have been just as shocked as you would have been. The Israelites had come to the Jordan River in hopes of crossing it, because it ran between them and where God was leading them. But the Jordan River was no stream and it was impossible to cross. So God told Joshua that if the priests carrying the Ark of the Covenant led them into the river, he would help them cross the Jordan by completely stopping it from moving. In fact, from where the priests stepped, he split it down the middle and sent the river going in opposite directions! (Kind of like what had happened to the Red Sea four decades earlier!)

When God has a plan for his people, not even impassable obstacles can stand in their way. Joshua and the Israelites had faith and God rewarded them.

GO TO THE EXTREME

• **The** Jordan River is 223 miles long and today is one of the borders for Israel. It is also the world's lowest river below sea level. It empties into the Dead Sea, which is the lowest point on the earth's surface.

• **The** Jordan River is not navigable—meaning boats can't sail up and down it—but it is used for irrigation in the dry desert area of Israel.

• **If** you were an Israelite born after passage through the Red Sea, you may have doubted God's ability to stop the flow of the Jordan.

JOKE ALERT!

Comments overheard at the edge of the Jordan River, just before the priests stepped in:

• *"Water you saying?"*
• *"Just go with the flow."*
• *"We can't see without our flood lights!"*
• *"H 2 oh oh!"*
• *"I forgot my floaties."*
• *"Is he joshin' us again?"*

1 1 3

Read the story in Joshua 3.

All the Time in the World

The sun stood still and the moon stayed in place until the nation of Israel had defeated its enemies. . . . The sun stayed in the middle of the sky, and it did not set as on a normal day.

Joshua 10:13 (NLT)

When you're having fun, a day can seem like it went by in a second. Sometimes there just isn't enough time in the day to do everything you want. If around noon the sun froze in the sky, what would you do with your time? You'd never have to go to bed and things that close at night (like amusement parks) would always be open!

God causing the sun to stand still for Joshua wasn't so he could prolong his bedtime or stay at an amusement park for a while longer; God did it to keep a promise. God had made the Israelites a powerful people, and when their neighbors became jealous, they teamed up to attack the Israelites. Joshua needed time on the battlefield, more time than there is in a day. God told Joshua that he would not only give him strength, he would give him more time as well. Joshua led the Israelites into battle the next day and in the midst of the fight, God held the sun still in the sky until Joshua had defeated all those who opposed him.

The word *can't* isn't in God's dictionary. He will keep his promises to us even if he has to stop the sun itself. With God we have all the time in the world!

GO TO THE EXTREME

- **The** sun is about 92.5 million miles away from earth—yet it is the star that is closest to the earth.

- **The** sun is so big that one million planet Earths would fit inside of it.

- **The** Aztecs believed that the sun died every night and could only be brought back to life by human blood. So every year they sacrificed 15,000 men to appease their sun god, Huitzilopochtli. Most of the victims were prisoners taken in wars.

JOKE ALERT!

Speaking of counting the hours, minutes, and seconds, the Israelites were way ahead of their time. Second Samuel 13:34 (KJV) tells us that a young man "kept the watch."

114

Read the story in Joshua 10.

Ax Me Again

"Where did it fall?" the man of God asked. When he showed him the place, Elisha cut a stick and threw it into the water ct that spot. Then the ax head floated to the surface.
2 Kings 6:6 (NLT)

If you've ever done any basic scientific experiments, you know what floats and what doesn't. Oil separates from water and floats. Corks float. You can even make a small needle float by using surface tension. However, solid iron ax heads simply don't float. For them to do so would defy the natural laws of physics (the science of matter and energy) and gravity (a force which pulls two objects toward each other).

But God can do anything.

Elisha's disciples decided to make a bigger meeting house because there were so many of them. For this construction project, one of the disciples borrowed an ax to help cut down the trees by the Jordan River. In the process, the ax head flew off the handle and landed in the river. This might not seem like a big deal, but God gave the Israelites a rule about loans: if you owe someone and can't pay them back, you might just end up as a slave for payment. This guy obviously didn't have the money to replace the ax. If he did, he could have bought and used his own ax. But iron tools were rare in Israel during ancient times. This ax would cost a bundle!

In his distress, he went to the only man who—with the help of God—could perform a miracle. It wasn't a big miracle like raising the dead or curing someone's disease, but this miracle saved a man from slavery and possibly death. By making the ax head float so the man could retrieve it, Elisha gave the man new life.

GO TO THE EXTREME

- **Most** axes weigh about four or five pounds, although some can weigh much more, especially if it's a large axe for cutting trees. You certainly wouldn't expect something that heavy to float.

- **The** density of mercury is higher than the density of iron, so a piece of iron will float in mercury, no matter what its shape is. But it certainly won't float in water!

- **Ships** are made of iron and are very heavy. But they float because they have a lot of air inside of the hull, and the air displaces more water without weighing more. Therefore, ships floats.

Read the story in 2 Kings 6:1-7.

The Original Star Trek

After hearing the king, [the wise men] went on their way. And there it was—the star they had seen in the east! It led them until it came and stopped above the place where the child was.
Matthew 2:9 (HCSB)

One of the greatest things to see in God's universe is a meteor shower: streaks of light fill the night sky as meteoroids burn up in the earth's atmosphere. Sometimes when you watch at night, you might see just one meteor—and sometimes we call it a "falling star." The rest of the time, however, you just see all of the stars every single night, various constellations moving across the night sky as the earth orbits around the sun.

The three wise men had probably seen a meteor shower before, and probably their share of "falling stars," so movement in the sky wasn't new to them. So what was different about this star? Instead of streaking across the sky, this star seemed to be traveling somewhere. Interested in where the star was going, they set out on a journey to follow it. To their surprise it led them to a little child. Realizing that this was a special child, they immediately fell to their knees and presented him with gifts. A traveling star that was only noticed by three men wound up guiding them to Jesus!

It must have taken a lot of patience to find that one star among all the rest, even if it was moving. Then, if that wasn't enough, they followed it not knowing where it would take them. God sure chose the right men for the job!

GO TO THE EXTREME

- **Even** before the time of Jesus people used stars for navigation. The oldest known star chart is thought to have been made around four thousand years ago!

- **Meteor** streams are the particles left by comets in their orbit around the sun. Meteor showers are created by cosmic debris that enters the earth's atmosphere at very high speeds.

- **On** any night, any location, a few meteors can be seen each hour. Take a look at the night sky tonight. Wait awhile. See what you can see.

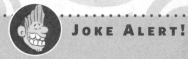

JOKE ALERT!

The wise men could have called themselves **STARS**:

Serious
Trek to
Acclaim
Royal
Savior

Read the story in Matthew 2.

Storms with a Chance of Sun

Suddenly a furious storm came up on the lake, so that the waves swept over the boat. But Jesus was sleeping. The disciples went and woke him, saying, "Lord, save us! We're going to drown!" He replied, "You of little faith, why are you so afraid?" Then he got up and rebuked the winds and the waves, and it was completely calm.
Matthew 8:24–26 (NIV)

When in the safety of your home, storms can be really cool. In fact, if it wasn't for mom you'd probably run out the door so you could play in the rain. Even with thunder that rattles the house, having your parents around makes things less scary.

In the middle of the lake the disciples weren't feeling too safe when a storm started to churn the water around their boat. Jesus and the disciples had left land earlier after a tiring miracle-filled day. When they got out onto the water, Jesus fell asleep and out of nowhere a storm appeared. Had this been a small storm the disciples probably wouldn't have worried, but when waves started to crash onto the deck of the boat the disciples began to fear for their lives. Thankfully Jesus wasn't as easily scared. After being awakened and alerted by his disciples that they were all going to die, Jesus calmly stood up, lifted his hands, and said, "Silence! Be still!" (Mark 4:39, NLT). At that very moment the sun came out and the storm immediately disappeared.

Weathermen have the ability to tell us when a storm is approaching, but it takes God to stop one from happening. The next time there's a storm, remember that there is always a sun shining behind those dark clouds.

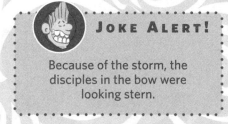

JOKE ALERT!

Because of the storm, the disciples in the bow were looking stern.

Go to the Extreme

• **Thunderstorms** can create gusts of wind that can start more storms up to 100 miles away. Even the smallest thunderstorm can generate millions of gallons of water.

• **The** type of cloud that causes thunderstorms is a cumulonimbus cloud. These clouds can be more than 12 miles high.

• **Because** light travels faster than sound, you can see lightning before you hear the thunder that caused it. If you want to know how far away the storm is, count the seconds between a lightning flash and the next sound of thunder, then divide by five. The result will give you the distance in miles that the storm is away from you.

Read the story in Matthew 8:23–27.

All Leaves and No Fruit

As [Jesus and the disciples] passed by in the morning, they saw the fig tree withered away to its roots. And Peter remembered and said to him, "Rabbi, look! The fig tree that you cursed has withered."
Mark 11:20-21 (ESV)

When the fall season starts and the trees lose their leaves before winter, it is a slow process. Depending on where you live in the country, on your way to school you'll notice the leaves changing colors; and then after a month or so the leaves will be on the ground and the trees' branches empty. Wouldn't it be weird if instead of it happening slowly, all the trees lost their leaves overnight? One day everything is green and the next day it's winter!

A tree on the road that Jesus was taking to Jerusalem experienced instant winter firsthand. Jesus was on his way to Jerusalem with his disciples when he found a fig tree that wasn't bearing any fruit. When he saw this he cursed it by saying, "May no one ever eat fruit from you again." After leaving Jerusalem the next day, they passed by the tree and it had withered and died overnight! The disciples were amazed at what Jesus had done, but he explained that anything is possible with complete faith.

Although killing a tree for not bearing fruit seems harsh, it demonstrated to the disciples that being productive and having faith are important parts of life.

GO TO THE EXTREME

• **Fig** trees belong to the genus of ficus and are evergreen trees—they keep their leaves in every season.

• **While** the roots of most trees go one to two feet deep (with them usually spreading out in a large area), a wild fig tree in South Africa holds the record for the deepest tree roots. Its roots reach down an amazing 400 feet!

• **The** fig tree was in the Garden of Eden. Adam and Eve covered themselves with fig leaves (Genesis 3:7).

JOKE ALERT!

Here's something you *won't* find in the Bible:

*As the disciples stood that morning, after breakfast, one said to another, "Let us leave?"
(get it? "lettuce leaf"?).*

"No," replied another, "I'll go out on a limb and say it's a fig."

118

Read the story in Mark 11:13-14.

GREAT Escapes

Many action movies and books are beloved because of the great escapes that occur. We're kept on the edge of our seats, wondering how the hero or heroine will escape from the villain or a trap set by the villain. Will the bomb go off while he's there? Can she escape from the handcuffs and stop the runaway train? The closer that person is to death, the greater the tension we feel as we read or watch.

You don't have to head to the movie theater or your Blu-ray player to catch the latest thriller. The Bible has some hair-raising, true life escapes, where people cheated death by a hair. But many had the help of the ultimate escape artist: God.

Fleeing a Father-in-Law

Jacob outwitted Laban the Aramean, for they set out secretly and never told Laban they were leaving.
Genesis 31:20 (NLT)

GO TO THE EXTREME

- **Having** more than one wife was common in Bible times. In fact, King Solomon had 700 wives—some of them married for purposes of alliances with other countries. Still, it was a problem, for the Bible talks about how they were foreign women who led him into idol worship. For all his wisdom, Solomon wasn't very smart . . .

- **According** to the U.S. Bureau of Labor Statistics, the average person changes jobs every four years. Jacob worked for his father-in-law five times as long!

- **The** idols Rachel stole were probably "teraphim," small wood or metal "gods" that people kept in their homes for protection. Sometimes they were passed on in the family as part of an inheritance— which might be why Rachel took them!

How would you feel if your parents said you could go to a friend's house after you cleaned your room, but when you finished, they told you that you had yet another chore to do? Pretty unfair, right? What if the list of things you had to do kept getting longer each time you completed a task?

Jacob wanted to marry Rachel, Laban's youngest daughter, so he agreed to work seven years to earn her hand in marriage. Laban instead gave Jacob his oldest daughter, Leah, and made him work seven *more* years for Rachel. Then, he made him work more years to earn flocks, but kept changing which livestock would be Jacob's "wages." Altogether, Jacob worked twenty years for Laban. Throughout all of this, God continued to bless Jacob, and finally told him to take his wives and leave.

So Jacob packed up his wives, belongings, and flocks and left—without telling Laban! Rachel took some idols from Laban without telling Jacob. When Laban realized that Jacob and the idols were gone, he chased after them. He caught up, but Jacob pointed out to him the injustice he had suffered and convinced him to let God's blessing serve as proof that he deserved to be free from Laban. Since Rachel had hidden the idols, Laban had little to make a case with, so he agreed. They built a rock tower to symbolize their agreement to leave each other alone.

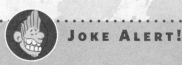

JOKE ALERT!

Possible titles for Jacob's autobiography:

- *I Led Two Wives*
- *Escape from Lost Wages (Las Vegas)*
- *In-laws and Outlaws*
- *I Saw Esau, Esau Me*
- *Idol Hands*

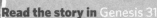

Read the story in Genesis 31.

Eyes on the Spies

When they left, they went into the hills and stayed there three days, until the pursuers had searched all along the road and returned without finding them.
Joshua 2:22 (NIV)

Picture this: You're playing the game *Steal the Bacon* in the woods. Your team picks you to run across and scout out where the other team's bacon is. You might be captured, but if you can get back, you can tell your team what the other side looks like.

In Joshua 2, Joshua sent two spies into Canaan to check out the city of Jericho. The two spies went to the home of Rahab, a prostitute in Jericho. (They went there probably because it would arouse the least suspicion.) It also helped that Rahab's house was built into the wall of Jericho. But the king of Jericho found out about these two unknown men and sent word to Rahab to turn the men who were there over to him. Imagine how the spies felt when they overheard that! But Rahab lied and said the men had already left. Actually, she had hidden them on her roof. The king sent men out to pursue the spies who were *still* inside the city!

Before Rahab helped the spies escape, she made them promise that she and her family would be spared when Israel attacked. They agreed that as long as she did not tell what they were doing, her family would be treated kindly by the Israelites. She then let them down the city wall with a rope and told them to wait three days in the hills until the men who were pursuing them had returned. Then they were able to make a clean getaway to tell Joshua that the enemies would be easily defeated. Later, in honor of Rahab's good deed, only Rahab and her family were saved when Jericho fell. (For more on that story, see "The Fall of a Wall," in Ballistic Battles, page 13.)

GO TO THE EXTREME

- **During** the American Revolution, the Culper Ring was a group of spies who gave information about the British to George Washington.

- **The** word *spy* comes from the Old French word *espie*, which means "watcher."

- **Rahab** ends up in the ancestral line of Jesus Christ—check it out in Matthew 1:5! How cool is that?

JOKE ALERT!

Laconic Limerick:
Rahab welcomed the spies,
the two brave Israelite guys.
Under flax she hid them,
then farewell she bid them,
her red rope proving her wise.

1 2 1

Read the story in Joshua 2.

Live and Let Die

Ehud escaped while the servants waited. He crossed over [the Jordan] near the carved images and reached Seirah.
Judges 3:26 (HCSB)

What's the longest time of punishment you've ever faced? The Israelites, no matter how many times they were punished, kept sinning against God's law, so God punished them over and over again. This time, he allowed them to be taken under foreign rule for eighteen years. Can you imagine being grounded for that long?

The Israelites had grown tired of being oppressed by Moab, so they prayed to God to help them. He gave them Ehud, a left-handed man. So, what's the big deal about his being left-handed? You'll see in just a minute. The Israelites sent him to give a tribute to Eglon, king of Moab. When Ehud told Eglon that he had a secret message, Eglon demanded that all of his servants leave the room. Once they were alone, Ehud revealed the "secret message"—a double-edged sword a foot and a half long hidden under his clothing. A left-handed assassin was totally unexpected! (For more about this story, check out "Message Received" in Gross and Gory, page 100.)

After doing what he came to do, Ehud escaped, locking the doors behind him. When the servants found the doors locked, they assumed that the king was in the ancient version of the restroom. They soon realized that the doors had been closed a little too long for that, though, so they unlocked them to find Eglon dead. Meanwhile, Ehud was gathering the Israelite troops for an assault to defeat Moab.

GO TO THE EXTREME

- **Between** 10–15 percent of the world is left-handed.

- **In** Ancient Hebrew, left was seen as symbolic of the power to shame society and bring about misfortune or the wrath of the gods.

JOKE ALERT!

Possible titles for Ehud's best-selling book about his exploits as a judge of Israel:

- *Left for Dead*
- *How to Get Ehud (ahead)*
- *Moabig a Deal*
- *I Took a Stab at It*
- *I'd Had a Belly-full of Eglon*
- *Excuse Me While I Scratch My Leg*

Read the story in Judges 3:12–30.

INCREASE YOUR BIBLE TRIVIA KNOWLEDGE!

WANT TO LEARN MORE ABOUT THE BIBLE? HERE ARE SOME PAGES WITH TONS OF BIBLE FACTS AND STUFF YOU PROBABLY DIDN'T KNOW...BUT IT'S REALLY COOL. SO IN CASE YOU'RE EVER ASKED, YOU CAN SURPRISE PEOPLE WITH AMAZING BIBLE FACTS!

BIBLE ANIMALS:

These aren't all the animals mentioned in the Bible, but you can get the idea that the critters of Bible times were like the ones we see today. IF SOME NAMES LOOK UNFAMILIAR, LOOK THEM UP!

Adder	Crane	Hart	Locust	
Ant	Cuckoo	Hawk	Mole	
Ape	Dog	Heifer	Mountain goat	
Asp	Donkey	Hen	Moth	
Badger	Dove	Heron	Mouse	
Bat	Dragon	Hind	Mule	Snail
Bear	Dromedary	Hornet	Nighthawk	Sparrow
Bee	Eagle	Horse	Osprey	Spider
Beetle	Elephant	Hyena	Ostrich	Stork
Behemoth	Fallow deer	Ibex	Owl	Swallow
Bird	Ferret	Insects	Ox	Swan
Boar	Fish	Kangaroo	Partridge	Swine
Buffalo	Flea	Kid	Peacock	Tortoise
Calf	Fox	Kine	Pelicans	Turtledove
Camel	Frog	Kite	Pigeon	Unicorn
Caterpillar	Gazelle	Lamb	Quails	Viper
Cattle	Gnat	Leopard	Ram	Vulture
Chameleon	Goat	Leviathan	Raven	Weasel
Chamois	Gopher	Lice	Roe	Whale
Cormorant	Grasshopper	Lions	Serpent	Wolf
Cow	Hare	Lizard	Sheep	Worm

INCREASE YOUR BIBLE TRIVIA KNOWLEDGE!

BIBLE FOODS:

There must have been lots of crazy foods and munchies way back in Bible times. We're sure there were many more that people enjoyed, but here are a few that are mentioned in the Bible. We still eat most of these today in some sort of recipe!

TASTY FRUITS AND NUTS-N-HONEY

- Apples
- Almonds
- Dates
- Figs
- Grapes
- Honey
- Melons
- Olives (olive oil)
- Pistachios
- Pomegranates
- Raisins

SAVORY SPICES

- Anise
- Coriander
- Cinnamon
- Cumin
- Dill
- Garlic
- Mint
- Mustard
- Salt

EAT YOUR VEGGIES

- Beans
- Cucumbers
- Gourds
- Leeks
- Lentils
- Onions

M-M-MEATS AND FISHES

- Calf
- Dove
- Eggs
- Fish
- Goat
- Lamb
- Oxen
- Partridge
- Pigeon
- Quail
- Sheep
- Venison

GRAINS AND DAIRY

- Barley
- Bread
- Butter
- Cheese
- Corn
- Curds
- Flour
- Millet
- Milk
- Wheat

BIBLE COLORS AND BIBLE JEWELS:

Colors are mentioned throughout the pages of the Bible. You've probably heard the story of Noah's ark and the rainbow. Colors play an important part of the stories in the Bible. Also, there are many precious metals, stones, and jewels mentioned in both the Old and New Testaments. Here are some that are still valued today!

COLORS

Amber
Black
Blue   Grey
Brown   Purple
Copper   Scarlet
Crimson   Vermillion
Gold   White
Green   Yellow

JEWELS

Amethyst
Beryl
Carnelian
Chalcedony
Chrysolite
Crystal
Emerald
Gold
Jacinth
Jasper
Pearl
Ruby
Sapphire
Sardonyx
Silver
Topaz

BIBLE PLANTS, TREES, AND FLOWERS:

Even though the stories of the Bible took place in a different part of the world from where you live, there are many plants, trees, and flowers that we have in our own surroundings today. Look at the ones mentioned in the Bible below and see how many you recognize or can even find in your own neighborhood!

Acacia	Calamus	Ebony	Nettle
Almond	Camphire	Elm	Oak
Aloes	Cane	Fig	Olive
Amber	Cedar	Fir	Onion
Apple	Chestnut	Flax	Palm
Ash	Cinnamon	Garlic	Pine
Bay tree	Cockle	Gopher wood	Pomegranate
Boxtree	Coriander	Gourd	Poplar
Bramble	Cypress	Grass	Reed
Bulrush	Date	Hay	Rose
		Hazel	Rosin
		Hemlock	Rush
		Herb	Rye
		Hyssop	Saffron
		Jacinth	Sycamore
		Juniper	Tares
		Leek	Teil tree
		Lentils	Terebinth
		Lily	Thistle
		Mandrakes	Thorn
		Melons	Tree of Life
		Millet	Tree of Knowledge
		Mint	of Good and Evil
		Mulberry	Vine
		Mustard	Wheat
		Myrrh	Willows
		Myrtle	Wormwood

BIBLE KINGS AND QUEENS:

So many names...so hard to remember, or even pronounce them all! Lots of the kings and queens in the Bible were great and did many wonderful things. Some were evil and were punished for all their wicked deeds. Here are just a few of the names that you may have heard of before or seen in this book. Look them up in your Bible.

KINGS

Saul
David
Solomon
Herod
Nebuchadnezzar
Hezekiah
Ahab
Hazael
Uzziah

Agrippa
Rehoboam
Hehoram
Hehu
Manasseh
Josiah
Zedekiah

QUEENS

Bathsheba
Candace
Queen of Sheba
Abigail
Ahinoam of Jezreel
Esther
Jezebel
Vashti
Zibiah

INCREASE YOUR BIBLE TRIVIA KNOWLEDGE!

BIBLE BATTLES AND WARFARE:

Victories and defeats! Blood & gore, and so much more! The Bible has all the excitement and action of any major motion picture about war that's ever been made. No, there were no lasers, aliens, or bombs, but the battles were just as fierce! Here are some of the weapons and equipment that were used as "deadly force."

Armor

Arrows

Artillery

Axe

Battering ram

Battle-ax

Battle-bow

Bow

Chariot

Dart

Goad

Hammer

Javelin

Jawbone

Knife

Mace/hammer

Quiver

Sling

Spear

Stones

Sword

Trident

INCREASE YOUR BIBLE TRIVIA KNOWLEDGE!

BOOKS OF THE BIBLE:

You probably already know that the Bible is one great big book! But it consists of 66 shorter books, 39 in the Old Testament and 27 in the New Testament. We've listed them here. Try to read some verses from a book of the Bible every day and you'll be surprised that you can read the entire thing in a year! That's quite an accomplishment.

OLD TESTAMENT

Genesis	Esther	Micah	Zephaniah
Exodus	Job	Nahum	Haggai
Leviticus	Psalms	Habakkuk	Zechariah
Numbers	Proverbs		Malachi
Deuteronomy	Ecclesiastes		
Joshua	Song of Solomon		
Judges	Isaiah		
Ruth	Jeremiah		
I Samuel	Lamentations		
II Samuel	Ezekiel		
I Kings	Daniel		
II Kings	Hosea		
I Chronicles	Joel		
II Chronicles	Amos		
Ezra	Obadiah		
Nehemiah	Jonah		

NEW TESTAMENT

Matthew	Galatians	Titus	III John
Mark	Ephesians	Philemon	Jude
Luke	Philippians	Hebrews	Revelation
John	Colossians	James	
Acts	I Thessalonians	I Peter	
Romans	II Thessalonians	II Peter	
I Corinthians	I Timothy	I John	
II Corinthians	II Timothy	II John	

PLAGUES OF EGYPT:

Have you ever watched the movie *The Ten Commandments*? It's been around for years, but is still a favorite for people who love stories from the Bible, history, and a great blockbuster adventure. For the most part, it follows the story of Moses, and his life from a baby Hebrew boy, to prince of Egypt, to shepherd, to mighty prophet of God! Below are the ten plagues that God told Moses Egypt would suffer because of Pharaoh's hardened heart toward the Israelites.

Plague of Blood (Ex 7:14-25)

Plague of Frogs (Ex 8:1-15)

Plague of Gnats (Ex 8:16-19)

Plague of Flies (Ex 8:20-32)

Plague of Death of Livestock (Ex 9:1-7)

Plague of Boils (Ex 9:8-12)

Plague of Hail (Ex 9:13-35)

Plague of Locusts (Ex 10:1-20)

Plague of Darkness (Ex 10:21-29)

Plague of Death of the Firstborn (Ex 11:1—12:32)

The Ultimate Gate Crasher

Samson lay till midnight, and at midnight he arose and took hold of the doors of the gate of the city and the two posts, and pulled them up, bar and all, and put them on his shoulders and carried them to the top of the hill that is in front of Hebron.
Judges 16:3 (ESV)

Have you ever watched the World's Strongest Man contests on TV? A few dozen men every year compete to see who is the strongest of the strong, lifting and carrying things that would be way too heavy for most people. They lift cars, pull airplanes, flip monster truck tires—lots of things that seem impossible until you see them do it.

The ultimate strongman of the Bible was Samson! If you read "A Deadly Date" in Dastardly Villains (page 79), you know that Samson's "kryptonite" was women. (In other words, when Superman encountered kryptonite, he lost his powers. When Samson encountered women, he seemed to get really dumb.) On one particular night in Gaza (one of the main cities of the Philistines, Samson's enemies), he decided to go on a date. When the people of Gaza found out, they waited for him outside to kill him the next morning. But Samson got up in the middle of the night before they expected him to leave, ripped the city gate out of the ground, and carried it to the top of a hill outside the city!

GO TO THE EXTREME

- **According** to one source, the gate Samson carried may have weighed as much as 4,000 pounds. That's more than most cars! He may have carried the gate 20 miles, which would make Samson unbeatable in any World's Strongest Man contest!

- **One** example of a strong man in our day would be the late Louis Cyr from France. He was able to lift as much as 4,300 pounds, and could lift even a 430-pound barrel of cement using only one arm!

- **Ryan** Kennelly, a U.S. power lifter, holds the world's record for bench pressing 1,075 pounds.

1 2 3

Read the story in Judges 16:1–3.

David's Great Escapes

Saul tried to pin him to the wall with his spear, but David eluded him as Saul drove the spear into the wall. That night David made good his escape.
1 Samuel 19:10 (NIV)

Nobody likes a bully. They push people around and steal lunch money—not cool! David had several encounters with a bully. Unfortunately for him, the bully was the king of Israel!

GO TO THE EXTREME

• **Harps** have been around since ancient Egypt—2500 BC.

• **There** is a dance troupe that actually has a dance routine with spears. They are the DESNA Ukrainian Dance Company of Toronto.

• **In** order to throw a spear hard enough to stick into a wall (as Saul did), you would need to have a certain technique. You would have to throw across your body, aim at the center of your target, and center your body on the target. This was not some idle throw by Saul—he had to stand up and really throw hard! David was fortunate to get out of the way in time.

By this point in the Bible, David has already killed Goliath for Saul. Because of David's success in battle, though, Saul was jealous of him and wanted to kill him. Jonathan, Saul's son and David's best friend, convinced Saul to let him live. David once again went to war and fought heroically, which made Saul jealous again.

While David was playing his harp one night, Saul tried to pin him to the wall with a spear. David escaped from the palace, but Saul sent men to watch his house and kill him the next morning. Michal, David's wife, warned him that if he didn't run for his life that night, they would kill him. She helped him escape by lowering him out of a window. Then she took a household idol and laid it on the bed with a garment around it and goat's hair at the head! This bought David enough time to work with Jonathan to come up with a survival plan. And—spoiler alert!—he survived!

JOKE ALERT!

Here's something you *won't find in the Bible:*

When the guards went to arrest David, they saw the lump under the covers and asked, "Statue David?" Then, when they saw the goat's hair, they exclaimed, "Stop kiddin' around!"

Read the story in 1 Samuel 19.

Revenge or Forgiveness?

Saul chose 3,000 elite troops from all Israel and went to search for David and his men near the rocks of the wild goats.

1 Samuel 24:2 (NLT)

Suppose there was somebody you knew who always tried to embarrass you. Then one day, the tables were turned, and you somehow had the chance to embarrass that person. Would you do it?

Saul, even after agreeing to stop trying to kill David, *still* wanted him dead. One day, as Saul was leading his army of three thousand men to find David, he took a restroom break. He decided to go into a nearby cave—the cave that David happened to be hiding in! While David could see Saul, Saul had no idea that David was there. Here was David's chance for revenge. But David knew that he would be sinning against God if he harmed the man God anointed as king. Instead of killing or threatening Saul, David sneaked up to Saul and cut off a corner of his robe. And Saul didn't even notice!

When Saul left the cave, David followed him out. He explained to Saul that he could have taken his life, but chose to let God be the judge between them instead of taking matters into his own hands. He showed Saul the piece of robe he'd cut. Saul felt guilty about how he had treated David—but he later tried to kill him again!

JOKE ALERT!

Here's something you won't find in the Bible:

In the cave, David not only cut off part of Saul's robe, but as a practical joke he also tied his sandal laces together.

GO TO THE EXTREME

- **The** cave David was hiding in was located in a place called the Crags of the Wild Goats.

- **Some** of the caves in that area are huge—able to hide hundreds of men all at once. This worked out well for David and his army that had to keep running and hiding.

- **The** tassels at the corner of Saul's robe that David cut off represented Saul's authority, which may be one of the reasons David felt bad about what he had done.

Read the story in 1 Samuel 24.

Breakfast of Champions

Then [Elijah] was afraid, and he arose and ran for his life and came to Beersheba, which belongs to Judah, and left his servant there.

1 Kings 19:3 (ESV)

What do you like to eat for breakfast? Breakfast is a very important meal. Not only does it replenish the nutrients that your body used while you were sleeping, but it also provides you with the energy you need to start each day.

Elijah had just defeated all of the false prophets of Baal, who were servants of Jezebel, the queen of Israel at the time. Jezebel, the wife of Ahab, was a wicked queen. She wanted revenge against Elijah for defeating the prophets of Baal and Asherah on Mt. Carmel. When she sent a threatening message to Elijah, he had to run for his life.

Jezebel's threats depressed Elijah. (You'd probably feel the same way if you were him.) God sent an angel to bring bread and water to Elijah. Elijah ate and drank, but then he hit the proverbial snooze button by falling asleep again. The angel came back again and woke Elijah up to eat and drink to prepare for his journey. When Elijah had finished eating and drinking this time, he felt strengthened and went on his journey to Horeb to hear the voice of God—a journey that took him forty days and forty nights!

GO TO THE EXTREME

- **A** recent poll lists scrambled eggs as the favorite breakfast food of most Americans.

- **The** snooze button was actually invented in the 1950s by Lew Wallace, who also wrote the book that inspired one of Hollywood's most famous biblical epics—*Ben-Hur!*

- **Bread** is one of the main food groups necessary for life. Each American consumes, on average, 53 pounds of bread per year. That's a lot of toast!

JOKE ALERT!

Why couldn't the surviving prophets of Baal catch Elijah when he ran?

Answer: *They were de-feet-ed."*

126

Read the story in 1 Kings 19:1–8.

Most Wanted in Damascus

Their plot became known to Saul. So they were watching the gates day and night intending to kill him, but his disciples took him by night and lowered him in a large basket through [an opening in] the wall.

Acts 9:24–25 (HCSB)

Imagine having all of your old friends turn on you to the point of trying to kill you. Now imagine that they were watching to make sure you couldn't escape. How could you possibly get out?

Paul, also known as Saul, had just experienced a life-changing conversion to Christianity. This happened on the road to Damascus, the city where he planned to arrest Christians. Because of this, his former Jewish allies wanted nothing more than to kill him. He had been one of their leaders; now he was leading their most-wanted list! They watched and waited for him to try to escape so they could kill him, but he learned about the plot against him. One night, his followers got him out in a basket through the window like a midnight picnic. And what a sweet picnic it was—Paul got out of town safely to meet with the rest of the disciples in Jerusalem!

JOKE ALERT!

Why did Paul have a hard time escaping from Damascus?

Answer: He was such a basket case!

GO TO THE EXTREME

- **Baskets** had been in use for thousands of years already by the time Paul needed one—possibly as early as 8000 BC.

- **J.** Edgar Hoover, who once headed the FBI, started the Ten Most Wanted Fugitives program in 1950.

- **There** are lots of baskets in the Bible—Moses was hidden in one; lots of people had dreams about things in baskets; and when Jesus multiplied bread to feed over 5,000 people, there were twelve baskets full of food left over!

1 2 7

Read the story in Acts 9:19–25.

Sleepwalking Out of Jail

Suddenly an angel of the Lord appeared and a light shone in the cell. He struck Peter on the side and woke him up. "Quick, get up!" he said, and the chains fell off Peter's wrists.
Acts 12:7 (NIV)

Have you ever noticed how many movies and TV shows there are about prison escapes? The old classic *Escape from Alcatraz* comes to mind. A group of men spent years planning and preparing for one attempt to escape their cells, chipping away at the walls with spoons, past the guard towers, and across a mile and a half of the San Francisco Bay to the California coastline. It was based on a true story, even down to the ending. No one knows if they survived!

In Acts 12, Peter found himself in a similarly inescapable prison—he was guarded 24/7 by four squads of four guards each. While he was locked up, the church prayed that God would save him. They feared that King Herod would have him executed, which he probably intended to do. The night before Peter's trial, an angel woke him up. That's right. An angel had to wake him up! He was sleeping between two guards. Talk about trusting God despite this fearful situation! His chains fell off, and the angel led him past the guards and through the gates, which opened up for them!

The whole time, Peter wondered whether or not he was still asleep. When the angel left him outside the city, he realized that he was indeed awake—God had set him free. He went to tell the other disciples, and the servant girl was so excited to hear him that she forgot to let him in the first time! Talk about a close call!

GO TO THE EXTREME

• **The** majority of modern-day prisoners who escape are recaptured within one day.

• **A** prisoner once escaped from a prison by helicopter that some of his friends on the outside hijacked. He probably jumped from the prison roof and grabbed onto the skids of the helicopter! He didn't get away, though. He was recaptured and sent back to prison for an extra seven years.

• **Another** prisoner escaped when, in broad daylight, two of his friends drove an 18-wheel truck through four prison fences. The truck was followed by a car driven by—wait for it!—the prisoner's own mother.

JOKE ALERT!

Speaking of escaping, here's some airplane travel advice straight from the Bible:
"Pray ye that your flight be not in the winter, neither on the sabbath day" (Matthew 24:20, KJV).

Read the story in Acts 12:1–18.

Ruining an Ambush

Paul's nephew told him, ". . . There are more than forty men hiding along the way ready to ambush him. They have vowed not to eat or drink anything until they have killed him. They are ready now, just waiting for your consent."
Acts 23:20–21 (NLT)

Do you ever feel like adults just don't listen to you? Even when you know that you are right about something, sometimes adults still won't accept advice from children or teens.

Thankfully for Paul, the commander in charge of guarding him was willing to listen to a young man. Paul was being held in prison, and the Jews were once again plotting to kill him. They claimed to want him brought before the Sanhedrin to find out more about him. Really, they planned to murder him before he arrived! Paul's nephew found out about the plot and warned Paul. Paul sent him to tell the Roman commander. Incredibly, the commander was willing to listen to him. Because of the courage of Paul's nephew, the commander was able to move Paul safely away from the would-be killers!

GO TO THE EXTREME

- **Many** fish, snakes, and reptiles are considered ambush predators. They rely on the element of surprise rather than physical advantages (size, strength, speed) to kill their prey.

- **The** first ninjas (*shinobi*), Japanese spies and assassins, might have started around the fourteenth century.

- **The** Bible says that a group of 40 men were in on the plot to kill Paul. They had taken an oath not to eat anything until they killed Paul. Hmm . . . I wonder what happened to them.

JOKE ALERT!

More travel advice from the Bible. This verse proves that people who are afraid to fly are right:

Jesus said, "Lo, I am with you always" (Matthew 28:20, KJV). ("Low" as opposed to "high.")

Read the story in Acts 23:12–45.

CREEPY Places

A **dank, garbage-strewn alley** crawling with rats. A dark dungeon filled with straw and old bones. A lonely road in the middle of nowhere. The dentist's office. The bottom of your gym locker. What do these places have in common? Glance up at the title again. That's right. You know them when you see them or try to avoid seeing them. (Okay, we're just kidding about the dentist's office. . . .) They're the places that haunt your dreams or make the hair stand up on the back of your neck. You shudder even at the thought of going there. These are places you wouldn't want to visit even on the brightest day, and certainly never at night.

The Bible has stories of places even scarier than your dentist's office or the bottom of your locker. And you can be sure, if you went to these places, you wouldn't receive a free toothbrush. In fact, some of these places involve a one-way trip—no turning back. Don't blame us if you get goose bumps.

What Are You Babbling About?

That is why it was called Babel—because there the LORD confused the language of the whole world. From there the LORD scattered them over the face of the whole earth.
Genesis 11:9 (NIV)

- **The** Linguistics Society of America states that there are 6,809 distinct languages in the world.

- **The** Bible was written in three languages: Hebrew, Aramaic, and Koiné Greek.

- **The** Tower of Babel was a *ziggurat* (rising building), which is like the Egyptian pyramid. Ziggurats were used for religious purposes, but pyramids were used as tombs.

Up until the Tower of Babel was built, the world had only one language. If you had been alive then, you could have traveled all across Europe, Asia, and Africa, with no problems understanding the people. Imagine that—no language barriers,

You might be wondering why God decided to confuse everybody with different languages, which suddenly divided everyone into little groups who only understood each other. Well, if you read the whole passage, you'll see that the people's intentions weren't exactly noble. They weren't just trying to build a cool tower for awesome views of the nearby Tigris and Euphrates rivers. What they really wanted was worldwide fame for their accomplishment and the feeling that nothing could stop them—not even God.

The tower would have been a marvel (a wonderful thing), but it was a monument to the people, not to God. God decided it would be better for the people to move on and settle all over the world rather than stay in one area near the tower. So he confused their language!

"Hey Joe, hand me the hammer."
"Che?"
"Er will einen hammer."
"什麼?"

What chaos must have followed as people desperately tried to find others who spoke the same language! Calling attention to your achievements isn't a bad thing. Just don't let their importance take the place of God in your life.

JOKE ALERT!

How do we know that Adam could run fast?

Answer: *He was the first in the human race.*

Read the story in Genesis 11:1–9.

Got Fire Insurance?

We are about to destroy this city completely. The outcry against this place is so great it has reached the LORD, and he has sent us to destroy it.
Genesis 19:13 (NLT)

Note to self: When God sends angels to tell you he's going to destroy your home, rent a U-Haul immediately!

Back in the days of Abraham, not too long after the flood, there were two cities full of people who were just plain evil. The cities were named Sodom and Gomorrah. So one day, God decided he had heard enough about the sin in those towns. He would destroy them, but not before getting Abraham's nephew, Lot, and his family out of town.

The angels told Lot what was coming—burning sulfur raining down from the sky—and he tried to save others. (If you knew your town was going to be incinerated, you'd probably try to save people too, right?) When Lot told of the coming doomsday to the two guys who were supposed to marry his daughters, they thought Lot was joking When the angels told him to run for the hills, Lot was so scared he couldn't move—the angels had to grab him and his family and pull them to safety! Still, only Lot and his daughters made it to safety, and they left a pillar of salt (Lot's wife) behind (see the story "An Awful A-Salt" in What a Way to Go, page 22).

The next day Abraham saw smoke rising from where the cities had been. Total wipeout. God punished evil, but at the same time, showed mercy to Lot. Lot must have been grateful to those angels for being his personal fire insurance policy.

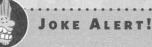

JOKE ALERT!

Possible reasons Lot's wife turned and looked back when leaving Sodom:

- *She thought she left the iron on.*
- *The kids double-dared her.*
- *She thought the angels had said "pillar of the community."*
- *She thought Lot was lost, and she wanted to ask for directions.*
- *She forgot to use the bathroom before leaving.*

GO TO THE EXTREME

- **Sulfur** burns at approximately 5,000 degrees Fahrenheit. So the "burning sulfur" (Genesis 19:24) that fell from the sky was incredibly hot!

- **Archaeologist** Ron Wyatt is credited with finding the remains of the cities of Sodom and Gomorrah on the western side of the Dead Sea in Israel. Most of what he found was ash, but embedded in the ash were balls of sulfur, surrounded by burn rings.

- **Approximately** 4,000 people in the United States die each year in house fires. Having a working smoke alarm dramatically increases your chances of surviving a fire. Tell your parents to make sure you have at least one smoke alarm in your house.

Read the story in Genesis 19:12-29.

Too Hot to Handle

They have built pagan shrines to Baal in the valley of Ben-Hinnom, and there they sacrifice their sons and daughters to Molech. I have never commanded such a horrible deed; it never even crossed my mind to command such a thing. What an incredible evil, causing Judah to sin so greatly!
Jeremiah 32:35 (NLT)

The valley of Ben-Hinnom, just south of Jerusalem, was where some very terrible things happened. When the people turned away from God and started worshiping other gods like Molech, they did horrible acts like sacrificing their own children to that god—something the true God never asked of his people. Scary, right? This practice was such an abomination to God and to the people of Israel that this valley was later referred to as hell, or, in Greek, *Gehenna*.

GO TO THE EXTREME

• **About** 500 million people live on or very near to volcanoes. There are even major cities close to active volcanoes. Popocatapetl (pronounced poh-poh-kah-teh-peh-til) is a volcano less than 50 miles from Mexico City, Mexico.

• **The** earth has more than 1,500 active volcanoes. When they erupt, the temperature of the molten rock is over 2,000 degrees!

• **The** loudest sound ever heard was caused by a volcanic eruption at Krakatoa, Indonesia in 1883. The sound was so loud that it was heard in Australia, which was over 3000 miles away.

The valley later became a place where trash and the bodies of dead animals were burned up—a kind of garbage dump. The heat of continual fires and the horrible smell of the smoke made most people stay as far away from it as possible.

Because this place was so horrible, this valley became associated with hell—an unquenchable fire with punishing heat and terrible odors in the smoke.

Thankfully, this valley no longer burns with garbage or anything else. Today, to have Gehenna on earth would be like living on the edge of a volcano. You would experience intense heat from the constant flame, terrible odors, and always having to worry that your house could burn down. If you lived like that, you would indeed be like the living dead. Worse, though, is that hell is real. God has made every person with an eternal (forever) soul. Even though our bodies die, our souls go on living forever. We can make one important choice in our lives which will decide whether our soul spends eternal life in heaven or in hell. Choose Jesus!

JOKE ALERT!

Here's something you *won't* find in the Bible:
The people of Jerusalem were constantly looking for a government Baal-out.

1 3 4

Read the story in Jeremiah 32:32–35.

No to Nineveh!

Everyone must call out earnestly to God. Each must turn from his evil ways and from the violence he is doing. Who knows? God may turn and relent; He may turn from His burning anger so that we will not perish.
     Jonah 3:8–9 (HCSB)

Suppose you lived near the worst prison on earth, and someone told you that you have to go inside and teach all of the criminals how to be good. Sounds impossible, right? Maybe even scary? What would you say? "No way, I'm not going in there! They'll eat me alive!"

That's how Jonah felt when God told him to go preach repentance (being sorry for their sins) to the people of Nineveh. The book of Nahum (3:1–4) gives a good description of how horrible and bloody this city was. The people were so cruel and violent that when God told him to go there, Jonah went in the completely opposite direction! He hopped on a boat, got tossed overboard, was swallowed by a big fish, and was puked up on the beach. It took all of that to make him finally go to Nineveh. So, smelling of salt water and fish guts, Jonah preached to the Ninevites.

And the big surprise? The people actually repented! From the king all the way down to the slaves, everyone was sorry for their sins. God liked this and decided to forgive them. God used a stinky preacher to help a whole city full of people turn over a new leaf.

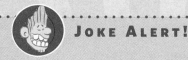

JOKE ALERT!

Other possible reasons that Jonah resisted going to Nineveh:

1. He didn't like his passport photo.
2. He would lose his deposit on his upcoming weekend fishing trip.
3. At a crossroads, some joker switched the Nineveh and Tarshish directional signs.
4. He was allergic to sackcloth and ashes.
5. The ship to Tarshish was offering "a whale of a deal!"

GO TO THE EXTREME

- **Jonah** walked through the entire city of Nineveh in three days and his message reached over 120,000 people.

- **Nineveh** was located near present-day Mosul, Iraq. Even though it was once an enormous city, there are only ruins today.

- **Assurbanipal,** one of the kings who ruled in Nineveh, had a library that contained over 20,000 tablets with cuneiform (a kind of picture) writing.

135

Read the story in Jonah 1—4.

Graveyard Shift

When Jesus climbed out of the boat, a man possessed by an evil spirit came out from a cemetery to meet him. This man lived among the burial caves and could no longer be restrained, even with a chain.
Mark 5:2–3 (NLT)

Have you ever considered what it might be like to live near a cemetery? When you really think about it, it's just a well-kept park with flowers and trees. And it's very quiet. You'd never have to worry about the neighbors being too loud!

But would you ever want to live *in* a cemetery? The thought of that might just give you the willies. In Bible times, when people died, they weren't buried underground. Natural caves in hillsides were used (sometimes more were dug) to place bodies, and then stones were stacked to cover the entrance. The stones were put there to keep wild animals out, and to prevent the stink of the dead bodies from wafting into town on the breeze. Talk about a creepy place to call home! But that's exactly where the man in this account lived.

We don't know his name, but the man was demon-possessed and the townspeople wanted nothing to do with him. He had no place to go except the graveyard caves. At least there he couldn't hurt anyone but himself.

When Jesus saw his sad situation, he made the demons leave the man. Back in his right mind, the man was able to change his address. Jesus told him to go home to his family—his living relatives—and tell his story.

GO TO THE EXTREME

• **In** the city of Manila, Philippines, more than 10,000 families live in the enormous Manila North Cemetery because they don't make enough money to rent an apartment or buy land for a home.

• **The** Mount of Olives in East Jerusalem has been used as a Jewish cemetery for over 3,000 years and holds approximately 150,000 graves.

• **The** oldest known cemetery dates to 5000 BC and contains about 100,000 skeletons. It is located in southeastern Iran in the region where Iran, Afghanistan, and Pakistan meet.

JOKE ALERT!

Why do most cemeteries have walls or fences around them?

Answer: *Because people are dying to get in.*

Read the story in Mark 5:1-20.

You Take the High Road

A man was going down from Jerusalem to Jericho and fell into the hands of robbers. They stripped him, beat him up, and fled, leaving him half dead.
Luke 10:30 (HCSB)

Travel in the ancient world was hazardous. Traveling alone was even worse. People didn't carry first-aid kits. If you got into trouble you couldn't whip out your cell phone and call for help. This is why most people traveled in caravans (large groups) because, as everyone knows, there is safety in numbers.

The distance between Jerusalem and Jericho was about 17 miles. If you're on foot, the journey takes just under seven hours. One stretch of this road was known as the "Way of Blood" because so many people were robbed and killed there. Yikes! Yet this was the road of choice for many because the other road went through Samaria. Not a bad place, but, sadly, the Jews didn't like the people there, so they avoided it.

Say you were told that you had a choice between two roads: One would take you through a town full of people whom you don't like (and they don't like you either) and the other would take you through an area populated by muggers. Which road would you choose?

Jesus used this parable (a story which teaches truth) to help people learn to get along with others. He knew that everyone had either heard of this "Way of Blood" or they had actually traveled it. He wanted them to put aside their differences and stop putting themselves in danger just to avoid people they didn't like.

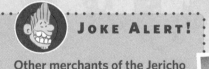

JOKE ALERT!

Other merchants of the Jericho Road Mall, in addition to the inn:

- *Body by Samson and Hair by Delilah*
- *Goliath's Big and Tall Shop*
- *Esther's Queen-Sized Apparel*
- *John B's Health Foods*
- *Zacchaeus R. Block Tax Preparation*

GO TO THE EXTREME

- **The** road between Jerusalem and Jericho was built by the Romans during Jesus' childhood. In some areas, paving stones still exist on the road, although most of the stones were stolen for building purposes.

- **The** world's most dangerous road is the North Yungas Road in Bolivia. Two hundred to three hundred travelers die on this road each year.

- **The** Inn of the Good Samaritan is a Turkish building located on the highway halfway between Jerusalem and Jericho. It is not the actual inn of the parable, but rather a museum and tourist trap selling souvenirs.

137

Read the story in Luke 10:30–37.

Gone to Golgotha

Carrying the cross by himself, he went to the place called Place of the Skull (in Hebrew, Golgotha).

John 19:17 (NLT)

While not telling us exactly where Golgotha was located, the Bible does give us a few clues to the location of this creepy place. It was outside the city gate, near a heavily traveled road. It was only a short distance from the tomb in the garden where Jesus' body later was placed.

GO TO THE EXTREME

• **Crucifixion** was the chief form of punishment in the Roman world for around 800 years, from 600 BC to AD 400.

• **The** ancient historian Josephus wrote of only one known survivor of crucifixion—a man who was taken down before he died. Christians, however, know of one man who rose from the dead after crucifixion: Jesus Christ.

• **In** modern history there are instances when crucifixion was used as the means of death. The Japanese banned Christianity, and to punish those who broke that law, they crucified some Jesuit and Franciscan missionaries at Nagasaki in 1597.

Since no one is sure of the exact location of Golgotha, you can't visit the place where Jesus and many men before and after him were crucified. No one even knows for sure what this place looked like. Some people say the hill was shaped like a skull, which is why they called it the Place of the Skull. Others say the name came from people associating death with skulls.

This was the place where hundreds, maybe thousands of people received the death penalty by the gruesome method of crucifixion. In fact, crucifixion was so gory, the people began to protest. It was finally banned by the Roman emperor Constantine I in AD 337.

JOKE ALERT!

"What did you learn in church today?" Mom asked her five-year-old.

"We sang a song about a bear with a problem" answered little Suzie. "And we learned his name!"

Intrigued, Mom asked, "Really? What's the song?"

"Gladly, the Cross-eyed Bear," she answered.

Read the story in John 19:17.

Field of Blood

They decided to use the money to buy the potter's field as a burial place for foreigners. That is why it has been called the Field of Blood to this day.
Matthew 27:7–8 (NIV)

When **Judas Iscariot was** overcome with remorse for accepting thirty pieces of silver to betray Jesus, he returned the coins to the temple. The priests, however, knew the money was payment for murder (because they were the ones who paid him!). They could not accept "blood money" (money used to purchase the death of a person), so they used it to buy land on which to bury the poor and foreigners.

The land they bought was rich with clay and had been owned by a pot-maker, so it was known as a "potter's field." The "potter's field" in this account, although its location is in dispute today, was also known as "Aceldama," which is an Aramaic word meaning "field of blood." It was called this because of the awful condition of Judas's body when he was buried there. Acts 1:18 describes what occurred after Judas hanged himself (Matthew 27:5). His body began to decay as it hung from the rope. Eventually, his corpse fell, and his body split open when it hit the ground—he literally burst apart. Gross.

JOKE ALERT!

Some people think Judas's last name, or at least his nickname, was "Scaredy Cat" (Iscariot). Here are some possible last names of other New Testament people:

Mark Down

Luke Warm

Pilate Here

Theophilus Mess

Barnabus Stop

Phoebe Sting

Titus Over

Rhoda Construction

GO TO THE EXTREME

• **The** term "potter's field" comes from an ancient description of a piece of property that was rich with clay. Those in the business of making earthen vessels for a variety of purposes—potters—would purchase this land and have an abundant supply of clay for their business.

• **Pottery** is dishes, plates, cups, and cooking pots made out of clay. Making dishes and pots out of clay is good for two reasons: clay is cheap and easy to get, and pretty much anybody can make a useful container out of it.

• **The** thirty pieces of silver of Judas's time is equivalent to $8,000 today.

1 3 9

Read the story in Matthew 27:1–10; Acts 1:16–19.

Hellfire

[This] is the way it will be at the end of the world. The angels will come and separate the wicked people from the righteous, throwing the wicked into the fiery furnace, where there will be weeping and gnashing of teeth.
Mathew 13:49–50 (NLT)

Okay, just to be clear, no matter what some people might try to tell you, hell is real. How do we know hell is a real place? Because the Bible tells us it is. The Bible is God's Word, and God never lies. So what is hell really like?

Well, since no one on earth has gone there to visit and come back to tell us, we have to believe the description of hell given by Jesus in the parable of the rich man and Lazarus in the book of Luke (Luke 16:19–31). When the rich man died, he went to hell (not because he was rich, but because he was mean to people), and he could see someone he knew—Lazarus—in heaven. The flames were so hot and the rich man was so uncomfortable, he begged for Lazarus to bring him just one drop of water to cool his tongue!

Hell is a place where the maggots never die and the fire never goes out (Mark 9:48). Imagine all of the smoke from never-ending fires. Revelation 14:10–11 tells us that those in hell will never get relief from the flames and smoke. The pain and suffering will go on *forever*.

Not a pretty picture. In fact, it's downright horrible, disturbing, and scary! Why would anyone want to go there?

Thankfully, you don't have to go there. Ever. When Jesus died on the cross he went into hell to take the keys to the place from Satan himself. Because he rose from the dead, Jesus has the power to keep people from going there. All you have to do to avoid hell is believe in Jesus as your Savior. When you do that, you don't ever need to be afraid of that awful place.

GO TO THE EXTREME

- **Hell** is mentioned more than 60 times in the Bible, depending upon which translation from the original Hebrew, Aramaic, and Greek you read.

- **Many** scary movies about hell have been made in Hollywood, yet none of them give the viewer an answer to the question, "How can I avoid hell and go to heaven?"

- **There** is a Hell, Michigan, a Hell, California, and a Hell, Arizona (which is a ghost town!).

Read the story in Luke 16:19–31.

Abysmal Abyss

The angel threw him into the bottomless pit, which he then shut and locked so Satan could not deceive the nations anymore until the thousand years were finished. . . .
Revelation 20:3 (NLT)

The bottomless pit mentioned in the verse above is also called the "abyss" in other places in Scripture (like in Luke 8:31 when the demons begged Jesus not to send them to the "abyss"). An abyss is a deep, immeasurable space, gulf, or cavity; a vast chasm. Can you imagine falling into a hole and never landing? You just fall and fall and fall and. . . . Can't imagine it? Maybe because it just doesn't make sense. Since human beings have never seen a hole without a bottom, it's hard for us to believe such a thing exists but it does. The good thing is that God created this abyss not for us, but for Satan.

The abyss is the prison where God will put Satan for a thousand years. (Some believe this is a literal 1000 years; others think it's figurative, symbolic—either way, it's a long time.) He'll be chained up, tossed in, and not allowed to "land" until the thousand years are up. During those thousand years, Jesus Christ will be King of the world and no one will be deceived by Satan. He'll be totally powerless as he falls, bound up in chains. He'll be serving the longest prison sentence ever!

GO TO THE EXTREME

• **The Abyss** was a 1989 science fiction movie about an undersea trench populated by aliens.

• **In** 2009, a robot sub explored Challenger Deep, an abyss within the Mariana Trench that reaches 36,000 feet beneath the waves. That's more than six miles!

• **In** October of 2004, a team of explorers set a new caving depth record of 6,824 feet in the world's deepest known cave called *Krubera*, located near the coast of the Black Sea in the Republic of Georgia. It took the team two weeks to reach the bottom of the abyss.

JOKE ALERT!

Signs of the end-times *not* recorded in Scripture:

• *Spam will be served in fine restaurants everywhere.*

• *Professional athletes will agree to play for minimum wage.*

• *Things will feel itchier.*

• *There will be a dramatic increase in belly-button lint.*

• *The newest NFL franchise will be awarded to Babylon.*

Read the story in Revelation 20.

BACK to Life

When someone is dying, doctors use all kinds of equipment to help save that person's life. One of the pieces of equipment they might use is the defibrillator—a machine that virtually shocks a person in cardiac arrest back to life.

In Bible times, defibrillators didn't even exist. (The process of defibrillation wasn't developed until around 1899, thanks to two Swiss physiologists.) A dying person simply. . . died. But sometimes an amazing thing would happen. The dead person came back to life! No, this isn't a horror story. We're talking about real people who came back to life through the power of a God who didn't need a defibrillator or any other equipment.

Get ready for the amazing stories of the dead who walked, talked, and sneezed. And we promise you won't have nightmares after reading them!

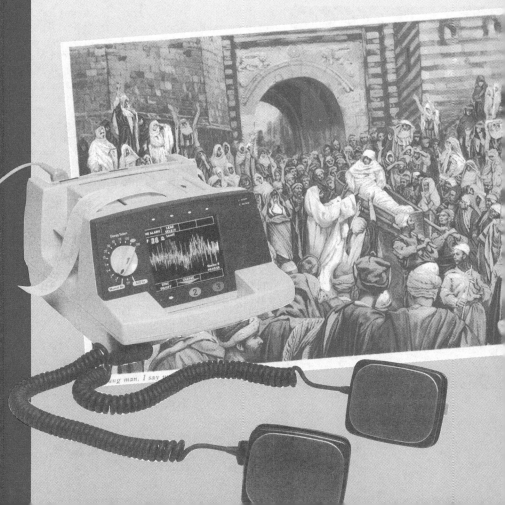

ung man, I say

A Weighty Resurrection

[Elijah] stretched himself out over the child three times and cried out to the Lord, "O Lord my God, please let this child's life return to him."
1 Kings 17:21 (NLT)

If you're playing football with your friends and three or four of them all piled on top of you, you'd understand how it feels to have a lot of weight crushing you. Well, one prophet in the Bible actually lay across a kid—not to crush him or take the breath out of him, but to actually bring it back!

For a long time, there was a drought in Israel, which made food and water difficult to find. Elijah, a man who loved God and tried to get Israel to turn back to God, was staying in Sidon with a widow and her son. God had sent Elijah out of Israel because King Ahab and his wife, Jezebel, wanted to kill him.

Elijah helped the widow and her son get food to survive, and they had come to trust him. The widow was beginning to think that God really was with this strange guy. Then one day, her son—her only other family member—suddenly died. The widow was heartbroken and mad at Elijah. If he had such an "in" with God, why had God allowed her son to die?

Elijah was sad too. So he took the dead boy in his arms, carried him upstairs, and laid him on a bed. Elijah prayed . . . and then he did something weird: he stretched himself out on the boy three times! Sort of breathing his own life into the boy. And instead of squashing him, it actually helped. God heard Elijah's prayers, and the boy came back to life!

GO TO THE EXTREME

• **The** average weight of a National Football League player is 248 pounds, but an offensive tackle could weigh as much as 318 pounds. Do the math: How much weight would be on top of you if you had three offensive linemen tackle you?

• **Hard** to believe, but no player has ever been killed by a hit in the NFL, although certainly plenty of injuries have occurred!

• **This** is not the last time a prophet in the Bible will lay on someone to bring him back to life! (See the next story.)

JOKE ALERT!

Possible ancient talk show subjects (if they had talk shows):

• *Did Adam have a belly button?*

• *What's with all this talk about Babel?*

• *Goliath—giant headache*

• *Women who act like Jezebel and the men who fear them*

• *Elijah—lying down on the job?*

• *Haman's hang-ups*

1 4 4

Read the story in 1 Kings 17:17–24.

Gesundheit!!

The boy sneezed seven times and opened his eyes.
         2 Kings 4:35 (NIV)

Sneezing is just never really a nice, subtle thing to do. Usually it is accompanied by all manner of grossness, and means we need to get someone a tissue or at least not touch what he or she touched. But in one story in the Bible, a sneeze was the best sound ever!

One day as Elisha was worshiping God, he saw a friend of his a long way off on her way to meet him. He knew something was wrong, because she was riding her horse at breakneck speed.

When she got to him, she threw herself at his feet and said to Elisha, "Did I ask you for a son, my lord?" . . . "Didn't I tell you, 'Don't raise my hopes'?" (2 Kings 4:28, NIV). Elisha had no idea what she meant, but then she explained: the child Elisha had prayed she would have had suddenly gotten a terrible headache and died that very morning. The woman wondered why Elisha would pray that God would give her a son, only to have God let the boy die a couple of years later. It seemed like a mean trick to play.

Elisha didn't understand it either, but he ordered his servant to run as fast as he could to the woman's house and lay Elisha's staff on the boy. The staff was a symbol of Elisha's God-given power. But it didn't work.

So when Elisha arrived, he closed himself in a room with the boy, prayed, and then it happened again: the prophet of God stretched himself out on the boy once, got up and walked around, and then stretched himself out on the boy again.

Suddenly, the boy sneezed seven times . . . and opened his eyes! The best sneezes ever!

GO TO THE EXTREME

• **A** twelve-year-old girl from England holds the world record for most consecutive sneezes: she sneezed every minute for a while. Later her sneezes slowed down to every five minutes, but lasted for 977 days!

• **Sneezes** have been clocked at over a hundred miles per hour!

• **A** sneeze can launch particles up to twelve feet away! Ewwww!

Read the story in 2 Kings 4:18-37.

Totally Cool!

Little girl, I say to you, arise.
Mark 5:41 (ESV)

Have you ever wanted something really badly? Wanted it so badly, you'd even do something all your friends would think is totally uncool just to get what you wanted?

In Jesus' day, the Pharisees were the religious in-crowd: they were the cool ones, the people everybody wanted to be. And the Pharisees hated Jesus because he didn't care how cool they were.

GO TO THE EXTREME

- **The** Pharisees were the law-keepers of the day. Unfortunately, they were also the law-adders. They didn't just worry about God's law, but they also added over 600 other laws that all the people were expected to keep!

- **Some** notable Pharisees in the Bible include Nicodemus (John 3) and Paul (Acts 26).

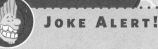

JOKE ALERT!

Here's something you *won't* find in the Bible:

From this moment on, the disciples could see things right and keep their spiritual balance by remembering this event . . . using their Jairus-scope.

Jairus was a Pharisee. But one day, his daughter got so sick he knew she was going to die. The doctors couldn't do anything, nobody could help her. Jairus was desperate. Then he had a thought: Jesus! Jesus was the only person Jairus had ever heard of who actually healed people.

He found Jesus in a crowd and begged him to come heal his daughter. Jairus knew his friends would be shocked to see him falling at the feet of Jesus, but he thought it would be worth the humiliation if Jesus could save his little girl.

Jesus looked into his eyes, and Jairus knew he would help. But then suddenly, a servant ran up, and Jairus knew the worst had come: "Your daughter is dead." The words were like a blow to the stomach—he couldn't breathe. But before he could say anything, Jesus looked at him again: "Do not fear, only believe," he said (Mark 5:36, ESV).

Then Jesus went to Jairus's house, took the little girl by the hand, and said "Little girl, I say to you, arise." To Jairus's delight, she sat up immediately.

Sometimes being totally uncool is totally worth it.

Read the story in Mark 5:21–43.

Not So Fast!

The dead man sat up and began to talk, and Jesus gave him back to his mother.
Luke 7:15 (NIV)

What would you do if you got up one morning and there was no food in your house? What if you found out that you had no way of getting more food either? You'd be pretty upset, right?

That's pretty much how the woman in this story was feeling, only she was terribly sad too because her only son had just died.

In Jesus' day, women usually relied on men to work and bring home money and food for the family. This woman had lost her husband, and then a bit later, she lost her only son. Widows were not able to own land, a source of money and food, so they were forced to depend on family or charity to survive. Not only did she not have any family, she also didn't have any way of getting food. She was hopeless and desperate.

But as the funeral procession moved out of her town to the burial site, Jesus happened to be walking by. He didn't see a husband or other sons with her and knew she was in trouble. So he walked up to her and gave her hope, saying, "Don't cry" (Mark 7:13, NIV). This must have been confusing for her. But then as Jesus touched the stretcher the dead young man was lying on, he said, "Young man, I say to you, get up!" (7:14, NIV).

The people following the funeral were amazed when the young man suddenly sat up and started talking! What an unexpected miracle! They began praising God because of what Jesus had done.

JOKE ALERT!

Not a good motto for a doctor:
*When you are at death's door,
I will pull you through.*

GO TO THE EXTREME

• **In** 2009, a Brazilian family was in the middle of a funeral service when the man they thought they were burying walked in alive!

• **Embalming** of dead bodies has been done since the days of ancient Egypt. The Egyptians embalmed bodies because they believed it necessary to enter the afterlife. During the American Civil War, bodies were embalmed so they could be shipped back to their families for burial. Embalming is still done today, because it preserves the body and gives a more pleasing appearance for a viewing in the casket.

147

Read the story in Luke 7:11-17.

Return of the (Stinky?) Mummy

When [Jesus] had said these things, he cried out with a loud voice, "Lazarus, come out." The man who had died came out, his hands and feet bound with linen strips, and his face wrapped with a cloth. Jesus said to them, "Unbind him, and let him go."
John 11:43–44 (ESV)

It's great to have a best friend. That person is important to you, and you're important to that person. You expect that person to come through for you, no matter what, to have your back, to stand up for you. You'd be pretty upset otherwise.

Mary, Martha, and Lazarus were all really good friends of Jesus. So when Lazarus got sick, Mary and Martha sent a message to Jesus to come right away.

Jesus, who prayed all the time so he could know what God wanted him to do, knew that he needed to wait to go to Lazarus. By the time he got to Mary and Martha's house, Lazarus had died. In fact, he had been dead and buried for four days by the time Jesus arrived.

Both Martha and Mary were pretty disappointed in Jesus. "If you had been here, my brother would not have died," Martha said (John 11:21, ESV). Jesus saw their sorrow, and he wept with them.

Then he went to Lazarus's tomb and told a few of the men with him to roll away the stone that blocked the tomb's entrance. Of course that caused people to comment. A dead body smells horrible when it starts to decompose. If you've had meat go bad in your refrigerator, you get the general idea. A dead body is worse.

In any case, Jesus insisted, and once the stone had been moved, he called out, "Lazarus, come out." The people stood staring, and suddenly, out came Lazarus, all wrapped up like a mummy, but fully alive! Many of those who saw this believed that Jesus was the Son of God.

GO TO THE EXTREME

- **Dr.** Pamela Dalton was hired by the U.S. military to create a non-violent weapon to disable enemies: it's a stink bomb that they call "stench soup."

- **Our** word *mummy* comes from an Arabic word for black gooey stuff. You can only imagine why . . . .

- **During** the late 1800s, rich party-throwers in England purchased mummies and unwrapped them to entertain guests!

(1 4 8)

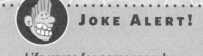

JOKE ALERT!

Life verse for someone who doesn't use deodorant:
"Lord, by this time he stinketh" (John 11:39, KJV).

Read the story in John 11:1–44

Lost and Found

[Jesus] showed them his hands and his side. Then the disciples were glad when they saw the Lord.
John 20:20 (ESV)

Have you ever hidden something special in a secret place and then gone back to find it, only to discover it's missing? Frustrating, isn't it? And sometimes sad too, if it was something you really cared about. But it's even more awesome when you find it!

Frustration and sadness must have been some of the feelings Mary, Peter, and John had when they went to Jesus' tomb three days after he was crucified.

Mary woke up early in the morning to go to the tomb, but when she got there, the heavy stone had been rolled to the side and the tomb was empty. When she told Jesus' disciples, Peter and John went racing down the streets to see it.

Were they angry, thinking someone had tampered with the tomb of their Lord? Mary seems to have been, because she asked the gardener (well, she thought he was the gardener) what he had done with the body. Where could it have gone?

They saw for themselves that the tomb was empty—in fact, Jesus' grave clothes were folded and piled up neatly in the corner! They didn't know what to make of it, but they were scared. Something weird was happening, and after what the authorities had done to Jesus, the disciples were afraid something was going to happen to them, too.

Locked in a room out of fear, the disciples waited for news. Suddenly, Jesus stood right there in the room with them! Nobody knew how it had happened, but there he was. They touched his hands, his side—he was real. And he was alive! Awesome indeed!

GO TO THE EXTREME

- **Estimates** have been made that the stone used to seal Jesus' tomb weighed as much as two tons. That's about the weight of your family car.

- **Crucifixion** upside-down was the penalty for tampering with any tomb—such as Jesus' tomb—that had the Roman seal on it. No wonder everyone was worried about the tomb being empty!

- **Intense** debate has surrounded a burial cloth known as the "Shroud of Turin." Some argue that it is the face cloth that had been on Jesus' head (mentioned in John 20:7).

JOKE ALERT!

The resurrection proved conclusively that Jesus was who he claimed to be—God in the flesh, the Messiah. Here are some reasons to know a religious leader is *not* the Messiah:

- *While trying to walk across the surface of the swimming pool, he had to be rescued from the deep end.*

- *He's only able to turn conversation into whine.*

- *He's dead.*

149

Read the story in John 20:1-23.

An Awakening in Joppa

[Peter] gave [Dorcas] his hand and helped her up. Then he called in the widows and all the believers, and he presented her to them alive.
Acts 9:41 (NLT)

Have you ever known someone who was really generous and kind? Someone who just enjoyed giving special things to people and helping them?

Dorcas was this type of woman. She lived in a town called Joppa, and she was a seamstress. Because the clothes people wore took a long time to make, clothing was pretty valuable. Everything was handmade. Imagine all the pin-pricks—yowch! But evidently Dorcas liked doing this kind of work, because she had sewn clothes for many of the poor widows in Joppa.

GO TO THE EXTREME

- **In** Jesus' day, their outer clothing layer—called a cloak—was often made of animal hairs. The hairs had to be twisted together to make yarn, and then they made cloth out of the yarn. Imagine how long that would take!

- **Machines** to make clothing weren't invented until the late 1700s or early 1800s.

- **Mother** Teresa, a woman who helped the poor just as Dorcas did, established nearly six hundred helping headquarters throughout the world during her lifetime.

One day, Dorcas suddenly got sick and died. The believers in Joppa were heartbroken: they had all lost a loving friend. So when they heard that Peter was in a neighboring town, they sent for him immediately. They knew he was an apostle and had healed many people through God's power.

Peter agreed to go with them. When he arrived and saw what a difference Dorcas had made in the lives of the townspeople, he went into the room where Dorcas lay.

Next, Peter asked everyone to leave the room. (You could say all of the mourners were waiting outside "on pins and needles.") Peter prayed and then told Dorcas to get up. She opened her eyes and did just as Peter said. Because of Dorcas's popularity in the town, news of the miracle spread quickly throughout Joppa, and God used it to help lots of people believe in Jesus.

Read the story in Acts 9:32–42.

A Deadly Snooze

> Seated in a window was a young man named Eutychus, who was sinking into a deep sleep as Paul talked on and on. When he was sound asleep, he fell to the ground from the third story and was picked up dead.
>
> Acts 20:9 (NIV)

Ever fall asleep in church? Imagine if it killed you! That's what happened to a young man named Eutychus.

Many people gathered to listen to Paul talk about Jesus and the Scriptures. Eutychus was among them, and apparently he was feeling sleepy. You'd probably be sleepy too if you were listening to a sermon until midnight!

Thinking some cool night air might wake him up a bit, Eutychus found a window and sat down in it. Maybe it worked at first, but not for long. Before he knew it, Eutychus was fast asleep. Maybe he jerked in his sleep, maybe he shifted positions to get more comfortable. The fact is, he fell out of the window, and the window was three stories up!

He was pronounced dead at the scene, but then Paul walked over, lifted him up in his arms, and Eutychus came back to life. This event encouraged all the believers. It was another reminder of God's love and power.

Maybe falling asleep in church won't kill you, but be sure to get enough sleep the night before so that you can listen, sing, and worship God—no matter how long the preacher talks!

GO TO THE EXTREME

- **Narcolepsy** is a health problem where people fall asleep suddenly at random times. (Eutychus didn't have narcolepsy though, he was just really tired.)

- **By** today's standards, three stories is about thirty feet—yikes! Stay away from open windows when you're tired!

- **In** World War II, an airman named Alan Magee is said to have survived a 22,000-foot fall from his bullet-riddled airplane. But the fall didn't kill him. He was found on the floor of a railroad station, and people assumed that the glass ceiling of the building somehow absorbed his fall.

JOKE ALERT!

Laconic Limerick:

People were packing the place.
When Paul spoke, that was often the case.
But not feeling too well,
young Eutychus fell,
and they suddenly met face-to-face.

151

Read the story in Acts 20:7-12.

More Super than Superman

For the trumpet will sound, and the dead will be raised imperishable, and . . . this mortal body must put on immortality.
1 Corinthians 15:52–53 (ESV)

Did you know that you are, in some ways, immortal? That's right. The Bible says that when Jesus returns to earth at the Second Coming, we will all be raised from the dead, immortal.

Because God is all-powerful, he rules over all things, and the Bible says that the last enemy he will destroy is death itself. Jesus' resurrection was the first sign of the end of death.

Just as Jesus rose from the dead by the power of God, you will too. And on top of that, you'll have a snazzy new body as well. The Bible doesn't tell us much about that body, but it won't get sick or sore or achy or tired ever again.

After Jesus had risen from the dead, he walked through locked doors. Maybe we'll be able to do that too—who knows? Pretty cool, huh?

The important part though is that you believe that you're a sinner and Jesus' death paid for your sins to bring you into his family. This is the key to spending your immortality celebrating with Jesus.

GO TO THE EXTREME

- **Probably** the most famous immortal superhero is Superman. The first Superman comic book was released in 1938.

- **The** Flash, a superhero who first showed up in comic books in 1940, is said to be able to move so fast that he can go right through a wall without breaking it.

- **There** are over 22,000 known viruses on the earth, and the number is always increasing. None of them will hurt us when Jesus comes back.

JOKE ALERT!

Sign in a nursery:
"We will not all sleep, but we will all be changed"
(1 Corinthians 15:51, NIV).

1 5 2

Read the story in 1 Corinthians 15:35–56.

TOUCHED by an Angel

People have been fascinated by angels for ages. There have been television shows, movies, and multitudes of books about angels. You could probably name several books or TV shows you've seen. (We won't quiz you.) It's fascinating to think that someone previously unseen could suddenly appear before your startled eyes.

Sadly, some people find it easier to believe in angels than to believe in God. But angels are the messengers and helpers of God. The Bible doesn't say how many angels there are. But we know there are different classifications of angels: messengers; archangels (leaders of angels); cherubim (six-winged angels worshiping before the throne of God); seraphim (the angels seen by the prophet Isaiah). An angel didn't make a move without the permission of God. (Well, most of them didn't, as you'll see if you keep reading.) In the Bible there are many stories of people who encountered angels. Sometimes they didn't realize they were actually talking to an angel! But each time a person was touched by an angel, something amazing happened. On the following pages, see how many different types of angels you can spot.

WrestleMania in the Middle of the Night

He said, "Your name shall no longer be called Jacob, but Israel, for you have striven with God and with men, and have prevailed."
Genesis 32:28 (ESV)

Imagine that you had to step into the wrestling ring with a sumo wrestler—you know, one of those super-heavy guys. You'd probably be thinking, "I'm toast," or something like that, right?

Jacob had a wrestling match that may have made him feel similarly. One night, in the middle of the night, while Jacob was preparing to face his brother Esau, an angel came and wrestled with him until morning. Jacob must have been pretty strong to hang in there for so long!

One tiny detail tells us how amazingly strong the angel was: he touched Jacob's hip and put it out of joint—just one little touch and Jacob was limping for a long time.

But Jacob held on, determined, and as the sun started to rise, Jacob clung to the angel and would not let the angel go until he blessed him.

The angel agreed to bless Jacob and changed his name to Israel, which would become the name of the nation God made from Jacob's family. Remember—Jacob was the grandson of Abraham, the one God promised would have a family more numerous than the stars in the sky!

GO TO THE EXTREME

• **The** heaviest Japanese sumo wrestler weighed 580 pounds!

• **It** takes a huge amount of force to dislocate a hip. In fact, in a healthy person, it's usually only caused by something like a high-energy collision, such as being hit by a car or an NFL linebacker.

• **The** average adult male needs 2500 calories a day, but since an hour of wrestling could burn as many as 1000 calories, Jacob may have burned more than 6000 calories during that night of wrestling!

154

Read the story in Genesis 32.

JOKE ALERT!

Laconic Limerick:
Caught in a wrestling grip
He held on without a slip
Jacob was game
So he got a new name
And a memory jog in his hip.

Angel Foretells Strongest Man in the World!

He will take the lead in delivering Israel from the hands of the Philistines.

Judges 13:5b (NIV)

Think you're God's gift to your family? Samson had evidence to prove that he was! Before he was born, an angel showed up and told his parents so.

Manoah and his wife were unable to have children. One day an angel showed up and told her to start eating a special diet because she was going to give birth to a baby boy. Then he said some other strange things: her son should never cut his hair, drink wine, or eat anything "unclean" (such as pork).

These special rules would make him a Nazirite, a person set apart to God. Manoah's son was supposed to follow these rules his whole life. The angel said God would use this boy to begin to deliver Israel from the oppression of the Philistines. Samson would grow up to become the strongest man in the Bible.

When she told her husband, Manoah understood that this would be a big responsibility, so he prayed that the angel would come back and teach them how to raise the boy. The angel did come back and repeated all the same things to Manoah, and then encouraged him to offer a sacrifice to God. When he did, an amazing thing happened. As the flames were blazing up from the altar, the angel ascended in the flames up to heaven!

Clearly, Manoah and his wife knew for certain that this angel was from the Lord, and they fell to the ground and bowed their faces in the dust.

GO TO THE EXTREME

- **Other** Nazirites in the Bible: John the Baptist and Paul.

- **Wood** burns around 1500 degrees Fahrenheit . . . that's a hot flame that angel ascended in!

- **The** heaviest weight a person has ever bench pressed is 1075 pounds— that's about the weight of an adult male polar bear.

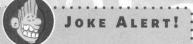

JOKE ALERT!

Here's something you won't find in the Bible:

The angel told Manoah how to raise Samson in order to teach him Nazi-rite from wrong.

1 5 5

Read the story in Judges 13.

The Beautiful Angel

How you have fallen from heaven, morning star, son of the dawn!
Isaiah 14:12 (NIV)

Who's the most beautiful person you know? Did you know that the Bible tells us that of all the angels, Satan was the most beautiful?

Crazy, huh? Like people, angels can fall prey to self-centeredness, at least that's what the story of Satan tells us.

God created him, and his name was Lucifer, which means "shining one," or "morning star." Not usually what you think of when you hear the word "devil" or "Satan." Usually we picture a red, horned guy with a spiky tail and pitchfork.

Well, he was beautiful, and perhaps it was his own beauty that caused him to think of himself as equal to—or maybe even more powerful than—God. He wanted to take over heaven and have everyone worship him instead of God.

So God easily and instantly removed him from heaven. The Bible says he was thrown down into the pit of the dead, where he and everyone else who loves themselves more than God will eventually wind up.

Scary stuff, huh? The Bible tries to make it clear what a crazy thing it is, in the face of the beauty and wonder of God, to love ourselves instead. Not only does it seem really foolish, it's also not good for us in the long run!

GO TO THE EXTREME

- **Venus** is the brightest planet in the sky, and you can see it in the morning and the evening. That's why it is perhaps the most famous morning star.

- **Our** picture of Satan as a red guy with horns, a pointy beard, tail, and pitchfork may have began as early as the 1400s.

- **There's** a real animal called a Tasmanian Devil. It looks like a small dog; when stressed, it releases a really bad smell.

JOKE ALERT!

Why does Satan walk funny?
Answer: *Because he has deviled legs (deviled eggs).*

Read the story in Isaiah 14:9–15.

On the Fast Track

"Don't be afraid," he said, "for you are very precious to God. Peace! Be encouraged! Be strong!"
Daniel 10:19 (NLT)

Once you've eaten a meal, it doesn't take too long before your body starts sending you signals that it would like some more food, please. Grrrooowwl, goes your stomach and you start thinking, *Gotta get a snack!*

So imagine fasting for twenty-one days. Fasting is when you don't eat food so you can focus all your body's energy on reading the Bible, talking to God, and thinking about him. But imagine having only water fcr three weeks! How wild would the smell of pizza make you then?

Daniel had been fasting for three weeks because he was sad about the fact that the men of his people (including Daniel himself) had been taken away from their homeland and forced to live in Babylon.

One day, an amazing angel showed up to encourage Daniel about the future of the nation of Israel. This angel told Daniel about how angels are fighting with the powers of Satan. God appointed a powerful angel named Michael (an archangel) to protect Daniel's people, and in the end, everyone who loves God will be delivered.

The angel encouraged Daniel and showed him that in the heavenly realms, God had sent angels to fight for his good.

GO TO THE EXTREME

- **A** lady in India, named Irom Sharmila, has been on a hunger strike for the last eleven years! (She has had *some kind* of nutrition, of course.)

- **Rumbles** in your tummy are caused by muscles tightening and loosening in your digestive system.

- **How** to end a fast? How about a hot-dog-eating contest? The world record holder ate 62 in ten minutes!

JOKE ALERT!

Here's something you won't find in the Bible:

Often those who fast are allowed to have some sort of nourishment, thus the expression "fast food."

157

Read the story in Daniel 10—12.

I'm Gonna Have a What???

And behold, you will conceive in your womb and bear a son, and you shall call his name Jesus.
Luke 1:31 (ESV)

Think of something you would never expect to have in the next few months. A million bucks? Your own private island? Complete power over your parents and siblings? You know, something that seems pretty impossible to get.

Well, Mary, a girl who was maybe 14 or 15, never expected to have a baby anytime soon. She wasn't married or anything! But one day, an angel named Gabriel showed up and told her, sure enough, she was going to have a baby.

Knowing that babies didn't come from storks, Mary of course was curious as to how this was going to happen. Gabriel explained to her that God's Spirit was going to help her have a baby boy—in only nine months!

GO TO THE EXTREME

• **There** are more than 5000 and counting paintings of Gabriel delivering his news to Mary.

• **Thirteen** was the legal age for marriage in biblical times.

• **The** largest species of stork can be almost five feet tall and have a wingspan of 10 feet!

The next thing Gabriel said must have really made her wonder: he said that the boy she would birth would be a King and would rule over the people of Israel forever!

Mary's response shows how much she loved and trusted God. She said, "I am the servant of the Lord; let it be to me according to your word" (Luke 1:38, ESV).

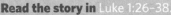

JOKE ALERT!

After Sunday school, Lindsey proudly displayed to her parents the picture she had drawn in class. It looked very much like an airplane with passengers, so her father asked what the picture represented.

"It's the flight to Egypt," answered the girl.

"I see," said his father, "and this must be Mary and the baby Jesus."

"Yes!" Lindsey answered enthusiastically.

Pointing to a rotund figure in the back of the plane, Dad asked, "Who's this?"

"That's Round John Virgin!"

(1 5 8)

Read the story in Luke 1:26–38.

From Counting Sheep to Wide Awake

The angel said to them, "Don't be afraid, for look, I proclaim to you good news of great joy that will be for all the people."

Luke 2:10 (HCSB)

Ever count sheep in your mind to help you fall asleep? It's supposed to help, but since we don't see sheep on a real regular basis, it does seem a little random, right? One-sheep, Two-sheep, Three-sheep . . .

Back in Bible times, raising sheep was as common a business as running a fast-food restaurant. Some sheep were raised to become sacrifices in the temple. A group of shepherds near Bethlehem, who were probably watching a flock of sheep for the temple had the shock of their lives one night! Bright light beamed down on them, and they suddenly heard the voice of an angel announcing the birth of the most important person in all of history. Next, the angel told them where to find Jesus. After that a huge crowd of angels appeared and started singing praises to God!

This was indeed, the most hopeful day of human history, and one that fulfilled a prophecy by the prophet Micah (Micah 5:2). Jesus' birth marked the beginning of his sacrifice to clear away all our sins and give us his pure, spotless record.

JOKE ALERT!

Bursting through the door after his first Christmas pageant rehearsal, little Edmund exclaimed, *"Wow—I get to be a shepherd, and I learned all about angels."*

"Really," responded Mom. "What did you learn?"

Edmund answered, "Well, the leader is Harold, and he keeps trying to find Gloria!"

GO TO THE EXTREME

• **The** world's oldest sheep was named Lucky, and lived to be 23 years old—twice the normal age for sheep.

• **One** of the top tips for falling asleep quicker? By threes, count backward from three hundred: three-hundred, two-ninety-seven, two-ninety-four . . . zzzz.

• **One** of the brightest moments in a night sky is when there's a full moon and it's closest to earth in its orbit. It happens about once every year and a half.

Read the story in Luke 2:1–20.

Knock, Knock . . . Who's There?

She saw two white-robed angels, one sitting at the head and the other at the foot of the place where the body of Jesus had been lying.
John 20:12 (NIV)

An old riddle asks, "Who's buried in Grant's tomb?" People often think for a while and then give up: "I don't know—who?" Grant, of course! It's his tomb, after all. (There, now if you didn't know that, you can be smarter than all your friends for about a minute.)

If someone asked that of Jesus' tomb though, the answer would be a lot less obvious, since he certainly isn't there!

Mary found this out firsthand when she went early Sunday morning, a few days after Jesus' crucifixion. Instead of finding Jesus in the tomb, she found a wide-open tomb, with two angels sitting in it. Beside them was a folded stack of the cloths that had been wrapped around Jesus when he was buried.

The angels didn't say much, but what they did say hinted at the exciting fact Mary was about to discover. "Woman, why are you crying?" is all they said. Angels should have known that if Jesus *was* dead, there was cause for weeping. Their question hints that they knew something Mary didn't know.

Moments later, as Mary saw Jesus face-to-face, she discovered the amazing fact the angels had already known: Jesus was alive!

GO TO THE EXTREME

• **One** of the biggest tombs in the world is called the Daisen Kofun. It is the tomb of the Japanese Emperor Nintoku and is 1,594 feet long!

• **The** Church of the Holy Sepulchre in Jerusalem was built on the site of Jesus' tomb.

• **The** oldest chartered cemetery in the U.S. is the Grove Street Cemetery in New Haven, Connecticut. The first burial there took place in 1797.

JOKE ALERT!

Why might a building be called "House of Angels"?

Answer: *Because of all the wings.*

Read the story in John 20:1-18.

Angels Everywhere!

*And night will be no more. They will need no light of lamp or sun, for the Lord God will be their
light, and they will reign forever and ever.*
Revelation 22:5 (ESV)

Breaking a record can be fun. John's book of Revelation sets the record in the Bible
for most angels seen by a person. Revelation has tons of angels!

John saw angels who were in charge of specific churches throughout the world and
angels who were in charge of the winds, sun, earth, and sea. At one point, he saw more
angels than he could count, surrounding God's throne and singing praises to God.

He also saw angels who had frightening jobs. For example, seven angels had special
trumpets. When they blew them, awful things happened—from fire burning up a third
of the earth, to insects with a scorpion's bite scuttling
over all the land.

After many terrible sights, an angel came to John
and showed him the most mind-boggling sight of
all: the New Jerusalem in heaven. Unlike any other
city imaginable, New Jerusalem shone with all the
radiance of God and was made of clear crystal. This
city represented the promise of heaven—no pain, no
sorrow, no meanness, and no selfishness.

GO TO THE EXTREME

• **Some** scorpion stings
feel like a wasp sting, but
there's one scorpion in the
Sahara Desert that's as
poisonous as a Cobra!

• **Some** medieval scholars
actually debated the
question of how many
angels could dance on the
point of a needle!

JOKE ALERT!

Here's God's message to a church
through one of his angels, by
way of a . . . Laconic Limerick:
God will give the churches their due.
Judgment will fall on some too.
If they stay true to form,
Laodicea's lukewarm.
Watch out, here comes a spew!

161

Read the story in Revelation 21—22.

HOORAY for Healing!

I **f you've ever been** sick, you know how good it feels to get well again (especially if it means not having to take any more icky-tasting medicine). In our day, we have many choices about doctors to call or medicines to buy at the pharmacy. But in Bible times, doctors were few and far between. Medicines were costly (just like today). Diseases could be easily spread. That's why there are so many rules about cleanliness in the Law of Moses—to prevent the spread of disease.

Many times in the Bible, however, God miraculously healed people or gave individuals the power to do so. The power to heal showed that the healer was a man of God. In the New Testament, healing was also a sign that the long-promised Savior had come. As you read these stories, feel free to give a hooray or two for the amazing God who showed he could do anything.

Really? A Mud Bath?

Naaman became angry and stalked away. "I thought he would certainly come out to meet me!" he said. "I expected him to wave his hand over the leprosy and call on the name of the LORD his God and heal me!"

2 Kings 5:11 (NLT)

Ever watched an elephant or hippo have a mud bath? Did it make you want to close your eyes and turn your head? Maybe watching this animal made you want to jump in and join the fun.

Naaman, an army commander, was a leper. Leprosy was one of the worst skin diseases imaginable. It was very contagious and painful. He wanted to be healed, but he had no idea that muddy water would be involved.

GO TO THE EXTREME

• **Did** you know that chinchillas clean their fur by taking baths in dust made of fine pumice?

• **On** June 22, 1969, an oil slick and debris in the Cuyahoga River caught fire in Cleveland, Ohio. A river on fire! This shocking event helped lead to the passage of the Clean Water Act in 1972.

• **Spa V** at the Hotel Victor in South Beach, Florida is the world's most expensive spa. If you like to take a bath in Evian water and you have at least $5000, head on over.

Elisha was a prophet at this time. Naaman heard through a slave that Elisha could heal him. When Naaman arrived with his fancy horses and chariots and bags of gold and silver at Elisha's door, Elisha sent a messenger to tell Naaman to wash in the Jordan River seven times. He would then be healed.

The Jordan River wasn't the cleanest river in the world. Naaman stomped off. He was an important commander in the army, not an animal who needed a mud bath! But his officers convinced him to follow Elisha's instructions, and after seven dips in the muddy river, Naaman became a man with healthy skin and a new attitude.

Who knew what a mud bath could do?

JOKE ALERT!

Laconic Limerick:
Naaman, a desperate man,
said to Elisha, "Please do what you can."
When seven times he went in,
so clear was his skin,
that he quickly became a God-fan.

Read the story in 2 Kings 5:1–16.

Sit! Stay! Go!

I myself am a man under authority, with soldiers under me. I tell this one, "Go," and he goes; and that one, "Come," and he comes. I say to my servant, "Do this," and he does it.
Matthew 8:9 (NIV)

Some dogs never learn much in obedience school. They don't want to sit or stay, even with the reward of a dog treat—or two or three. Mostly they want to run around chasing other dogs.

The Roman centurion in this story, however, understood the idea of obeying commands, being "under authority." He was a soldier—the leader of one hundred men. He came to Jesus one day and asked Jesus to heal his servant. Even though Jesus agreed to go, the centurion wasn't yet finished. In response to Jesus' willingness, he humbly explained that he wasn't worthy to have Jesus enter his home! Yet he had the faith that Jesus could heal his servant.

This is one of the few times in the Bible where Jesus is described as being "amazed." Consider the setting. The Romans were in charge in Judea. A Jewish man or woman had to do whatever a Roman person told him or her to do. But this Roman soldier was different. He recognized that Jesus was special.

This soldier would definitely get a good grade in God's obedience school, don't you think?

JOKE ALERT!

How did this government become so large and in charge of the known world?

Answer: *Because they were roamin' (Roman) all over.*

GO TO THE EXTREME

- **The** roads the Romans built were some of the best in the ancient world. The Appian Way (Via Appia), the most well-known Roman road, was built in 312 BC and still exists today.

- **A** battalion in the U.S. Army is a military unit of around 300–1,200 soldiers. This unit is further divided between two and seven companies, and typically led by either a lieutenant colonel or a colonel.

- **A** typical Roman soldier's gear and weapons weighed about 66-100 pounds.

1 6 5

Read the story in Matthew 8:5-13.

Hand-to-Hand Healing

[Jesus] said to the man, "Stretch out your hand." And the man stretched it out, and it was restored, healthy like the other.
Matthew 12:13 (ESV)

Try wadding up a piece of paper into a tight ball. Then undo your ball. What do you see? How does your paper look now compared to how it looked before you squished it into a ball?

GO TO THE EXTREME

• **The** human hand has 27 bones. The wrist alone has eight bones.

• **A** child who breaks a bone might be back to normal in just a few weeks, but an adult who breaks a bone might take six to eight weeks to heal.

• **The** Pharisees made up a lot of rules for their Sabbath. In fact, they had thirty-nine different sections of rules—very different from God's guidelines for the Sabbath (Exodus 20:8–11).

One day Jesus met a man whose hand didn't look quite right. Maybe it had been broken, maybe it had been burned, or maybe it just grew differently from his other hand. Before he could do anything for the man, the Pharisees (the religious leaders who didn't believe in Jesus) jumped in to ask Jesus a question about healing on the Sabbath. Instead of answering with a "yes" or "no," Jesus asked the Pharisees a question they couldn't answer: "Which one of you who has a sheep, if it falls into a pit on the Sabbath, will not take hold of it and lift it out?" (Matthew 12:11, ESV).

Jesus then reached out and healed the man's hand. Suddenly, it looked like a new hand! Imagine if your wadded-up piece of paper suddenly looked brand-new, with no wrinkle-lines. Amazing! Impossible? God can do the impossible.

JOKE ALERT!

Comments overheard in the crowd at this healing:

"What's it gonna take, an arm and a leg?"

"Let's give the man a hand!"

"These guys aren't being fair, you see." (Pharisee)

"Those stretching exercises really work!"

166

Read the story in Matthew 12:9–14.

Spitting Allowed?

[Jesus] took him away from the crowd privately. After putting His fingers in the man's ears and spitting, He touched his tongue.
Mark 7:33 (HCSB)

No **Spitting Allowed! A** sign in a Hong Kong train station sends a clear message with a big red *X* drawn over a person who is spitting. Don't do it! How interesting that Jesus chose to heal someone by doing something we consider gross—and in some places today, like the trains in Hong Kong, is against the law.

One day some people brought to Jesus a man who could not hear and could not speak well and begged Jesus to heal him. Jesus listened to them and then pulled the man away from the crowd.

Now, we might expect that Jesus would pray for this man or maybe put his hands on his head. But, no! Jesus put his fingers in the man's ears. And then he spat on his fingers and touched the man's tongue. Then Jesus said, "Be opened!" (Mark 7:34, HCSB). Instantly, the man could hear everything and could speak perfectly.

Don't you wonder what word this man spoke first? And don't you wonder why Jesus chose this way to heal?

JOKE ALERT!

Here's something you *won't* find in the Bible:

Later people would say of this man, "He's the spitting image of Jesus."

GO TO THE EXTREME

• **Llamas** sometimes feel the need to spit. Mostly they do it to other llamas as a way to say, "Back off!" Sometimes, though, when a llama has been mistreated by a person, it may spit at that person.

• **The** blue-ringed octopus secretes venom through its saliva.

• **Every** July since 1974, people from around the world gather in Michigan for the International Cherry Pit Spitting Championship. Did you know that the world record for Cherry Pit Spitting is currently 100 feet, 4 inches?

SPITTING ON SIDEWALKS PROHIBITED

Read the story in Mark 7:31-37.

From Doubt to Faith

When Jesus saw that the crowd of onlookers was growing, he rebuked the evil spirit. "Listen, you spirit that makes this boy unable to hear and speak," he said. "I command you to come out of this child and never enter him again!"

Mark 9:25 (NLT)

You may know someone who has epilepsy, a medical condition that happens when a person's brain produces sudden bursts of electrical energy. These bursts disrupt other brain functions and affect a person's movements or actions. Well, in this story, a father brought his son to Jesus. The boy had symptoms that many people with epilepsy would recognize. Sometimes the boy would fall to the ground unable to speak and begin foaming at the mouth.

The frightened and concerned father begged Jesus' disciples to heal his son. Unlike people today with epilepsy, this man's son was possessed by an evil spirit. The disciples couldn't make the evil spirit go away. So the doubtful father turned to Jesus.

Jesus knew that the father doubted his ability. After reminding him that God could do anything, Jesus commanded the evil spirit to leave the boy. It immediately obeyed!

This shows that we don't have to have faith in our *faith*—our ability to believe Jesus! Jesus helped a doubting father to have rock-solid faith in the Savior.

GO TO THE EXTREME

- **What** do Vincent van Gogh, Charles Dickens, and Sir Isaac Newton have in common? They all had epilepsy.

- **An** Austrian physicist named Hans Berger was the first to measure the electrical activity in the human brain.

- **The** human brain has about 100 billion neurons (cells that transport electrical impulses).

JOKE ALERT!

This was a faith-to-faith encounter!

Read the story in Mark 9:14-29.

If You Had Three Wishes . . .

"Go," said Jesus, "your faith has healed you." Immediately he received his sight and followed Jesus along the road.
Mark 10:52 (NIV)

Ever play the "Three Wishes" game? You and your friends take turns saying what you would wish for if someone gave you three wishes. A puppy? A best friend? A million more wishes?

Jesus met a man named Bartimaeus one day who had one big wish. This blind beggar waited with lots of other people outside the city of Jericho. As he heard Jesus coming, he began to shout, "Son of David, have mercy on me!" (Mark 10:48, NIV).

People in the crowd tried to shut him up. But Bartimaeus would not stop. He wanted to talk to Jesus, no matter what. Jesus heard Bartimaeus and asked him what he wanted. There was only one thing—to see.

Jesus spoke a few words, and, you guessed it, Bartimaeus received his wish. He could see! A wish come true!

GO TO THE EXTREME

- **In** 1930, the first state law was passed that granted blind pedestrians protection and the right-of-way while carrying a white cane.

- **Did** you know that qualified volunteers help train puppies to become Seeing Eye dogs? They teach puppies good house manners and basic obedience then give them to an organization that specifically trains them to help the blind.

- **The** Braille alphabet was developed by Louis Braille, a blind man who lived in France.

JOKE ALERT!

Laconic Limerick:
Blind Bart shouted his plea
"Son of David, have mercy on me!"
To Jesus he came
and was never the same
following the One he could see.

1 6 9

I Just Want to Say "Thanks"

And as he entered a village, he was met by ten lepers, who stood at a distance and lifted up their voices, saying, "Jesus, Master, have mercy on us." When he saw them he said to them, "Go and show yourselves to the priests." And as they went they were cleansed.
Luke 17:12–14 (ESV)

Don't forget to say thank you!" Ever get tired of that parent reminder about anything from a ride home from school to half a peanut-butter sandwich from your brother?

One day Jesus came to a village and heard a group of lepers (people with a skin disease) standing together and shouting at him for mercy. They wanted Jesus to heal them.

In Bible times, people who had leprosy had to stay away from other people so the disease wouldn't spread. If a leper thought his leprosy had gone away, he was supposed to present himself to a priest, who could declare him clean. Instead of saying a word or touching them, Jesus simply told them to show themselves to the priest.

As the lepers obeyed Jesus and turned to go on their way, they looked at their skin. It began to look better and better. Then it looked normal. They were healed!

One of the lepers got so excited about his new skin that he ran back to Jesus and began praising God. Yet this one leper, a Samaritan, was the only one who said thanks.

GO TO THE EXTREME

- **Many** lepers live in danger of losing limbs. The leper starfish, an echinoderm, can lose a limb and grow a new one. This process is called regeneration.

- **Your** skin cells constantly shed. You get new skin every 30 days.

- **Did** you know that skin is our largest organ? Adults have eight pounds of it!

JOKE ALERT!

An organization of lepers could have been entitled **PARTS**:

People

Admitting

Really

Terrible

Sores

Read the story in Luke 17:11-19.

Lend Me Your Ear?

Then one of [the disciples] struck the high priest's slave and cut off his right ear. But Jesus responded, "No more of this!" And touching his ear, He healed him.
Luke 22:50–51 (HCSB)

Ever get so excited that you do something before you even think about it? Like running out the door to see a friend and forgetting that you are still in your pajamas? Peter, one of Jesus' disciples, did things like that.

On the night of his arrest, Jesus took the disciples to the Garden of Gethsemane. He spent time praying. The disciples fell asleep. And then, just as they were waking up, a crowd of people approached. They were led by Judas, one of Jesus' disciples who had decided to betray Jesus.

What would you have done if you had been there? Peter, usually a man of impulsive action, pulled out his sword and sliced off the ear of Malchus, the slave of the high priest!

Quickly, Jesus reached out, touched the man's ear, and made it whole. This was his last act of healing before he would perform the greatest healing ever—dying on the cross to cure the "sin sickness" of everyone.

GO TO THE EXTREME

• **John** Mark, the writer of the Gospel of Mark, was present that night in the garden. The Bible mentioned that he was so frightened, he ran away completely naked! (See Mark 14:51–52.)

• **An** earwig is a nocturnal parasite that feeds on plants and insects. Many people believe the rumor that earwigs like to burrow in the ears of people and lay eggs in their brains. Not true!

• **A** collection of Japanese swords was sold at Christie's auction house in New York for $8 million in 1992.

JOKE ALERT!

Overheard in the garden, just before the arrest of Jesus:

• *"Malchus, you're such a cut-up!"*
• *"This place is earie."*
• *"I thought I was joining a club. I didn't know I was supposed to bring one."*

171

Read the story in Luke 22:49–53.

Jumping for Jesus

Then Peter said, "Silver or gold I do not have, but what I do have I give you. In the name of Jesus Christ of Nazareth, walk."
Acts 3:6 (NIV)

How many steps do you think you take every day? Ever tried counting? Peter and John, two of Jesus' disciples met a man one day who could not take any steps. In fact, he had never walked.

Peter and John had just watched Jesus die on the Cross. And then they were so surprised when they saw that Jesus was alive again. They saw him with their own eyes and heard him promise that the Holy Spirit would come upon them. That promise came true on the day we call Pentecost. So, when Peter and John saw this crippled man at the Beautiful Gate of the Temple, they knew that the power of God now lived inside of them. They knew that they could give this man much more than just a few coins. In Jesus' name, they could give this man something much better—the ability to walk! So they told him to get up and walk. And that's exactly what the man did!

Now that is something worth jumping about, don't you think?

GO TO THE EXTREME

• **Did** you know that pure gold is too soft for day-to-day use as money and is typically hardened by being mixed with copper, silver, or other metals?

• **Instead** of being made of silver, today's quarters are "clad," which means coated. The inner core is pure copper and the outer covering is copper mixed with nickel.

• **Speaking** of leaping, in September 2011, Mike Powell, an American athlete, broke the record for the long jump at 8.95 meters (29.4 feet).

172

Read the story in Acts 3:1–13.

SPECIAL Effects

What was the last movie that made you go "Whooooaaa" because of the special effects? Thanks to ever-changing technology, special effects in movies are the best ever. Computer generated graphics can almost make you believe that what you're seeing is the real thing.

In Bible times, the only special effects were those God produced. He didn't need cameras, computers, or a Hollywood budget. All he needed was an audience and sometimes a willing prophet to show forth his glory. These events made a special impact on those who saw them. Get ready for some of the most eye-popping, exciting stories in the Bible. Lights, camera. action!

Walls of Water

Moses stretched out his hand over the sea. The LORD drove the sea [back] with a powerful east wind all that night and turned the sea into dry land. So the waters were divided, and the Israelites went through the sea on dry ground, with the waters [like] a wall to them on their right and their left.

Exodus 14:21–22 (HCSB)

The Israelites had been through a lot in the days prior to this trek to the Red Sea. They had seen Egypt buckle under plagues (widespread misery); experienced the shadow of the angel of death in the first Passover; and loaded all of their belongings onto donkeys and carts, as they left the only home they had ever known. And then, with their backs against a sea and the Egyptian army closing in, they panicked.

You'd think that, after all they had seen God do for them in Egypt, another miracle would be no surprise. After all, God brought them out of slavery. He wasn't about to let them die in the wilderness! But that's what they were afraid of. They blamed Moses and whined about having left Egypt—and they did this even as God placed himself between them and the soldiers, as a visible cloud or pillar of fire.

God told Moses what to do. Moses raised his hand over the sea and told around 2.5 million people to get moving. No time to waste! As they walked the dry land between two 60-foot walls of water, did they see fish, whales, or other creatures swimming by? Did they step carefully around crabs and coral reefs? If you had been there, would you have picked up a shell or two as a souvenir of your trip across the Red Sea?

GO TO THE EXTREME

- **The** Red Sea lies between the Mediterranean Sea and the Indian Ocean. It's about 1,400 miles long and between 100 and 220 miles wide. The Israelites most likely crossed at the northern end, in a portion now called the Gulf of Suez, where it's only 20 miles wide.

- **The** Red Sea most likely gets its name from the tiny sea plants that tinge its waters red when they are in bloom.

- **For** all of Israel to cross in one night, the opening in the Red Sea would have been between five and eight miles wide.

JOKE ALERT!

Possible reasons the Israelites spent forty years in the desert after crossing the Red Sea:

- *Their chariots got poor mileage.*
- *The map was written in hieroglyphics, and they had it upside down.*
- *They kept stopping at scenic overlooks to take pictures.*
- *The kids kept asking, "Are we there yet?"*
- *They didn't have exact change at the wilderness tollbooth.*

Read the story in Exodus 14.

Samson Brings Down the House

Samson prayed to the LORD, "Sovereign LORD, remember me again. O God, please strengthen me one more time. With one blow let me pay back the Philistines for the loss of my two eyes."
Judges 16:28 (NLT)

Have you ever wanted to pay someone back for something they did to you? That's what Samson wanted. Even though God tells us we should forgive those who do bad things, he allowed Samson to have revenge upon the Philistines. So how did he get into a mess in the first place?

Samson was a Nazirite and a judge of Israel. God told him that as long as he never cut his hair, he would be blessed with superhuman strength. Well, if you read "A Deadly Date" in Dastardly Villains (page 79) you know that Samson's own girlfriend, Delilah, tricked him by shaving his head! Now bald, he had no more strength. The Philistines captured him, gouged out his eyes, and put him in chains. This would have been the end of Samson except for one thing: his hair grew back.

Samson probably plotted his revenge as he felt his hair growing and his strength returning. His opportunity came when his arch-enemies were having a party and called him in to make fun of him. He prayed to God and asked for enough strength to bring down the temple and destroy everyone there, including himself. God granted his plea and used him to punish some very wicked people.

Sadly, he did this not for God, but for himself. In the end, revenge destroyed Samson. Remember, it's better to forgive and live.

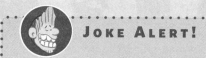

JOKE ALERT!

Some things biblical moms might have said to their kids:

Joseph's Mom—"Joey, you're such a dreamer!"

Moses' Mom—"Look both ways before crossing the Red Sea."

Samson's Mom—"What's it gonna take—an eye?"

Solomon's Mom—"Oh, you think you're so smart!"

Paul's Mom—"Why is it you can write letters to everyone else but never to your mother?"

GO TO THE EXTREME

- **The** temple that Samson destroyed was not a temple to the one true God, but to a pagan god named Dagon, who was said to be half man, half fish.

- **The** 1,100 pieces of silver that Delilah received for giving up Samson's secret is equal to about $300,000 today.

- **The** average amount of human hair growth per year is about six inches.

175

Read the story in Judges 16:23–30.

A Flash in Front of the Mob

GO TO THE EXTREME

• **A** Catholic religious order was founded on Mt. Carmel in the twelfth century. The monks who live in the monastery there are called *Carmelites*.

• **On** January 11, 2011, what looked like fire falling from the sky turned out to be a meteor. People from five states (Arkansas, Oklahoma, Florida, Mississippi, and North Carolina) reported seeing a flash of light and hearing a sonic boom.

• **The** prophets of Baal demonstrated typical behavior for ancient pagan religions such as yelling, wild dancing, and cutting themselves in order to draw blood.

The fire of the LORD fell and burned up the sacrifice, the wood, the stones and the soil, and also licked up the water in the trench.
1 Kings 18:38 (NIV)

Elijah was the only true prophet of the Lord left in Israel. The evil queen Jezebel ordered that all of God's prophets be put to death, but God protected Elijah. Jezebel and her husband, King Ahab, worshiped a false god named Baal. Because they worshiped Baal, they expected everyone in Israel to do the same. God wasn't pleased about that, so he sent Elijah to set things straight.

Elijah issued a challenge: the false prophets, all 850 of them, should meet him on Mt. Carmel for a showdown. Sacrifices would be offered, and the first group to receive fire from their god would get bragging rights.

The prophets of Baal yelled, danced, and even cut themselves on purpose. They did this *all day long*, but . . . silence. No answer, no fire.

Then it was Elijah's turn. Just to avoid any hint of cheating, he had people pour 12 buckets of water over the sacrifice. The meat, the wood, and the stones were soaking wet, and the water filled the trench around the altar. Then Elijah prayed a simple prayer.

God answered right away and proved to the people that he is real and Baal was just a phony.

JOKE ALERT!

April Fool's Day pranks *not* recorded in Scripture:

• *To alleviate stress on the ark, Shem, Ham, and Japheth put the two skunks under Noah's cot.*

• *Moses parted the Red Sea just as Aaron jumped off the diving board.*

• *Elijah first sent the prophets of Baal to Mount Chocolate.*

1 7 6

Read the story in 1 Kings 18:16-39.

Elijah's Ticket Home

As they were walking along and talking, suddenly a chariot of fire appeared, drawn by horses of fire. It drove between the two men, separating them, and Elijah was carried by a whirlwind into heaven.

2 Kings 2:11 (NLT)

Elijah was a pretty special guy. God granted him amazing power. In fact, earlier in 2 Kings, we learn that Elijah struck the Jordan River with his coat and the waters parted (just like the Red Sea). God immediately answered his prayer on Mount Carmel and protected him many times from harm. Elijah was so special to God, he was one of the only two people in the Bible who never died.

You read it right. Elijah didn't die. He was given a first-class ticket to ride on God's personal chariot in a whirlwind right up to heaven. Wow!

Three times Elijah told his servant Elisha to stay put, but three times Elisha was determined to stay with his mentor and friend. Finally Elijah asked Elisha what was so important that he stuck to him like Velcro. Elisha admitted his desire to be just like Elijah—he wanted the same God-given abilities and power as a prophet of God.

Apparently this request pleased both Elijah and God. Not only did Elisha get to see the chariot of fire, but when he went back to the river, he was able to part the waters *just like Elijah!*

Chariots . . . horses . . . a whirlwind. These things all represent power. Chariots and horses of fire aren't just power—they're God's power. Talk about going to the extreme!

JOKE ALERT!

Elisha's "group of prophets" (2 Kings 2:5, 7) could have been called SEERS:

Special
Envoys
Explaining
Righteous
Stuff

177

GO TO THE EXTREME

- *Chariots of Fire* is a 1981 British movie. It tells the true story of two athletes in the 1924 Olympics: Eric Liddell, a Scottish Christian who runs for the glory of God, and Harold Abrahams, an English Jew who runs to overcome prejudice.

- **The** strength of the whirlwind God created for Elijah would be equal to an F2 tornado. The wind speed necessary to lift a man from the ground is between 113 and 157 miles per hour.

- **Elijah,** Elisha, and Moses were all given the power to divide water. Since Baal, the fish-god, supposedly controlled water, many of Elisha's miracles involved water. Elisha's power over water showed that God was the one in control, not Baal.

Read the story in 2 Kings 2:1–12.

Striking (Olive) Oil

Elisha said; "Borrow as many empty jars as you can from your friends. . . . go into your house with your sons and shut the door behind you. Pour olive oil from the flask into the jars, setting each one aside when it is filled.". . . Soon every container was full to the brim!

2 Kings 4:3–4, 6 (NLT)

GO TO THE EXTREME

- **Olive** oil is obtained from olives (*duh!*), which grow on trees mainly in the Mediterranean Basin. It is commonly used in cooking, cosmetics, and soaps and as a fuel for traditional oil lamps.

- **The** world's most expensive olive oil is made in Greece. Special Koroneiki olives are harvested by hand, cold pressed, and bottled by hand. A 500ml bottle sells for $200.

- **Extra** Virgin Olive Oil (EVOO) is made by placing the olives in a vat and allowing them to crush the oil from each other by their own weight. The oil drips through the bottom of the vat through screens. This first pressing is bottled.

Say your dad owes his friend some money. Maybe he let your dad borrow money to help buy your new bike. Now he wants his money back, but your dad doesn't have enough to pay him. What happens next?

Well, in ancient times, the law said that if you owed someone money and couldn't pay, the other person could make you become his slave. And that's not all—they could take your *whole family* as slaves!

That's the kind of trouble the widow was in. She was in debt and the bill collectors were threatening to take her sons away. What could she do about it? She had nothing of value to sell, just a little jug of olive oil in the house.

Enter Elisha. He told the widow to borrow as many empty jars as she could find. This miracle was to meet the need of the widow and her two boys. He didn't do some big, public miracle here; rather, he helped them recognize God's power as the oil multiplied in front of them.

After selling the oil the widow had enough money to pay her debtors and enough extra to live comfortably with her sons.

JOKE ALERT!

Regardless of what some may say, this was *not* the conversation Elisha began at the widow's house:

Elisha, knocking at the door: *"Knock, knock!"*

Widow: *"Who's there?"*

Elisha: *"Olive."*

Widow: *"Olive who?"*

Elisha, laughing (what a kidder): *"Olive you too. Now please open the door."*

Read the story in 2 Kings 4:1–7.

Hot Stuff!

One of the seraphim flew to me with a live coal in his hand, which he had taken with tongs from the altar. With it he touched my mouth and said, "See, this has touched your lips; your guilt is taken away and your sin atoned for."
                    Isaiah 6:6-7 (NIV)

Can you imagine being touched by a red-hot coal? Cattle, horses, and sheep are often branded as a sign of ownership. Branding is when a piece of metal is heated in red-hot coals. When placed against the hide of an animal, the metal burns a pattern in the skin permanently.

Go back and read the verse again and notice something: the seraphim (a fiery, six-winged angel) had to use tongs to pick up the coal—it was too hot for a fiery angel to touch it, yet it didn't burn or leave a mark on Isaiah's lips!

Isaiah knew he was no better than those around him. He wasn't proud. In fact, when he had a vision of the Lord, he was painfully aware of his sin when he said, "I'm doomed! I'm sinful! I have filthy lips and I live around people with filthy lips!" Isaiah knew he was unworthy to be used by God, but because of his humility, God cleansed his sin and made him a mighty prophet.

God used a red-hot coal as a way of showing his power over the physical world as well as the spiritual world—only God can forgive sins, and he can do it however he pleases.

GO TO THE EXTREME

• **Instead** of branding, many farmers now use ear tags to identify their animals. This helps because animals from different farms often graze together and farmers need to know which ones are which. Ear tags sound much nicer than a hot brand!

• **A** burnt lip caused by hot liquids or foods can leave behind a painful and unsightly reminder for about a week. A lip burn from a hot coal would cause third-degree burns and would result in permanent scarring.

• **Seraphim** (literally meaning "burning ones") are the fiery, six-winged beings who continually praise God while circling his throne. They are described in detail in Revelation 4:8 as having eyes all over, including under their wings.

JOKE ALERT!

Note: after this incident, the prophet *did not* utter, "I say, uh, tongs a lot!"

179

Read the story in Isaiah 6:1-8.

Break a Leg!

I did as I was told. In broad daylight I brought my pack outside, filled with the things I might carry into exile. Then in the evening while the people looked on, I dug through the wall with my hands and went out into the night with my pack on my shoulder.

Ezekiel 12:7 (NLT)

Before there were movies, live theater was the only way people could see a story acted out. Some of the greatest plays in history were put on by such famous people as William Shakespeare, Christopher Marlowe, Moliere, and Tennessee Williams. Look them up sometime. But right now let's look at a well-known actor, the prophet Ezekiel, and his playwright/director, God.

The book of Ezekiel has eight episodes of dramatic theater directed by God and performed by Ezekiel. Each of the plays was meant to cause the people of Israel to ask, "What does this mean?" and then help them understand what God planned to do to punish them for centuries of sinful behavior.

In one performance, Ezekiel had to shave his head with a sword, put his hair in three separate piles, and set one on fire. In another, he had to pack his bags in broad daylight, then when night came, dig a hole into the side of his house and sneak out, pick up his bags, and walk away. His longest performance involved lying on his left side for 390 days and then his right side for 40 days!

Each play was not just for entertainment, but to teach a lesson. Because of Ezekiel's faithfulness to his Divine Director, the people of Israel got the message loud and clear.

GO TO THE EXTREME

- **The Mousetrap** is a mystery play by Agatha Christie. It opened in London in 1952 and has been running continuously since then, with over 24,000 performances so far.

- **Stories** from the Bible came alive in the tenth century through medieval mystery plays. They focused on the representation of Bible stories in churches and included an accompanying song.

JOKE ALERT!

Do not try these at home:

- *Dropping a millstone (Judges 9:53)*
- *Catching 300 foxes (Judges 15:4)*
- *Touching your lips to a burning coal (Isaiah 6:6–7)*
- *Eating a scroll (Ezekiel 3:2–3)*
- *Shaving your head with a sword (Ezekiel 5:1)*

180

Read the story in Ezekiel 12:1–16.

Don't Play with Fire

"Look!" Nebuchadnezzar shouted. "I see four men, unbound, walking around in the fire unharmed! And the fourth looks like a god!"
Daniel 3:25 (NLT)

Have you ever been in so much trouble that you thought it would take a miracle to get you out of it? Shadrach, Meshach, and Abednego were in a heap of trouble, all because they stood up for their faith in God.

King Nebuchadnezzar thought his kingdom was the best thing on earth, so he decided to have a 90-foot tall statue made. Being so tall, it would be seen far, far away. But the king also demanded absolute loyalty from his subjects. He rounded them all up and demanded that they prove their loyalty by bowing down to the statue, or face death in the fiery furnace.

Shadrach, Meshach, and Abednego weren't about to bow to anyone but God, much less a statue! This made the king furious! He ordered that they be tied up and thrown into the furnace. The furnace was then stoked seven times hotter than usual. It was so hot, the soldiers who tossed in the bound boys died from the heat! Yet the flames had no effect on Shadrach, Meshach, and Abednego. God not only kept them safe from the fire, he was with them in the fire. When they came out of the furnace, their clothes smelled clean and fresh and not a hair on their heads was singed! This was a serious miracle, one that showed just how powerful God is!

JOKE ALERT!

Overheard quotes that you *won't* find in the Bible:

- *From a royal advisor: "Those three guys think they're so hot!"*
- *From King Nebuchadnezzar, speaking of the three men: "They're bound to know."*
- *From Shadrach, Meshach, and Abednego as they looked out of the furnace: "Statue King?"*

GO TO THE EXTREME

- **A** statue 90 feet tall would be about the height of an eight- or nine-story building.

- **Nebuchadnezzar's** furnace was most likely an industrial furnace used as a brick kiln or an ore smelter (for iron weapons).

- **Fire** dancing is a performance art that involves spinning a flaming staff or swinging burning balls on a chain or cord while dancing. It is very dangerous and only professionals who have practiced the art for many years should perform fire dances.

181

Read the story in Daniel 3.

Pork Soup

[Jesus] said to them, "Go!" So they came out and went into the pigs, and the whole herd rushed down the steep bank into the lake and died in the water.
Matthew 8:32 (NIV)

Imagine your town has a couple of crazy men who are so violent, no one can even go near them. They know they aren't wanted, so they live in the only place where the neighbors don't complain: the cemetery! Would you wonder why they were so scary, mean, and violent?

Jesus met two men like this. Only he didn't have to wonder what made them the way they were. He knew. As soon as he came near to the men, the demons inside of them began screaming, "Why are you interfering with us, Son of God?"

The demons knew who Jesus was and how much power he had over them. They liked where they were, causing trouble and making people's lives miserable. But Jesus had compassion on the men and decided it was time for them to have their lives and their sanity back. The demons begged to be sent into a herd of pigs. Jesus told them, "Go!" and instantly the men were in their right minds and the pigs went crazy! The entire herd began a squealing stampede right down a hill and into the lake.

Suddenly, everyone knew what was for dinner.

GO TO THE EXTREME

- **Some** pigs can grow up to almost 2,000 pounds.

- **Pigs** can run surprisingly fast, and can outrun most people as their top speed is around 15 miles per hour.

- **Pigs** don't usually run in a straight line; they zigzag in order to escape predators. So if you are chasing a running pig, stop and save your strength— wait for the pig to tire out.

JOKE ALERT!

Why couldn't the two men continue to live in the cemetery?

Answer: *They were dispossessed.*

182

Read the story in Matthew 8:28–34.

Come On In, the Water's Fine!

"Come!" [Jesus] said. And climbing out of the boat, Peter started walking on the water and came toward Jesus.

Matthew 14:29 (HCSB)

The next time you're getting ready to get into the bathtub, see if you can just step *on* the water instead of in it! That might be kind of cool if you could do it, but then, how would you ever get clean? You'd have to start taking showers for sure!

The disciples were out in the boat on the lake when a storm began to brew. The winds became fierce, causing high waves. They were far from shore, and in trouble, no doubt. Early in the morning, Jesus came out to the boat. On foot. Walking on the water. Yep, you read that right. He was *walking on the water*.

When the disciples saw this, they were understandably freaked out. At first, they thought they were seeing a ghost! But Jesus called out to them, "Don't be afraid!" (Matthew 14:27, HCSB). Peter wanted to be sure it was Jesus, so he asked for proof.

Jesus told Peter to come, and what do you know? Peter walked on the water toward Jesus! He must have been almost in shock when he realized he was walking over waves in the midst of a great storm. When he looked around, he got a little scared and began to sink. Jesus grabbed his hand and they both climbed into the boat, then the wind and waves stopped.

While it's no surprise that Jesus—the Son of God—walked on water, it's pretty neat that Jesus allowed Peter to do what no other human being had ever done before.

Go to the Extreme

• **Water** often has a really cool phenomenon called surface tension. It's like a very thin skin that covers the surface of calm water and very small, light objects are able to sit on this skin and not sink. Some bugs can skitter across water on the surface tension.

• **Basilisks** are lizards in the iguana family. They have large hind feet with flaps of skin between each toe. The fact that they move quickly across the water, aided by their web-like feet, gives them the appearance of "walking on water," hence the nickname, "Jesus Christ Lizard."

• **Liquid** Mountaineering is a new extreme sport in which people get a running start on land and, by taking very quick steps, are able to run on water for a few steps before sinking.

JOKE ALERT!

Note: Peter wondered what was going on, and then it began to sink in.

183

Read the story in Matthew 14:22-33.

The Spotlight's on Jesus

[Jesus] was transfigured before them, and his face shone like the sun, and his clothes became white as light. And behold, there appeared to them Moses and Elijah, talking with him.
Matthew 17:2–3 (ESV)

Suppose your best friend completely changed his or her style, maybe got a wild haircut or new clothes totally different from what he or she usually wears. How would you react? Jesus changed right before the eyes of his startled friends—Peter, James, and John. But the change wasn't about clothes or haircuts. Instead, these disciples were shown something amazing about Jesus, something that would make a great movie.

Out of all the disciples, Peter, James, and John were the ones closest to Jesus. One day, they went with Jesus up on a mountain. Nothing special about that, right? But suddenly Jesus started glowing! His clothes became blinding white as if a spotlight hit them or a gaffer (a person working in movies who specializes in lighting) turned bright lights on him. If that wasn't amazing enough, suddenly Moses and Elijah—people who lived during long, long ago in *Old Testament* times—appeared and had a conversation with Jesus!

A stunned Peter tried to make a suggestion about putting up tents for Jesus, Moses, and Elijah. But all heard a voice speaking: "This is my beloved Son, with whom I am well pleased; listen to him" (Matthew 17:5, ESV). Hearing the voice of God terrified the disciples. But when Jesus told them not to be afraid, he suddenly looked the way he always did.

Was this all just a weird dream? No. The three men saw Jesus as he really was: the Son of God who was the perfect reflection of God's glory. And no makeup or special effects were needed!

Go to the Extreme

- **The** brightest beam of light in the world is on top of the Luxor Hotel and Casino. This light beam has 315,000 watts! If you were in an airplane, you can see it 250 miles away!

- **Two** of the most expensive movies ever made are *Spider-Man 3* ($258 million) and *Avatar,* which probably cost around $280 million to make.

JOKE ALERT!

Why did Peter suggest putting up shelters on the mountain for Jesus, Moses, and Elijah?

Answer: *He thought the experience was in-tents.*

Read the story in Matthew 17:1–8.

Up, Up, and Away!

He was taken up before their very eyes, and a cloud hid him from their sight.

Acts 1:9 (ESV)

Ever been in a helicopter? Like a hummingbird, a helicopter can lift straight off the ground. It doesn't have to taxi down a runway like a plane. Thanks to tail rotors and the main rotors, it has the thrust to lift off the ground.

After Jesus rose from the dead, he knew that his time on earth was limited. He appeared to his disciples and reminded them to wait in Jerusalem for the coming of the Holy Spirit. He also gave them a special assignment: to make disciples of people from all nations. But suddenly, whoosh—Jesus started floating up in the sky! If you know about gravity, you know that what goes up must come down. But Jesus just kept on going toward heaven! The eleven disciples (minus Judas who betrayed Jesus) stood there gaping at him as he disappeared behind a cloud. (Wouldn't you?)

And that's not all! Two men popped up next to them. While they might have looked like men, they were angels with a special message: Jesus would someday leave heaven and return to earth.

Just like gravity: what went up will someday come down.

JOKE ALERT!

Laconic Limerick:
*The disciples were wondering why
as they watched him ascend in the sky.
But angels soon told
that they should live bold
and then with their Savior to fly.*

GO TO THE EXTREME

- **A** ruby-throated hummingbird can fly straight up, similar to a helicopter.

- **The** "human cannonball" is a performance where a person is shot out of a specially-designed cannon by way of compressed air or a spring. Someone shot out of a cannon can go as far as 200 feet and travel at 70 miles per hour.

- **The** Feast of the Ascension, celebrated by some churches, commemorates Jesus' ascension into heaven forty days after his resurrection. Ascension Day falls forty days after Easter.

185

Read the story in Acts 1:1–11.

Who Needs French Class?

Suddenly, there was a sound from heaven like the roaring of a mighty windstorm . . . tongues of fire appeared and settled on each of them. And everyone present was filled with the Holy Spirit and began speaking in other languages.
Acts 2:2–4 (NLT)

It seems like something out of a video game. Your objective: meet up with other believers before the sound of a windstorm hits. If you do so, you'll be filled with power. You will know you have powered up when a flame appears above your head and you can speak in a different language.

GO TO THE EXTREME

• **The** five most popular languages in the world are Mandarin, Spanish, English, Arabic, and Hindi.

• **If** you can speak more than one language fluently, you are a *polyglot*.

• **Fluency** in a foreign language takes around 200 to 500 hours of active study. Languages that are close to English and use the same alphabet (such as Spanish, French, Italian) take less time; languages that are very different and use an alphabet we have to learn (like Russian, Chinese, Polish) take more time.

But it wasn't a game. It really happened, long before animation or computer generated images, and it wasn't just a story from someone's overactive imagination!

All of the believers were gathered together. They were probably having a meeting to figure out what to do next, but what happened was out of their hands. The sound of wind roared through the place. A little flame appeared over each head. Suddenly, they could speak in many foreign languages!

The loud noise was heard by everyone in Jerusalem, and they came running to see what was up. When they heard the gospel, each in their own language, around 3,000 people believed and were baptized.

Talk about power! Loud noise, floating flames, fluency in a foreign language . . . that's better than any video game ever made!

JOKE ALERT!

Overheard in the crowd:

• "No wonder they call this the Windy City."
• "Did I hear pig-Latin?"
• "How much does a Penta-cost anyway?"
• "Now that's the Spirit!"

japanese

SPANISH

FRENCH

ITALIAN

(1 8 6)

Read the story in Acts 2:1–12.

Shed Some Light on the Subject!

As he was approaching Damascus on this mission, a light from heaven suddenly shone down around him. He fell to the ground and heard a voice saying to him, "Saul! Saul! Why are you persecuting me?"

Acts 9:3–4 (NLT)

Saul was a very devout Jew. He knew the law and he knew the Scriptures. When he was persecuting Christians, he really thought he was doing what was right. He believed that Christians were enemies of God who had to be stopped, and he was going to be the one to stop them.

One day, on his way to yet another town to put more Christians in jail, God stopped *him* in his tracks. A blinding light (literally!) blasted out of heaven and made Saul fall down. Then Jesus himself spoke. Wouldn't that be awesome? To have Jesus shine a light down onto you and speak to you? Out loud? And all of your friends hear it too? That's exactly what happened to Saul, but he didn't think it was cool—he was scared speechless. And he was now blind.

Everything he had believed to be true about Christians, and about Jesus, was suddenly turned upside down. Saul wasn't the good guy, Jesus was. The Christians weren't the enemies of God, Saul was. He was so shocked by this event that, when his friends got him to Damascus, he didn't eat or drink for three days.

When God sent someone to heal Saul's blindness, the first thing he did was eat. Then he headed out to tell everyone about Jesus.

GO TO THE EXTREME

- **Early** astronomers such as Galileo, Newton, and Cassini all suffered vision problems after staring directly at the sun, but none were completely or permanently blinded. The vision problems lasted for a few hours to a day.

- **Every** five seconds, one person in the world goes blind. An estimated 37 million in the world are blind.

- **Blindness** is both a cause and a result of poverty. Many people in developing countries are more likely to suffer from malnutrition, poor water quality, and poor sanitation. This places them at much higher risk of contracting eye disease which can lead to blindness.

JOKE ALERT!

The Paul weight-loss program:
Walk from Jerusalem to Damascus and suddenly feel light.

187

Read the story in Acts 9:1-6.

All Shook Up!

Suddenly, there was a massive earthquake, and the prison was shaken to its foundations. All the doors immediately flew open, and the chains of every prisoner fell off!
Acts 16:26 (NLT)

GO TO THE EXTREME

• **Scientists** have tried many different ways of predicting earthquakes, but none have been successful. On any particular fault (a crack in the earth's crust), scientists know there will be another earthquake sometime in the future, but they have no way of telling when it will happen.

• **An** earthquake freed prisoners in the Port-au-Prince prison during the Haitian earthquake in 2010. Haitian human rights attorneys said that 80 percent of those inmates were never charged with a crime, or they were imprisoned on false charges, just like Paul and Silas.

• **About** 80–90 percent of earthquakes occur in the Pacific Ring of Fire. Most are small and centered in unpopulated areas, causing little damage and few deaths.

When you hear about an earthquake, the stories on the news are usually about injuries, death, and people searching for the missing. Have you ever heard any good news about an earthquake? Imagine the news story that might have come out of this Bible passage about Paul and Silas: "Earthquake Sets People Free!"

That's right. There were no injuries, no deaths. Paul and Silas were just sitting in their cell singing praises to God, when all of a sudden, a really big quake hits! (To find out the reason they wound up in prison read, "Peril at Philippi" in Fortune-Telling and Magic page 48.) Every prison door was opened and all of the inmates' chains fell off. Paul and Silas were in the deepest, darkest part of the prison, and their feet were in stocks. Stocks are heavy bars placed across the feet so the prisoner can't even move. You might think this is the worst place to be in an earthquake, right? Paul and Silas couldn't even run for cover! But they didn't need to. God had sent the quake to help them, not to hurt them.

The jailer was so worried his prisoners had escaped that he was ready to kill himself. But Paul and Silas stopped him and told him about their amazingly powerful and merciful God.

JOKE ALERT!

Paul traveled (with Barnabas, Silas, and others) to many places. At one stop he evidently made an endorsement in the race for governor. He wrote:

"I have no man likeminded, who will naturally care for your state" (Philippians 2:20, KJV).

Read the story in Acts 16:16–33.

BIBLE Beasts

Got pets? What's your favorite kind of animal—pet or otherwise? Even if you don't have pets, you can see animals and insects everywhere: squirrels chattering from trees; birds singing and winging through the air; fish frolicking in the water; bees buzzing from flower to flower.

As soon as God created land and divided the seas, he created creatures to populate land, sea, and sky. Animals are the stars of many stories in the Bible. You can probably name at least one parable or a proverb from the Bible that mentions an animal. The God who knows every sparrow can be known through the many stories of animals within the pages of the Bible.

Stir up your favorite animal call (feel free to hoot like an owl or bark like a seal) and get ready for the beasts of the Bible in all of their glory.

Ssssee Serpent, Hear Serpent

Now the serpent was more crafty than any of the wild animals the LORD God had made.
Genesis 3:1 (NIV)

If you heard a snake talk, what would you do, besides run away? There was one snake in history that *could* talk. That snake—a serpent—was really Satan in disguise. When the serpent talked to Eve, she wasn't surprised that it talked. If only she had run away when it did. The serpent questioned the command that God had given Adam and Eve: to not eat the fruit from the tree of the knowledge of good and evil. First, he asked Eve if God forbade them to eat from any tree. When Eve added an extra rule that God hadn't given them—"You must not eat fruit from the tree that is in the middle of the garden, and you must not touch it, or you will die" (Genesis 3:3, NIV)—the serpent was quick with a lie.

After hearing that she wouldn't die, Eve plucked the fruit, ate it, and gave some of it to Adam. Because of their disobedience, Adam and Eve were expelled from the garden and the whole world was cursed. Everyone born afterward was born with a desire to sin. But God had good news, even as if he sadly forced the first people to leave the garden. A Savior would be born someday who would defeat the serpent once and for all.

GO TO THE EXTREME

- **The** snake that had the record of longest snake in the world was a reticulated python at the Columbus Zoo in Ohio. It was 24 feet long and weighed 300 pounds. It died in October 2010.

- **The** deadliest snake in the world is the Inland Taipan snake in Australia. Its bite can kill a person in 45 minutes.

- **The** corn snake is one of the most popular snakes people have as pets. This snake comes in a variety of colors.

JOKE ALERT!

How did Adam and Eve react after being expelled from the garden?
Answer: *They raised Cain.*

190

Read the story in Genesis 3.

The Floating Zoo

You are also to bring into the ark two of every living thing of all flesh, male and female, to keep them alive with you. Two of everything—from the birds according to their kinds, from the livestock according to their kinds, and from every animal that crawls on the ground according to its kind.

Genesis 6:19–20 (HCSB)

Have you ever had to feed an exotic pet? Some snakes require large rats for their dinners. Or how about feeding a lion enough meat to satisfy his daily hunger? Imagine having a boatload of animals to feed every day! When God promised to send a flood to wipe out most of the people and animals he had made, he gave Noah a new job: the world's first zookeeper. And it happened when Noah was 600 years old!

Why did God reach such a decision? Well, a group of fallen angels married some women on earth. Talk about bad marriages! And their kids were terrible. Soon, instead of obeying God, many, many people only wanted to do wrong things. God had only one man that he considered "good": Noah. God told Noah to build a huge boat and load it up with his wife, his three sons, and the sons' wives. In addition, God gave Noah the command in the passage above. (Perhaps you feel like singing "Rise and Shine" right now.)

Imagine being shut up in that ark for not just the 40 days and nights of rain but over 190 extra days. Imagine the sights, sounds, and smells! After the ark landed on Mt. Ararat, Noah had to wait until the floodwaters decreased.

Noah sent a raven to find dry land. When it returned, Noah sent a dove out twice. The second time, the dove returned with an olive leaf. That meant it had found dry land! Finally, God told Noah that his family and all of the animals could leave the ark.

GO TO THE EXTREME

- **The** Toronto Zoo is one of the world's biggest zoos with 5,000 animals.

- **The** San Diego Zoo and the Columbus Zoo are two top zoos in America.

- **The** ark was 300 cubits long—about the length of one and a half football fields. Can you imagine a football stadium riding a wild wave?

JOKE ALERT!

Where did Noah keep his bees?
Answer: *In the archives (ark hives).*

191

Read the story in Genesis 6:9—8:14.

Look out for Locusts!

If you refuse to let my people go, behold, tomorrow I will bring locusts into your country, and they shall cover the face of the land, so that no one can see the land.
Exodus 10:4–5 (ESV)

Some of the smallest creatures can cause the most devastation. No, we don't mean your young cousin who once broke your toys or messed up your room. We mean a small insect known as the locust. Some desert locusts may be three inches long, but when they swarm, watch out!

When God told Moses he would free the people of Israel from slavery, God knew that it would take ten plagues on Egypt to do the job. One of the plagues involved swarms of locusts. All Moses had to do was stretch out his hand toward Egypt. God sent swarm after swarm. *How bad could that be?* you might wonder. Locusts will eat anything green in sight.

Locusts weren't just in every field and pasture. They were in every house, every farm, everywhere! You couldn't even bake a loaf of bread without a locust ending up in the dough. (Mmm . . . locust surprise.)

In order for locusts to grow in numbers, there must be a large amount of rain. But the Creator of the world didn't need rain to whip up millions of locusts.

Go to the Extreme

• **Locusts—grasshoppers— are** considered good eating in many countries.

• **The** worst locust swarm migration in recent history happened in northwest Africa in 2004. Scientists estimate that one swarm of locusts had 69 billion locusts.

• **Cicadas** aren't really locusts, but they carry that name. Most of these interesting insects live for two to five years, but some, the "17-year locusts," start beneath the earth, and remain there until emerging 17 years later.

JOKE ALERT!

Egyptian weather forecast the night before the plague of locusts:
Quite swarm, with a 90 percent chance of pain.

192

The Donkey's Tale

Then the LORD gave the donkey the ability to speak. "What have I done to you that deserves your beating me three times?" it asked Balaam.
Numbers 22:28 (NLT)

When's the last time you had a good conversation with your pet? What? You say that's never happened, because animals can't talk? You're right, of course. We can talk to them, but if they answered back in words we could understand, we'd be shocked.

Yet that's exactly what happened more than two thousand years ago to a man named Balaam. He was a "prophet" from a country called Aram.

Balaam had a reputation for being able to bless and curse others. One day, King Balak of Moab asked Balaam to curse the Israelites. God spoke directly to Balaam, telling him not to curse them (Numbers 22:12). So Balaam refused the king's request. Balak continued to press, however, offering to make him very rich—still Balaam wasn't going to do what the king asked.

Eventually, however, when Balaam seemed to be determined to curse the Israelites, the Lord got his attention by allowing his donkey to talk to him.

The donkey turned away three times from the Angel of the Lord who was standing in the road with a drawn sword. Of course Balaam didn't know the donkey was saving his life.

This is the only time in the Bible such an event takes place. God delights in using unusual and surprising ways to accomplish his purposes and teach us lessons—even by a talking donkey.

GO TO THE EXTREME

- **The** smallest donkey is the Mediterranean Miniature donkey. This donkey is about 30 to 34 inches tall.

- **The** mammoth donkey is the largest breed of donkey in the world. They can grow up to 14 to 16 hands—56 to 64 inches—the size of a horse.

- **Probably** the most famous donkey in the Bible is the one that Jesus rode as he entered Jerusalem on Palm Sunday (Matthew 21:1-11). Now if that donkey could talk!

JOKE ALERT!

Possible names for Balaam's donkey (if you can't figure these out, ask Mom or Dad):

Kong (Donkey Kong)

Bray-lon Hotie (Don Quixote)

Jack Shane (Dankeschön)

Mr. Ed

Jaws (see the next story)

1 9 3

Read the story in Numbers 22:21-34.

Fiery Justice

[Samson] went out and caught three hundred foxes and tied them tail to tail in pairs. He then fastened a torch to every pair of tails, lit the torches and let the foxes loose in the standing grain of the Philistines.

Judges 15:4–5 (NIV)

Have you ever seen a field burning? Farmers sometimes burn old fields to clear them for growing new crops. Samson wasn't a farmer; he was a judge for Israel.

During the time of the judges—the special leaders in Israel who led their people in battle against their enemies—the people of Israel suffered at the hands of the Philistines. If you read "A Honey of a Riddle" in Puzzles & Riddles (page 34), you know that Samson told a riddle at a feast when he married a Philistine woman. When the guests decided to cheat by forcing the bride to find out the answer to the riddle, Samson took revenge against the Philistines. That didn't sit too well with his father-in-law, who gave Samson's bride to another man.

Revenge time again! Samson caught 300 foxes—an impressive amount—tied them together in pairs with a torch for each pair, and sent them into the crop fields of the Philistines. Samson's revenge led the Philistines to retaliate by burning his wife and her father. Samson couldn't let them get away with that. After he killed several Philistines, he later grabbed the jawbone of a donkey and killed a thousand men!

GO TO THE EXTREME

- **The** Romans in New Testament times would tie the tails of foxes together placing a firebrand in each pair. They would release them in the feast of Ceres to be hunted. The feast was to celebrate the goddess of corn. A very cruel form of entertainment!

- **There** are over thirty different breeds of foxes.

- **The** fox that Samson would have hunted was probably a red fox, which was about 24 inches long. They are harder to find in Jerusalem nowadays.

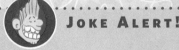

JOKE ALERT!

Samson's plan for fiery revenge was very *de-tailed.*

194

Relying on Ravens

You are to drink from the wadi. I have commanded the ravens to provide for you there.
1 Kings 17:4 (HCSB)

What's the weirdest food delivery you've ever seen? Maybe you gawked at a car shaped like a hotdog that delivered food to your neighbor's house. Maybe your cat dropped a mouse at your feet and wondered why you weren't appropriately grateful. But more than likely, you've never seen food delivered by ravens.

Elijah was one of God's prophets—one of the greatest in the Old Testament. He spoke God's messages in the time of King Ahab. Because Ahab worshiped false gods and continually made God angry, Elijah told Ahab that there would be no rain on the land until Elijah gave the word. With no rain, what happens? Crops don't grow. People starve. That includes prophets. But God didn't let Elijah go hungry.

First, he sent Elijah to a brook where he could get water to drink. Second, God explained that food would be delivered by ravens. You read that correctly. Ravens. Every day, like clockwork, the ravens delivered bread and meat to the hungry prophet in the morning and in the evening.

Next time you see a raven, think about how God can turn a bird into the best delivery service around.

Go to the Extreme

• **Some** ravens are actually 2.5 feet long. All are scavengers.

• **"The** Raven" by Edgar Allan Poe is one of the most well-known poems and certainly the work for which Poe is most known.

• **In** paintings depicting people in the early church, many were painted with ravens.

JOKE ALERT!

Elijah devoured the specially delivered food because he was *raven*-ous!

195

Read the story in 1 Kings 17:1-6

Too Horrible to "Bear"

Some small boys came out of the city and jeered at him, saying, "Go up, you baldhead! Go up, you baldhead!" And he turned around, and when he saw them, he cursed them in the name of the LORD. And two she-bears came out of the woods and tore forty-two of the boys.
2 Kings 2:23–24 (ESV)

At some time in your life, if you haven't already, you'll run up against a bully. Bullies come in all shapes and sizes. For many, their weapons are the cruel words they use. When they're punished for their behavior, most of us can't help rejoicing that justice has finally won out.

Sometimes a bully gets more than he or she bargained for. That's what happened when a group of kids decided to make fun of the prophet Elisha. Elisha had just become God's prophet when Elijah went to heaven. (For that story, read "Elijah's Ticket Home" in Special Effects, page 177.) When Elisha was headed toward the city of Bethel, the kids started calling him names. Well, Elisha didn't take that for long! If you read the Bible passage above, you can see the results. Judging by the fact that the bears attacked 42 of the kids, there may have been more than that number in the crowd. Just in case you're thinking that the punishment was too horrible to bear (get it . . . bear?), consider this: Elisha's curse showed God's judgment on those who disobeyed God.

This sad story shows the foolishness of mocking a prophet of God. God loves his children and will stand up for those who are mocked.

GO TO THE EXTREME

• **An** adult male grizzly bear can weigh over 700 pounds.

• **The** polar bear is the largest carnivore on land. An adult male polar bear can weigh up to 1500 pounds!

• **Grizzly** bears have been known to maul people. In July 2011, one grizzly bear attacked seven teens in Denali National Park in Anchorage, Alaska.

JOKE ALERT!

Laconic Limerick:
There once was a man with no hairs
who endured youthful mocking and stares.
But he was not deterred
and then had the last word,
as the boys became sport for the bears.

Read the story in 2 Kings 2:23–25.

Stronger than Leviathan

Can you catch Leviathan with a hook or put a noose around its jaw?
Job 41:1 (NLT)

What's the largest sea animal you've seen up close? A whale? A shark? In the Bible, one of the biggest sea animals was Leviathan. *What on earth is that?* you might wonder.

God mentioned Leviathan during a conversation he had with Job. In this conversation, God asked Job a series of rhetorical questions—questions that the one who is asking does not expect to be answered. The whole purpose for asking is to prove a point. After Job and his friends discussed the raw deal Job had been given—the deaths of all of his children; the destruction of his crops; his poor health—God had a point to prove to Job about his all-powerful nature and control over everything. He used Leviathan to teach Job. The way God describes Leviathan makes this sea creature sound invincible and almost dragon-like.

God knew there was no way Job could "catch Leviathan with a hook or put a noose around its jaw." Only God could do just that!

While scholars believe that Leviathan might have been a crocodile, the creature's exact nature wasn't the point of the lesson. As the creator of Leviathan, the elephant, and any other huge creature you can think of, God is more powerful.

GO TO THE EXTREME

- **The** Loch Ness monster is a sea creature believed to live in the Scottish highlands. But scientists call the Loch Ness monster a cyptid—a creature unlikely to be true.

- **The** komodo dragon is the largest type of lizard. Some can weigh 150 pounds.

- **The** largest crocodile in the world (so far) was caught in the Philippines in September 2011. It was 21 feet long and weighed a ton. It took 100 men to capture it.

JOKE ALERT!

Laconic Limerick:

Of all the world, he was best,
with wealth and family blessed.
Then hit with Satan's afflictions
and friends' derelictions,
whatever, Job passed the test!

197

Read the story in Job 41.

Hope from the Eagles

They who wait for the LORD shall renew their strength; they shall mount up with wings like eagles; they shall run and not be weary; they shall walk and not faint.
Isaiah 40:31 (ESV)

Hoping in God can be tough to do, especially when things don't go our way. A failed test grade or a broken friendship can make us feel as though God isn't near us anymore. Or it can be hard to hope in God when we have to do things we haven't done before. That can be frightening sometimes, but Isaiah has a comforting truth for those scary times.

The prophet Isaiah had a hard message to give to the people of Judah. They would be punished by God for their wrongdoings. For many years, they would live in another country far away from their homeland. But Isaiah also had words of hope. He used an eagle to make a point.

Ever see an eagle fly? An eagle doesn't have to constantly flap its powerful wings. It's built to soar on updrafts (upward movements of air). The person who waits for God and puts his trust in him is "built" to soar on faith. That's the hope Isaiah wanted his people to hold on to—the reminder that someday, they too will soar once more.

GO TO THE EXTREME

• **The** harpy eagle is the heaviest eagle in North America. The females are larger than the males. Some weigh 13 to 20 pounds. They have a wingspan of five to six feet.

• **An** eagle can fly over 10,000 feet.

• **The** golden eagle has a wingspan of six to seven feet!

JOKE ALERT!

How can someone recognize a "legal eagle"?

Answer: *Its claws (clause) have fine print.*

198

Read the story in Isaiah 40:27-31.

Pray Prey

> *When [Darius] got there, he called out in anguish, "Daniel, servant of the living God! Was your God, whom you serve so faithfully, able to rescue you from the lions?" Daniel answered, "Long live the king! My God sent his angel to shut the lions' mouths so that they would not hurt me, for I have been found innocent in his sight."*
>
> Daniel 6:20-22 (NLT)

The zoo is a popular place to visit. You get to see many strange, exotic, and exciting animals. One of the greatest things about a zoo is that you can see dangerous animals from a safe distance. Think about it: animals like lions, tigers, bears, and panthers are fascinating to observe, but would you really want to be in the same room as them, especially if they were hungry?

Daniel had to deal with this situation! Taken from his homeland of Israel, Daniel had become one of the advisors of Darius, the king of Persia. Daniel was very obedient to God, but some men envied him and wanted to get him in trouble. They tricked King Darius into making a law that would forbid anyone from praying to anyone other than the king himself! The punishment? A night with hungry lions.

Daniel was caught praying to God, and was taken to his punishment. Everyone expected him to die. However, God protected Daniel. An angel made sure the lions' mouths remained shut. They were as calm as house cats the whole night!

The worried Darius went to check up on Daniel the next day. He expected to see a pile of bones and some stuffed lions but instead was greeted by an unscathed Daniel!

When the men who tricked Darius were instead cast into the pit, they were eaten. Talk about an appetite!

GO TO THE EXTREME

- **An** adult lion can eat anywhere from 40–75 pounds of meat in one sitting!

- **A** lion's jaw cannot move side to side, like ours can.

- **After** eating a fulfilling meal, lions can sleep for as long as 24 hours!

JOKE ALERT!

Overheard near the pit:

Citizen: *"Daniel wouldn't bow now? Wow!"*

Envious advisors: *"Now for the mane event."*

Daniel: *"Love what you've done to the den."*

199

Read the story in Daniel 6.

Talk About a Fishy Situation

They took Jonah and threw him overboard, and the raging sea grew calm. . . . Now the LORD provided a huge fish to swallow Jonah, and Jonah was in the belly of the fish three days and three nights.

Jonah 1:15, 17 (NIV)

What's the worst punishment you can think of? No Internet? Doing chores? How about being grounded for three days in a squishy, dark, and slimy room? That's similar to how Jonah felt after being swallowed by the big fish.

But why did that fish come to swallow Jonah? Well, this was how God decided to punish him. You see, God gave Jonah specific instructions to go to a town called Nineveh with a message: repent or be destroyed. But Jonah didn't want to go. Nineveh was the capital city of the Assyrians: vicious, conquering people who treated others cruelly. Imagine how you would feel, having to tell a kid who beats up other kids at your school to stop being so mean. So Jonah took a ship to travel in the opposite direction of where God told him to go!

But God was ready for him. He sent a storm to batter the ship. Just before the ship could wreck, Jonah told the sailors to throw him into the sea. And then—*gulp!* Even though Jonah was spared from drowning, it was obviously not the best place to be. Take a look at Jonah 2 to learn how he deals with this fishy situation.

When God tells you to do something, you'd better get to it!

GO TO THE EXTREME

• **According** to some, the type of fish that swallowed Jonah was a sperm whale. Sperm whales have bottom teeth but no upper teeth, causing them to swallow their food whole!

• **The** sperm whale is the largest toothed animal in the world. It can grow as long as 60 feet or more.

• **A** baleen whale can grow to 110 feet and weigh about 420,000 pounds.

JOKE ALERT!

When asked why he was going to Assyria, what was Jonah's answer?

Answer: *"It's really Nine-veh business!"*

Read the story in Jonah 1.

Water Banking

Cast in a fishhook, and catch the first fish that comes up. When you open its mouth you'll find a coin. Take it and give it to them for Me and you.
Matthew 17:27 (HCSB)

Fishing can be lots of fun—if the fish are biting. But wouldn't it be shocking if you caught a fish and found a roll of twenty-dollar bills sticking out of its mouth?

The disciples had seen Jesus do many incredible things, but when it came time to pay their taxes they probably were a little skeptical of Jesus' money plans. After all, he was the son of a carpenter and a traveling homeless man, not exactly the first person someone would ask for money or financial advice. Yet Jesus told Peter that if he went fishing he would find the money they needed for their taxes inside the fish. Peter was a fisherman, so he had seen thousands of fish inside and out, but finding money in a fish seemed a little crazy. But Peter did what he was told, because he trusted Jesus over his own experience. Sure enough, Jesus came through again and inside the fish that Peter caught he found all the money needed to pay the taxes!

Peter had to humble himself to accept what Jesus told him to do. As someone who had fished just about every day of his life, he was a fishing expert. Jesus was a carpenter who didn't spend much time in and around boats and the sea. So when Peter did exactly what Jesus told him to do, it showed more than just obedience—it showed belief in Jesus as God.

GO TO THE EXTREME

- **There** are 25,000 known species of fish and it is estimated that about 15,000 species are still thought to be undiscovered!

- **The** Great Whale Shark is the largest fish in the world. It can grow to be as large as fifty feet long and weigh up to 50,000 pounds!

- **Because** of this story, a fish in Israel is called St. Peter Fish (known elsewhere as Tilapia).

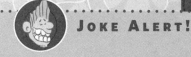

JOKE ALERT!

This incident occurred after a question by the official collectors of the Temple tax, but Jesus wouldn't take *debate* (the bait).

Read the story in Matthew 17:24–27.

Sheep Like "Ewe" or Me

If a man owns a hundred sheep, and one of them wanders away, will he not leave the ninety-nine on the hills and go to look for the one that wandered off?
Matthew 18:12 (NIV)

What do you know about sheep? They have wool, yes. Members of a herd tend to clump together, sure. Also, even the best sheep need a shepherd.

Jesus often spoke in parables—short stories that explained important truths about God. In many of these parables, the animal Jesus mentioned most was sheep. Why sheep? They're not glamorous or even remotely cool. But for Jesus, people were just like sheep. Before you check your ears for wool, consider Jesus' mission. He was the promised Savior—the one who came to save people from sin. So he called himself a "shepherd." This is the way God is described in Psalm 23. That's why Jesus told his disciples the parable of the lost sheep. He wasn't just talking about sheep that have a tendency to wander off. He was talking about people—real people just like you who needed to be found by a caring God. Like sheep, people are just as helpless, thus easy prey for predators.

Jesus' disciples would have known that a good shepherd would leave the rest of the herd—the ones who were already "found" and safe—to look for the lost sheep. That's what Jesus did.

GO TO THE EXTREME

• **The** Marco Polo sheep are the largest sheep in the world. Located in Afghanistan, these sheep have the largest horns of any sheep—up to six feet long.

• **Sometimes** llamas are used to guard sheep in pastures from predators.

• **In** 2009, the Royal Welsh Show—an agricultural event—had the biggest flock of sheep in the world: 2,948.

JOKE ALERT!

In New Testament times, why would shepherds refuse to hang glide?

Answer: *Because "they were sore [soar] afraid" (Luke 2:9, KJV).*

202

Read the story in Matthew 18:10–14.

Surprise in the Sticks

[Paul] shook off the creature into the fire and suffered no harm. They were waiting for him to swell up or suddenly fall down dead. But when they had waited a long time and saw no misfortune come to him, they changed their minds and said that he was a god.

Acts 28:5-6 (ESV)

Snakes are cool and scary at the same time. Even snakes that aren't poisonous are startling because of their surprisingly quick speed despite having no legs. We should have a healthy respect of snakes so that we're careful around them—no one wants to be bitten by a poisonous snake. We wouldn't have anything to worry about, though, if the poison didn't affect us at all. We could jump in snake pits with no fear.

Paul was simply trying to keep a fire burning and was gathering more wood. Suddenly a snake in the wood bit him. But God was watching over Paul. Although the snake was poisonous, Paul was fine. When all the people of the village saw what had happened, they thought he was a god! Who Paul was had nothing to do with him surviving that snakebite. God had protected him.

Paul was constantly faced with scary situations. He understood that nothing— snakes, spiders, or anything else we might be afraid of—is more powerful than God.

GO TO THE EXTREME

- **Every** year, 8,000 people in the United States are bitten by poisonous snakes, but only about twelve of them die from the bites.

- **All** snakes, poisonous or not, fear people and will try to escape contact with humans.

- **A** dead venomous snake can reflexively bite and inject its poison!

JOKE ALERT!

Other overheard comments around the fire on the island:

Guard, to one of the natives: *"Where can I get one of those famous Malta milks?"*

Woman, upon seeing the snake: *"Goodness snakes alive!"*

Anonymous man: *"Fangs for the memories."*

Friend of anonymous man: *"I hear Paul's a swell guy."*

Sociologist: *"That snake lived out in the sticks somewhere."*

Historian: *"Hmmm . . . the first incident of 'Snake-n-Bake.'"*

2 0 3

Read the story in Acts 28:1-6.

Eye of the Dragon

Then another sign appeared in heaven: an enormous red dragon with seven heads and ten horns and seven crowns on its heads. Its tail swept a third of the stars out of the sky and flung them to the earth.

Revelation 12:3-4 (NIV)

Got a favorite dragon story? Stories about dragons can range everywhere from knights and epic battles to Vikings and unlikely friendships.

A sense of fantasy and wonder isn't what the dragon of Revelation inspires. The book of Revelation is filled with difficult ideas, because it is a written description of a vision (a type of dream sent from God) that the apostle John (one of Jesus' close friends—see "The Spotlight's on Jesus" in Special Effects, page 184) had when he was an old man. The images John saw were events that would happen in the end times. This is why this book has creatures like a seven-headed dragon that you won't find anywhere else in the Bible. Not only does this dragon look fearsome with seven crowned heads and ten horns, but he also does something that dragons in fantasy stories could never do. His tail pulls stars down from the sky.

This dragon is a symbol—a word picture—for Satan. This dragon is the one who will control other evil beings: the antichrist and a false prophet of the antichrist. These rulers will someday cause trouble in the world. Pretty scary, huh? But you don't have to fear. If you check out "The Last Battle" in Ballistic Battles (page 19), you'll know the end of the story. Here's a preview: God wins!

GO TO THE EXTREME

• **Speaking** of mythical creatures, check out this verse in the King James Bible: "Will the unicorn be willing to serve thee, or abide by thy crib?" (Job 39:9). Your eyes aren't playing tricks on you. Scholars believe this "unicorn" was a type of wild ox.

• **The** Dragon Bridge in Ljubljana, Slovenia is known for its four dragon statues.

• **The** bearded dragon is a type of lizard in Australia. It has a cluster of spiny scales around its throat, which it uses for defense. These dragons are only about 13 to 24 inches long.

JOKE ALERT!

How do we know this creature got tired?

Answer: *It was draggin' throughout heaven and earth.*

204

Read the story in Revelation 12:1-6.

KOOKY Kings (and Queen!)

Ever had a teacher or a principal you thought was unfair? Perhaps this person made lots of weird rules that frustrated you or singled you out to be punished for something you didn't do. Having to obey that leader probably seems horribly unfair.

In Israel's long history, some kings (and at least one queen) were worse than others. The problem with living under their authority often meant being in trouble with God. Usually, when a king decided to worship idols, their people were encouraged to do the same. God would then punish his people for their sin by allowing them to be conquered by their enemies. As you read the stories in this section, you can decide which king (or queen) merits the title of "kookiest of all."

Unfair Pharaoh

Pharaoh gave this order to all his people: "Throw every newborn Hebrew boy into the Nile River. But you may let the girls live."
Exodus 1:22 (NLT)

It's a good thing you were born! After all, you wouldn't be here reading this book if you hadn't been born. Somewhere along the line your mom and dad had you, and here you are and you're reading about Pharaoh.

But you might *not* have been able to read about anything if you'd been a Jewish baby boy born under this particular Pharaoh back in Egypt. In fact, you might have been tossed into the Nile River. Yikes!

GO TO THE EXTREME

• **In** the United States, drowning is the second leading cause of death (after motor vehicle crashes) in children 12 and younger.

• **It's** surprising to learn that 19 percent of drowning deaths involving children occur in public pools with certified lifeguards present.

• **Some** important ways to be safe in the water include knowing how to swim (obviously), always swimming with a friend, making sure someone is watching you and can supervise, and being wise about where you go swimming.

This Pharaoh was a really bad guy. The Israelites had been in Egypt for a long time after Joseph's relatives had moved there centuries before (that story is at the end of Genesis). Now there were so many Israelites that Pharaoh was afraid they'd form an army and revolt. So he forced them into slavery. *Then* he ordered the midwives (women who help other women have babies) to kill all the baby boys. The midwives refused to obey that order because they feared God and wanted to obey him. So *then* Pharaoh decided to have all the Jewish baby boys thrown into the river.

How sad that must have been for so many Jewish mothers who loved their baby boys—just like your mom loves you. Pharaoh was not fair at all.

JOKE ALERT!

Why couldn't Pharaoh realize he was so nasty?

Answer: *He spent so much time in de-Nile.*

Read the story in Exodus 1:5–35.

A Tall Order

They again inquired of the LORD, "Has the man come here yet?" The LORD replied, "There he is, hidden among the supplies." They ran and got him from there. When he stood among the people, he stood a head taller than anyone else.
1 Samuel 10:22–23 (HCSB)

So who's the tallest person in your class at school? Maybe you? It's awkward to be tall for your age so that you tower over everyone else. What if being tall also made that person automatically president of the class? That might not be the best idea!

Saul was a really tall guy. He also, incidentally, became the first king of Israel—not because he wanted to be, or even that God wanted the people to have a king, but because the *people* said they needed a king so they could fit in with all the other countries around them.

Saul was a good soldier and military leader. He was thirty years old when God chose him to be Israel's king and the prophet Samuel anointed him. But when they went to get him for the ceremony, Saul was hiding among various supplies and bags and baskets. They had to drag him out and make him king!

God said he would be with Saul and help him with the kingdom, but Saul decided that being big and being king meant he didn't need to worry about God. He made some very bad choices that caused him to end up losing his kingdom.

Just being big doesn't necessarily make a person big in God's eyes. Saul found that out the hard way.

GO TO THE EXTREME

- **Various** kings in history have been reluctant to take the crown. For example, George VI of England did not plan to take the throne. However, when his older brother abdicated (refused to be the next king), George had to take the job. He ruled England from 1936 to 1952.

- **One** of the reasons George VI didn't want to be king was because he had a speech impediment (he stuttered, meaning he had a hard time getting his words out). More than 68 million people in the world stutter.

JOKE ALERT!

You won't find this in the Bible:
Behind his back, some people around the palace whispered that SAUL stood for
Seems **A**lways **U**nbelievably **L**ame.

Read the story in 1 Samuel 10.

That's One Way to Ruin a Kingdom...

[Jeroboam] placed these calf idols in Bethel and in Dan—at either end of his kingdom. But this became a great sin, for the people worshiped the idols, traveling as far north as Dan to worship the one there.
1 Kings 12:29-30 (NLT)

It's great fun to build sand castles at the beach. You can sculpt with buckets and bowls and any other kind of shape. But these sand castles—no matter how big or elaborate—will only last for a short time. Pretty soon the tide comes in and washes them away.

That's basically what happened to the great nation of Israel after King Solomon's death. He ruled over a time of great peace and prosperity. The nation could have stayed strong, but it didn't. Solomon started well, but then turned away from God and started worshiping idols. At that point, God told him that his kingdom would be divided. The twelve united tribes of Israel would be split apart—Solomon's son Rehoboam would get two tribes (read about that in "Pestered by Peer Pressure" on page 209), and a man named Jeroboam would get the other ten tribes.

God told Jeroboam: "If you will listen to all that I command you . . . I will be with you and will build you a sure house, as I built for David, and I will give Israel to you" (1 Kings 11:38, ESV). Problem was, Jeroboam *didn't* obey God. Instead, he made two golden calves and told all of his subjects to worship them. From that point on, his kingdom went from bad to worse. And it didn't have to be that way. All God had asked for was obedience.

GO TO THE EXTREME

• **Jewish** men were required to go to the temple three times each year (Deuteronomy 16:16). When the kingdom divided, the temple was in Rehoboam's land (which became known as the southern kingdom). Jeroboam set up these idols in the northern kingdom so the people wouldn't have to go to the rival nation to worship.

• **People** worshiped images of calves as signs of fertility and strength. The calf was a common god in the nearby nations.

JOKE ALERT!

Here are signs that *your* spiritual advisor is leading you in the wrong direction:

• He charges 15 percent commission on the offering.

• His goal is to be the next "American Idol."

• He says, "Sell all you have and give it to me."

Read the story in 1 Kings 11:26-40; 12:25-33.

Pestered by Peer Pressure

The king answered the people harshly. Rejecting the advice given him by the elders, he followed the advice of the young men.
1 Kings 12:13-14 (NIV)

When you have to make a big decision, who do you talk to? You probably talk to your friends and they give you all kinds of opinions. Hopefully, you talk to your parents too. And hopefully you take your *parents'* advice since they're older and know more than your friends do. Taking bad advice can cause problems, as one king discovered.

After Solomon's death, his son Rehoboam went to Shechem to be crowned king. He didn't know about the prophecy that his father Solomon's kingdom would be divided. Rehoboam thought he was going to continue his father Solomon's rule over everyone.

In the meantime, however, a man named Jeroboam had been told that he would get part of the kingdom. So after Solomon's death, Jeroboam led a group of people to speak to Rehoboam. They asked the new king if he would lighten the great load that Solomon had placed on the people (heavy taxes being part of the problem). Rehoboam talked to his father's advisors, who suggested that he follow what the people requested and lighten their burdens. Then Rehoboam talked to his buddies, and they told him to show his power and tell the people things were going to be even *worse* under him.

For some reason, Rehoboam thought his friends gave good advice and he took it. What followed was exactly what God had said through his prophet. Ten tribes refused to have Rehoboam as their king, so they followed Jeroboam as king. Rehoboam was left with just two tribes.

GO TO THE EXTREME

• **You've** probably experienced your share of peer pressure to be "cool." Statistics say that 30 percent of kids your age get offered drugs and 74 percent of high school kids are offered alcohol. Can you be "uncool" enough (and smart enough) to say no?

• **What's** the best advice of all time? It's in the Bible: "Trust in the LORD with all your heart; do not depend on your own understanding. Seek his will in all you do, and he will show you which path to take" (Proverbs 3:5-6, NLT).

JOKE ALERT!

Rehoboam's Regrets:
• *Attending the seminar on "How to Divide a Nation"*
• *Confusing "wise guys" with "wise men"*
• *Yoking around (1 Kings 12:14)*
• *Losing those revolting Israelites*

Read the story in 1 Kings 12:1-19.

A Weak Week King

GO TO THE EXTREME

> When Zimri saw that the city was captured, he entered the citadel of the royal palace and burned down the royal palace over himself.
>
> 1 Kings 16:18 (HCSB)

Can you imagine how cool it would be to be crowned king? But what if you got to be king for only a week? And what if, at the end of the week, you set fire to your house—with you still in it?

That doesn't sound very cool at all, does it? In fact, it sounds hot and painful.

Zimri was like one of those bad guys in the cop shows on TV that you hope gets in trouble in the end. He didn't start out in a royal family—he was never supposed to be king. He was an official in King Elah's army. But he turned on his king, murdered him, and took his place. Then it got worse. He killed all of Elah's family members (and even their close friends) to make sure no one tried to take the throne away from him. And that all happened in the first week—because, well, he was king for only a week.

You see, the Israelite army was off doing battle. When they heard that their king had been murdered, they decided to crown their commander (Omri) as king. Then they attacked the palace where Zimri was hiding out. When Zimri realized the army was out to get him, he set fire to the palace and killed himself.

Sad end to a bad guy.

- **Zimri's** reign as king has the distinction of being one of the shortest recorded reigns in history. Another very short reign was by Sweyn I of England who ruled for one month and nine days from 1013–1014.

- **William** Henry Harrison, ninth president of the United States, has the distinction of serving the shortest time in office. He was president for only 32 days before dying of complications from pneumonia.

- **According** to FEMA's (Federal Emergency Management Agency) Fire Administration, more than 3,000 people die each year in house fires. On average, more than two-thirds of the homes do *not* have smoke alarms.

JOKE ALERT!

Whatever happened to Zimri?
Answer: *He got fired!*

Read the story in 1 Kings 16:8–20.

Liar, Liar, Pants on Fire

The LORD has put a lying spirit into the mouth of all these prophets of yours, and the LORD has pronounced disaster against you.

1 Kings 22:23 (HCSB)

Nobody likes to hear bad news—especially if it's about themselves. Would you ever want to get called to the principal's office and have her tell you that you are in deep trouble because of your grades? Of course not! But what if she told you that your grades were great, and then you found out she had lied? You failed the school year and had to stay back. The truth would have been painful but much more helpful.

Ahab didn't really want to know the truth, so he surrounded himself with "prophets" who told him just what he wanted to hear. One time while Jehoshaphat was king of Judah and Ahab was king of Israel, Ahab suggested that they join forces against the Arameans. Jehoshaphat wanted to seek God's advice (he was actually a pretty good guy).

So Ahab gathered together four hundred prophets who all said the exact same thing: God would give them victory. Ahab liked that news! But Jehoshaphat was suspicious. Wasn't there someone else who prophesied? Grudgingly, Ahab brought in Micaiah, saying, "I hate him. He never prophesies anything but trouble for me!" (1 Kings 22:8, NLT).

At first, Micaiah pretended to play along. But then he told the truth—and it was indeed bad news for Ahab. Micaiah said Ahab would die.

GO TO THE EXTREME

- **Archery** was used by the ancient Egyptians as early as five thousand years ago.

- **Ancient** civilizations often used large numbers of archers in their armies. Hundreds of arrows shot into the air, aimed to rain down on opposing forces, were very effective against massed formations of enemy soldiers.

- **Archery** is a sport in the summer Olympics. Olympic archers use a recurve bow, which means the bow curves away from the archer to increase power. Arrows are propelled from the bows at speeds faster than 150 miles per hour.

JOKE ALERT!

Why didn't Ahab let the prophet's craftsmen out of prison?

Answer: *They couldn't make Baal (bail).*

Well, that wasn't going to happen, Ahab thought. So he went into battle disguised as an ordinary soldier. But a random arrow hit Ahab and he did indeed die.

Perhaps if Ahab had been willing to listen to the truth—not just what he wanted to hear—he might have lived much longer.

Read the story in 1 Kings 22:1–40.

A Gross Grandmother

When Athaliah, the mother of King Ahaziah of Judah, learned that her son was dead, she began to destroy the rest of the royal family.
2 Kings 11:1 (NLT)

Do you like spending time with your grandmother? Most of us expect a grandmother to be kind, bake cookies, and give presents at birthdays and Christmas. (Okay, some grandmothers don't bake cookies.) Queen Athaliah wasn't the cookie-baking kind of grandmother, however. She was the murdering kind.

Athaliah was the mother of King Ahaziah of Judah. After her son was killed by Jehu (see 2 Kings 9:27–29), Athaliah decided to grab the throne for herself. To do this, she had to kill her own grandsons! But she missed one. Joash was just a baby when his aunt, Jehosheba, ran off with him and hid him in the temple for six years while Athaliah ruled the land.

When Joash was seven years old, Josheba's husband, the high priest Jehoiada, crowned him king of Judah. He commanded the temple guards to keep the child safe during the coronation. Of course Athaliah found out about the coronation when the people started clapping and cheering. While Athaliah screamed about treason, Jehoiada ordered her to be put to death.

GO TO THE EXTREME

• **In** 2007, a 100-year-old woman—British grandmother, Peggy McAlpine—became the world's oldest paraglider.

• **Rifca** Stanescu of Romania became the world's youngest grandmother at the age of 23.

• **Mary,** Queen of Scots, was crowned queen when she was less than a year old.

JOKE ALERT!

According to legend, Athaliah couldn't speak too well—she was a really bad "grammer"!

212

Read the story in 2 Kings 11:1-16.

Fire Starter

Whenever Jehudi had read three or four columns of the scroll, the king cut them off with a scribe's knife and threw them into the firepot, until the entire scroll was burned in the fire.
Jeremiah 36:23 (NIV)

Have you ever worked with puppets? You know, either stuck a sock on your hand and made it talk, or created some elaborate caricature puppet with strings that move arms and legs? Puppets do as they're told. Someone has to control them.

King Jehoiakim of Judah was no more than a puppet ruler—his strings were pulled by Pharaoh Neco of Egypt who had killed his father in battle. Then Nebuchadnezzar king of Babylon defeated Pharaoh Neco, and Jehoiakim had a new guy pulling his strings.

In the fourth year of Jehoiakim's reign, God told Jeremiah to write down all of his messages to the people. That was a lot of messages! Jeremiah called his trusty scribe Baruch and dictated all of the messages he had given.

After he wrote it all down, Jeremiah sent Baruch to read the scroll in the temple to all the people. (Jeremiah couldn't go because the king had stopped him from prophesying there.) But that didn't stop God. The people heard Jeremiah's messages anyway. But then the king demanded that the scroll be brought to him. Then, he cut it up and burned it.

And what do you think God said? "Get Baruch to sharpen his pencil. We're gonna do it again!"

Burning the scroll didn't change the truth of God's words or stop his message to his people.

GO TO THE EXTREME

• **The** first emperor of China, Qin Shi Huang, wanted to control what people could read. He had all books burned—everything except those written by the emperor's own historians. Any local authorities who did not burn the listed books within thirty days ended their careers as slaves working on the Great Wall.

• **Some** very famous scrolls are the Dead Sea scrolls that were discovered near Jerusalem in 1947. They contain about 15,000 fragments of over 500 manuscripts. Some of them include parts of the books of Isaiah, Deuteronomy, and Psalms.

• **Early** scrolls were made of papyrus (a paper-like material produced from the papyrus plant) or vellum (animal skin) that had been prepared for writing.

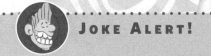

JOKE ALERT!

How could King Jehoiakim cut up the scroll?

Answer: *Because he was tear-able (terrible)!*

Read the story in Jeremiah 36.

Were You Born in a Barn?

Immediately the word was fulfilled against Nebuchadnezzar. He was driven from among men and ate grass like an ox, and his body was wet with the dew of heaven till his hair grew as long as eagles' feathers, and his nails were like birds' claws.

Daniel 4:33 (ESV)

Some superheroes have the power to change into some kind of insect or animal—with all of the cool characteristics that go with that creature. Spiders, wolf claws, fish scales.

GO TO THE EXTREME

• **A** disease called elephantiasis can cause grossly enlarged or swollen arms and legs. The disease is caused by parasitic worms transmitted by mosquitoes.

• **Some** people have to stay out of the sun because it will cause their skin to blister. No, they don't drink blood and sleep in coffins, but they do suffer from a rare disease that has vampire-like symptoms.

• **There** is a disease called Human Werewolf Syndrome. These people grow hair all over their faces and bodies, but they don't get sharp teeth and claws!

Nebuchadnezzar wasn't a superhero except in his own mind. He was the powerful king of Babylon, a nation that had conquered much of the known world and was an empire to be envied.

And that was the problem. Nebuchadnezzar became very proud. One afternoon, he went for a stroll on the palace roof. He was so impressed with himself and his power and dominion that he said to no one in particular, "Is not this the great Babylon I have built as the royal residence, by my mighty power and for the glory of my majesty?" (Daniel 4:30, NIV).

He had barely finished when God, who was listening, said, "You will be driven away from people and will live with the wild animals; you will eat grass like the ox . . . until you acknowledge that the Most High is sovereign over all kingdoms on earth and gives them to anyone he wishes" (4:32, NIV).

And immediately it happened. The once proud king of the world completely lost his mind. He chomped grass and crawled about as if he were an animal.

That was the hard way to learn a really important lesson: God is in charge.

JOKE ALERT!

Overheard in a speech to the people by Nebuchadnezzar after his episode as an ox:

• *"Be sure to check every claws."*

• *"But what could I dew?"*

• *"I had a very moooving experience."*

Read the **story** in Daniel 4:28–37.

Talk to the Hand

At that moment the fingers of a man's hand appeared and began writing on the plaster of the king's palace wall.
Daniel 5:5 (HCSB)

Some people just know how to ruin a party. In this case, it was just a *hand* that stopped a party.

Belshazzar wanted to have a party, so he invited thousands of the rich people of the land. He thought he'd try to impress everyone by bringing out the gold and silver goblets that his predecessor Nebuchadnezzar had taken from the temple in Jerusalem when he had attacked and destroyed the city. So someone went to find the goblets, and then everyone "drank the wine and praised their gods made of gold and silver, bronze, iron, wood, and stone" (Daniel 5:4, HCSB). Not a good idea.

That's when the party stopped, because the guests saw a human hand suddenly appear against the plaster wall and write some words. No one could understand the words, so the terrified king brought in all the wise men and astrologers and magicians, offering a big reward to whoever could interpret the writing. But no one could do it.

Except Daniel. Someone remembered that Daniel seemed to know everything, and so he was brought in to interpret the writing. Daniel explained that the words on the wall spoke of the coming destruction of the Babylonian Empire, starting right there in Babylon . . . that very night. (Read the rest of the story in "The Handwriting on the Wall" in Puzzles and Riddles, page 37.)

GO TO THE EXTREME

- **The** army that conquered Babylon that night entered by diverting the river that ran through the city and walking in on the dry riverbed.

- **Another** famous surprise attack occurred when the Greek army was laying siege to the city of Troy. Many years passed and the war dragged on. Finally, the Greeks constructed a huge horse and hid thirty men inside. Then they pretended to sail away, and the Trojan people pulled the horse inside the city. At night the men slipped out of the horse and opened the gates to let the Greek army in.

JOKE ALERT!

Laconic Limerick:
Brought into the packed banquet hall
Daniel the prophet stood tall.
Observing the hand,
he told what God planned,
and Belshazzar hit the wall!

2 1 5

Read the story in Daniel 5:1–12.

We Three Kings

Agrippa said to Paul, "Do you think that in such a short time you can persuade me to be a Christian?"
Acts 26:28 (NIV)

Ever have one of "those" days? Or maybe one of "those" weeks? Well, Paul was having one of those years. Actually it had been more than a year.

Paul had been arrested, basically, for being a Christian and speaking about Jesus. The rulers of the Jews were not very happy with him because they did not believe that Jesus was the Messiah. So they had him arrested, and that's how Paul had found himself in front of Felix, Roman governor of the province of Judea. Felix heard the case against Paul, but didn't want to do anything about it, so he kept Paul in prison.

Two years went by. Felix went back to Rome, and a new governor named Festus replaced him. Once again Paul's accusers were called to Caesarea to bring their case against Paul. Again, no one could seem to make a decision.

One day King Agrippa came to visit Festus, and Paul's case came up in their discussion. Once again, Paul was called out to tell his story and—you guessed it—he also shared the good news about Jesus.

Paul may have been in prison and in chains, but nothing could stop him from telling about his Savior.

GO TO THE EXTREME

• **In** many countries, people can be arrested for being Christians. In Uzbekistan, KGB officers raid the homes of Christians and confiscate their Bibles.

• **In** Somalia, Christians must practice their faith in secret. If caught, they could be kidnapped or killed. Islam is the only recognized religion.

• **In** Saudi Arabia, churches from any other religion than Islam are outlawed. A Muslim who converts to another faith is punished by death. Items such as the Bible, a cross, or any other religious symbol are prohibited by law.

JOKE ALERT!

Why didn't the king become a Christian?

Answer: *He couldn't get a-grip-pa on the truth.*

Read the story in Acts 24—26.

When G∘∘D GUYS Go Bad

You hear about it all the time in the news: people who failed. When someone others admire gives in to temptation, his or her failure is big news. But few things hurt worse than the discovery that someone you once trusted has betrayed you or failed in some other way.

The Bible has many stories of people who blew it big time. Some of the most well-known people in the Bible have painful, embarrassing pasts—maybe worse than anything you might see on the worst reality show. It's easy to point the finger at them or think, *How could they do that?* But these stories are a reminder that none of us is perfect. We're all human. Without God's help, many times we're all just a decision away from blowing it!

Me First!

"But are you really my son Esau?" he asked. "Yes, I am," Jacob replied.
Genesis 27:24 (NLT)

Funny thing about birthdays. You can't make them go backwards. Ever. Jacob and Esau were twins who seemed to fight a lot about birthrights. Esau came first, but Jacob came next, with his little hand on Esau's heel. In Bible times, the oldest son had the right to inherit more land than the younger sons. The firstborn also became the person in charge of the family. So you can see why the birthright was important.

The bad thing about this family is that their parents played favorites. Esau was the favorite of their father Isaac, while Jacob was their mother Rebekah's favorite. One day Isaac called for Esau. Isaac was old and blind and wanted to give Esau a blessing before he died. He asked Esau to prepare a meal of wild game the way Isaac liked it. Since Esau was a hunter, that was no problem. But Jacob wanted the blessing for himself. So his mother, Rebekah, helped Jacob fool his dad. She cooked a meal that tasted like something Esau would have made. Since Esau was a hairy man and Jacob wasn't, she helped Jacob cover his arms and neck with the hairy skin from a goat. Finally, she gave Jacob some of Esau's clothes to wear.

It worked! Although he had some doubts, Isaac gave his blessing to Jacob. You don't have to guess how Esau took it. He was furious enough to want to kill Jacob!

GO TO THE EXTREME

• **Did** you know that statistically people make eye contact at least half the time they are talking to someone? Some researchers believe that avoiding eye contact or looking down during a specific part of a conversation might be a sign of lying.

• **Frank** Abagnale, Jr., the subject of the 2002 movie, *Catch Me If You Can*, tricked people into believing he was an FBI agent, a pilot, a doctor, and other occupations. Some of this happened when he was just 16 years old! He also forged checks, gaining about 2.5 million dollars.

JOKE ALERT!

Esau's nicknames:
The Saw Man
See Saw
Harry
Fuzzy Wuzzy
Soupy Sales

Read the story in Genesis 27.

The Eyes Have You!

Looking this way and that and seeing no one, [Moses] killed the Egyptian and hid him in the sand.

Exodus 2:12 (NIV)

I have eyes in the back of my head!" Maybe you have heard your mom or dad use this phrase when you were right in the middle of doing something you probably shouldn't have been doing. Busted!

Moses, a 40-year-old man, thought he could be sneaky and do something without anyone seeing him. He lived as a prince in the palace of the Egyptian king, but he was not an Egyptian and he knew it. He was a Hebrew adopted by the daughter of the pharaoh. His people were slaves in Egypt.

One day he got angry when he saw an Egyptian mistreating a Hebrew. He decided to do something. He looked around quickly, then killed the Egyptian and buried his body.

The next day, Moses was out walking again and saw two Hebrew men arguing. When Moses tried to stop them, one asked Moses if he planned to kill him the way he killed the Egyptian! Busted!

When it comes to wrongdoing, God always sees.

GO TO THE EXTREME

• **The** Nile River, where baby Moses floated in a basket until he was rescued by Pharaoh's daughter, is considered the longest river in the world at over 4,000 miles long.

• **The** jumping spider has four eyes, with two toward the back of its head.

2 1 9

Read the story in Exodus 2:1-15.

To Wait or Not to Wait

[Aaron] took [the gold] from their hands, fashioned it with an engraving tool, and made it into an image of a calf.

Exodus 32:4 (HCSB)

GO TO THE EXTREME

- **Other** people in the Bible who had long waits: Jacob worked and waited for seven years to marry Rachel—and then had to work seven more years (Genesis 29:15-27); Joseph was wrongly imprisoned for two years (Genesis 41:1); the Israelites waited (and wandered) for forty years to enter the Promised Land (Numbers 14:34); after Paul began preaching about Jesus, he spent roughly five to six years in various prisons because of his faith. All that doesn't make waiting in line seem quite so bad, does it?

- **The** Israelites left Egypt as slaves, so normally would not have had gold jewelry to give. However, as they left Egypt, Moses told the people to ask the Egyptians for "articles of silver and gold" which were gladly given (Exodus 12:35-36). This was the jewelry that was melted down to make the idol.

Waiting for your turn on the computer. Waiting for the school day to be over. Let's be honest. Most of us do not wait well. We like action!

The Israelites did not wait well either. They had been waiting for Moses for forty days. He had gone to the top of Mount Sinai to talk to God. They began to wonder if Moses would ever come back. They wanted to *do* something. Finally, they asked Aaron to make them a god. The people who lived near the Israelites, worshiped gods in the shape of a bull. They wanted one too.

The interesting thing was, Moses was up on the mountain receiving the Ten Commandments, one of which said *not* to do this exact thing! But Aaron, Moses' brother and the man in charge, told the Israelites to hand over their gold jewelry. He melted the jewelry and fashioned it into a golden calf. Then he built an altar in front of the calf-statue and led the people in a celebration.

Moses came down the mountain and discovered the wild party. He was so angry he threw the carefully carved tablets containing God's commandments and broke them!

Aaron tried to blame the people, but like them he had only himself to blame. Moses had the calf melted down and the gold ground into powder. He then scattered the powder on water and forced the people to drink it!

JOKE ALERT!

Why was Moses the most sinful person in the Bible?

Answer: *He broke all the commandments at the same time (Exodus 32:19).*

2 2 0

Déjà Vu

The LORD said to Moses and Aaron, "Because you did not believe in me, to uphold me as holy in the eyes of the people of Israel, therefore you shall not bring this assembly into the land that I have given them."

Numbers 20:12 (ESV)

Déjà vu! **This French** phrase, which means "already seen" is a feeling you get when you think you've experienced something before. For example, a part of a conversation might remind you of a dream you once had. We often say "déjà vu all over again" when someone keeps doing the same thing over and over again.

That is exactly what the Israelites might have said when they camped at Kadesh in the Wilderness of Zin. They had been there many years earlier. And things hadn't gone so well then. What would happen now? The same old thing. Everyone was complaining.

Moses and Aaron went to talk to God about the situation. God gave Moses instructions: take your staff and speak to a rock. Water would come out.

So Moses and Aaron gathered the people. But then Moses let his anger get the best of him. Instead of speaking to the rock, he struck it twice with his staff.

God didn't let Moses get away with disobeying him. As punishment—after all the years he wandered in the desert with God's complaining people—Moses was not allowed to enter the Promised Land.

GO TO THE EXTREME

• **The** Sahara Desert, in North Africa, is the world's largest hot desert with temperatures ranging from 130 degrees Fahrenheit to below freezing (32 degrees Fahrenheit).

• **Dromedary** camels thrive in deserts, in part because they have bushy eyebrows and two rows of long eyelashes to protect their eyes. They also have one hump on their backs versus the two humps on the much less common Bactrian camel's back.

JOKE ALERT!

Laconic Limerick:

The Israelites were prone to pout
filled with questions and doubt.
Not feeling fine,
so sick of their whine,
Moses swung with his rod and struck out!

221

Read the story in Numbers 20:1–13.

Remind Me Again Who You Are

The Israelites examined their food, but they did not consult the LORD. Then Joshua made a peace treaty with them and guaranteed their safety, and the leaders of the community ratified their agreement with a binding oath.
Joshua 9:14–15 (NLT)

On a Friday morning at a Washington D.C. metro station, Joshua Bell, a world-famous violinist, wearing jeans and a T-shirt, played six classical pieces on a $3.5 million Stradivarius violin. Only seven people stopped to listen, and only one person recognized him.

During the time when Israel was in the middle of conquering Canaan, their leader Joshua also had trouble recognizing the truth about a whole group of people.

These men wore ragged clothes and worn-out, patched sandals. Their tired-looking donkeys carried old saddlebags filled with dry, moldy bread. They claimed to have come from a far distance and wanted a treaty with Israel.

Joshua made the decision by looking at their clothes and their food. He did not spend time talking to God about this situation or even thinking about the fact that God had told the Israelites never to sign a peace treaty with anyone. He made his own decision by offering a peace treaty with the people of Gibeon.

Three days later, Joshua discovered that these people, who looked like they lived far away, actually lived nearby! So much for, "What you see is what you get!"

GO TO THE EXTREME

• **The** Israeli–Egyptian Peace Treaty of March 26, 1979 is considered to be an event that opened a gateway to peace between Israel and the Arab world.

• **Today** we usually seal a promise with a handshake, the origin of which dates back as far as the fifth century BC. People usually shake with right hands, and it is considered inappropriate or even insulting to reject a handshake without good reason.

JOKE ALERT!

Here's something you *won't* find in the Bible:

From that time on, every year young children would dress up as beggars and go from tent to tent begging and saying, "Trick and Treaty."

222

Read the story in Joshua 9.

Just One More Little Thing . . .

Gideon made an ephod . . . and put it in Ophrah, his hometown. . . . It became a snare to Gideon and his household.
Judges 8:27 (HCSB)

Ever **wanted to be** a superhero? Spider-Man? Wonder Woman? Wouldn't it be great to save people from danger and bad guys?

Gideon was kind of an Old Testament superhero. He didn't leap tall buildings, but he did save the Israelites from their enemies, the Midianites.

For seven years the Midianites had burned the Israelites' crops and taken all of their animals. Then God helped Gideon to save the Israelites.

When the final battle was over and peace had returned to the Israelites, they were so happy with Gideon that they begged him to be their king. Gideon refused, but he had one moment of weakness. He told them to each give him a gold earring. Gideon took all the earrings, melted them, and made a golden ephod for himself. An ephod was a beautifully decorated, long, sleeveless shirt which the priests wore. It was considered holy.

He took it to his hometown where everyone could see it. Soon people started to come and stare at the ephod and even bow down to it. Earlier Gideon had told the Israelites that God should be the one who was most important to them.

Yikes! Seems like this hero should have followed his own advice.

JOKE ALERT!

Gideon wanted to take his golden rule!

GO TO THE EXTREME

- **Pyrite** is called fool's gold because its brassy yellow color is very similar to gold. Although it looks like gold, however, it is harder, less dense, and more brittle.

- **The** most expensive earrings in the world are a pair of diamond earrings worth $8.5 million. They were designed by Harry Winston.

- **Designer** Lizzy Gardiner made a dress out of gold American Express credit cards and wore it to the Academy Awards presentation in 1994.

223

Read the story in Judges 8:22–27.

"Not Me! Couldn't Be!"

- **Immaculate** Baking Company holds the world's record for the biggest cookie: 102 feet wide, weighing 40,000 pounds. This record was set in 2003.

- **The** biggest sacrifice of animals took place when Israel's first temple was dedicated by King Solomon: 22,000 cows and 120,000 sheep and goats (1 Kings 8:63).

- **Harry** S. Truman, the thirty-third president of the United States, kept a sign on his desk that said, *The Buck Stops Here.* That meant the president was responsible for any wrong actions, instead of trying to pass the blame to someone else.

When Samuel reached him, Saul said, "The LORD bless you! I have carried out the LORD's instructions." But Samuel said, "What then is this bleating of sheep in my ears? What is this lowing of cattle that I hear?"
1 Samuel 15:13–14 (NIV)

Remember the "Cookie Jar Game"?

Who stole the cookie from the cookie jar?

Who, me?

Yes, you!

Not me! / Couldn't be! / Wasn't me!

Then who?

Seems that Saul, Israel's first king, sometimes played a game like this.

God had commanded Saul to go and fight the Amalekites, a nation that did not follow God and constantly attacked and destroyed other nations. So Saul did as God asked him to do. Sort of. He (and his soldiers) saved the best sheep, goats, and cows to keep for themselves—something God had told them *not* to do.

When Samuel confronted Saul, Saul tried to explain how obedient he had been. But Samuel could hear the evidence for himself—the bleating of sheep and goats.

As Samuel reminded Saul, obedience is always better than any sacrifice that can be made. Because of Saul's disobedience, God gave his kingdom to someone else.

If you stole the cookie from the cookie jar, 'fess up!

JOKE ALERT!

Here's something you won't find in the Bible:
Saul said he was always tired because he had so many sheepless nights.

Read the story in 1 Samuel 15:1–26.

You Da Man!

Nathan said to David, "You are the man!"
2 Samuel 12:7 (ESV)

Nowadays when someone says, "You da man," that means you did something great. But in David's day, for a prophet to say, "You are the man" (the ancient version of "You da man"), meant anything but good.

God sent the prophet Nathan to tell David a story about two men—a rich man and a poor man. The poor man had a little lamb . . . and how he loved his little lamb! The lamb ate from the poor man's own plate, and the man often held it in his arms like a baby. Then one day, a guest arrived at the rich man's house. The rich man had many lambs, but he walked over to the poor man's house and took his only little lamb.

The story made David angry. The man who did such a thing should die, he declared. Busted! Nathan told him, "You are the man!"

You see, more than a year earlier, King David (the rich man) had arranged for Uriah (the poor man) to get killed in battle so David could marry Uriah's wife (just like the rich man took the poor man's only lamb that he loved so much).

God needed to get David's attention and point out his sin, which David seemed to have forgotten. Nathan's story hit David in his heart. He admitted his wrong before God and asked for his forgiveness.

JOKE ALERT!

Laconic Limerick:
When the king learned what had occurred,
judgment was his pronounced word.
Then Nathan told true,
"The villain is you!"
David's vision was no longer blurred.

GO TO THE EXTREME

- **In** 2009, a cade lamb named Deveronvale Perfection from Banffshire, Scotland, was sold by owner Graham Morrison for £231,000 ($392,000).

- **The** well-known nursery rhyme, "Mary Had a Little Lamb," was written by Sarah Josepha Hale and published in 1830. It was based on a true story.

- **The** most expensive wool in the world comes from the vicuña, an animal like a llama and an alpaca that lives in South America. Expect to pay close to $2000 to $3000 per yard.

Read the story in 2 Samuel 12:1–13.

Counting the Cost

After he had taken the census, David's conscience began to bother him. And he said to the Lord, "I have sinned greatly by taking this census. Please forgive my guilt, Lord, for doing this foolish thing."

2 Samuel 24:10 (NLT)

You got more than me!" It is hard to split a bag of M&Ms® so that everyone has the same number, isn't it?

King David decided one day that he needed to count all the people in Israel by taking a census. When his commander, Joab, asked him why, David did not answer Joab. Instead, he sent him and many other soldiers to walk to every city and count the people.

GO TO THE EXTREME

- **Tokyo** has the largest population of any city in the world: 32,450,000.

- **The** U.S. Census counts every resident in the United States. Article I, Section 2 of the Constitution states that it should take place every ten years.

- **Did** you know that, according to a census, the entire population of the U.S. in 1790 was 3,929,000? That is just a few people less than the population of the modern-day city of Los Angeles in 2010, where the census counted slightly over four million people.

They returned to the king and gave him their final count. The king was happy to know how many men he had who were strong enough to fight. And he was happy to know that he was in charge of all these people!

God was very angry with David for taking a census, instead of trusting him. God sent a prophet named Gad to give David a choice of punishments: three years of famine, three months of running from enemies, or three days of a plague. Which would you have chosen? David chose the plague. In three days, seventy thousand people died from it!

David learned the hard way that "I've got more than you" doesn't really make God happy.

JOKE ALERT!

Other alternate punishments rejected by David:

- *Three days of elevator music filling the palace*
- *A three-week visit from some noisy relatives*
- *Three years of camel-meals*

2 2 6

Follow-the-Crowd Disease

> The LORD was angry with Solomon, because his heart had turned away from the LORD God of Israel, who had appeared to him twice. He had commanded him about this, so that he would not follow other gods, but Solomon did not do what the LORD had commanded.
>
> 1 Kings 11:9–10 (HCSB)

Ever been tempted to follow the crowd? Even kings fall under that temptation sometimes. King Solomon was the third king of Israel, and he loved God and wanted to be the kind of king who led his people well. In fact, he asked God to give him wisdom so that he would be a good king. God gave him that and wealth besides. So far so good, right?

The problem for Solomon is that he had many wives—over one thousand! Many of these wives worshiped false gods. Solomon decided to worship the false gods as well!

He built a temple for God, but he also built himself a huge palace, which included a fancy throne decorated with gold. And he collected over 12,000 horses!

God wanted the king to remember what really mattered most—serving God. But Solomon got so caught up in doing what the people around him were doing that his ears and his heart stopped hearing God's voice.

Solomon definitely had a severe case of "follow-the-crowd" disease.

GO TO THE EXTREME

- **The** most expensive breed of horse in the U.S. is the Friesian or the Gypsy Vanner. You can get a foal (baby) for $10,000—$25,000. A world championship winning Quarter Horse might sell for $100,000.

- **Many** racehorse trainers put blinders on their horses. Blinders, either leather or plastic cups, attach to both sides of a horse's eyes and prevent it from seeing to the rear and, in some cases, to the side. Do you think a set of blinders might have helped King Solomon?

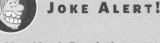

JOKE ALERT!

New Year's Resolutions of King Solomon:

1. To propose only twenty-seven times this year
2. To spend more time with his children—or at least get their names straight
3. To take better care of his cuticles
4. To stop horsing around
5. To write another song (see Song of Solomon)
6. To get a new vanity (see Ecclesiastes, KJV)

Read the story in 1 Kings 11:1–13.

When a Friend Fails

This very night, before the rooster crows, you will disown me three times.
Matthew 26:34 (NIV)

Got a best friend? A loyal friend is one of the best gifts you can have. But sometimes even loyal friends mess up. Peter, who was one of Jesus' best friends—one of the most loyal guys you could have around—messed up in a major way.

Jesus knew that he would soon be arrested and put to death. He wanted to celebrate the Passover with his disciples. At the meal that is now known as the Last Supper, he made a startling announcement: not only would one of his own disciples betray him, but also his close friend Peter would deny him!

Put yourself in Peter's shoes. He'd been everywhere with Jesus. He was the one who walked on water and saw Jesus transfigured. He saw some of the most amazing healings that some of the other disciples didn't see. Now here Jesus was telling him that Peter would deny knowing him!

And that's just what happened. When Jesus was arrested and brought on trial before Pilate and the religious leaders, Peter followed along. When a slave girl asked him if he knew Jesus, a frightened Peter said he didn't. Just as Jesus predicted, Peter denied knowing him—three times as a matter of fact. He felt just awful! But after Jesus' resurrection, Jesus asked Peter three times, "Do you love me?" Maybe that was Jesus' way of getting Peter to forget the past denials and remember the truth: Jesus still loved Peter and, yes, Peter loved Jesus.

Go to the Extreme

• **The** Passover is an eight-day celebration if you live outside Israel.

• **In** 1495–1498, Leonardo da Vinci depicted the disciples celebrating the Passover in *The Last Supper*—one of the most well-known paintings in the world. It is 15 feet by 29 feet.

JOKE ALERT!

Unrecorded denials of Peter when accused of being a disciple:

• *"I wasn't with Jesus. I was just waiting for a bus."*

• *"I was just sitting down to get a stone out of my sandal."*

• *"I was shopping for Roman candles when Jesus happened to walk by."*

• *"I was getting in line for the sale at Herod's."*

Read the story in Matthew 26:31–35, 69–75.

Topical I N D E X

A

Aaron 23, 44, 99, 220, 221
Abel 76
Abraham (also Abram) 12, 22, 52, 133, 154
Absalom 27
Abyss (bottomless pit) 141
Achan 14
Achish 16
Adam 190
Ahab 28, 29, 30, 80, 126, 144, 195, 211
Ahaziah 28, 212
Ai 14
Amalekites 16
Ananias and Sapphira 31
Animals (clean and unclean) 4
Apollos 74
Ark (Noah's) 191
Ark of the Covenant 25, 26, 90, 91, 113
Ascension of Jesus 185
Athaliah 212

B

Balaam 193
Barak 24, 66
Barnabas 47, 73
Bartimaeus 169
Baruch 213
Bears 196
Belshazzar 37, 215
Ben-Hadad 103
Boaz 58
Boils 105
Bread 2, 10

C

Cain 76
Communion 8

D

Daniel 36, 37, 60, 157, 199, 215
Darius 199
David 15, 16, 26, 27, 70, 71, 89, 90, 124, 125, 225, 226
David's Mighty Men 71
Deborah 24, 66
Delilah 79
Demons and demon-possession 48, 49, 136, 141, 182
Donkey (talking) 193
Dorcas 150
Dragon 204

E

Eagles 198
Eglon 100, 122
Ehud 100, 122
Eli 25, 88
Elijah 6, 28, 29, 30, 80, 126, 144, 176, 177, 184, 195
Elisha 29, 104, 115, 145, 164, 177, 178, 196
Elymas 47
Esau 218
Esther 72
Eutychus 151
Eve 190
Ezekiel 7, 59, 180

F

Famine 103
Fasting 5, 157
Felix 216
Festus 216
Fish 10
Flour 6
Foxes 194
Frogs 111

G

Gideon 67, 223
Golgotha 138
Goliath 15

H

Haman 72
Hannah 88
Heaven 19, 61, 96, 152, 161
Hell 140
Herod Agrippa 32, 216
Herod Antipas 83, 107
Herod the Great 82
Herodias 83, 107
Hezekiah 17, 92
Holy Spirit 185, 186
Hophni and Phinehas 25

I

Isaac 218
Isaiah 17, 35, 57, 58, 106, 179, 198

J

Jacob 53, 54, 56, 64, 120, 154, 218
Jael 24
Jairus 146
Jehoiada 212
Jehoiakim 213
Jehoshaba 212
Jehoshaphat 211
Jehu 29, 30
Jeremiah 213
Jericho 13, 121
Jeroboam 208
Jerusalem 18, 134, 137
Jesse 70
Jesus 8, 10, 19, 35, 38, 39, 40, 41, 84, 93, 117, 118, 136, 138, 146, 147, 148, 149, 152, 159, 160, 165, 166, 167, 168, 169, 170, 171, 182, 183, 184, 201, 202, 228
Jezebel 30, 80, 126, 144
Joash 212
Job 105, 197

John (apostle)..19, 61, 95, 172, 184, 204
John the Baptist...9, 38, 83, 94, 107
Jonah...135, 200
Jonathan..69
Joram...29
Joseph (Old Testament)...54, 55, 56, 64, 77
Joshua...13, 14, 65, 113, 114, 121, 222
Judas Iscariot...84, 139

K

Kedorlaomer...12

L

Laban..120
Last Supper..8
Lazarus..148
Leah...120
Leprosy..99, 170
Leviathan..197
Lions..199
Locusts..9, 192
Lot..12, 22, 133
Lot's wife...22

M

Manasseh..81
Manna..3
Martha...148
Mary (mother of Jesus)...93, 158
Mary (sister of Martha and Lazarus)..148
Mary Magdalene..160
Medium..46
Melchizedek..12
Micah..35, 159
Micaiah..211
Miriam..99
Mordecai..72
Moses............4, 23, 44, 65, 78, 86, 98, 99, 110, 111, 112, 174, 184, 219, 220, 221

N

Naaman..164
Nadab and Abihu..23
Naomi...68
Nathan..225
Nebuchadnezzar.................................18, 36, 37, 181, 214
Nineveh...135
Noah...191

O

Oil..6, 70, 178

P

Passover..2
Paul.............................47, 48, 49, 73, 74, 127, 129, 151, 187, 188, 203
Peter.......................31, 32, 128, 150, 171, 172, 183, 184, 201, 228
Pharaohs of Egypt...............2, 44, 55, 64, 78, 98, 111, 206
Pharisees...39, 146, 166
Pigs..182
Plagues (on Egypt)................9, 98, 111, 174, 192
Potiphar..77
Priscilla and Aquila..74

R

Rachel...120
Rahab...121
Ravens..195
Red Sea..174
Rehoboam...208, 209
Roman centurion..165
Ruth...68

S

Samson.............................34, 79, 101, 123, 155, 175, 194
Samuel..........................25, 46, 70, 88, 207, 224
Satan...105, 140, 141, 156, 204
Saul........................16, 46, 69, 70, 89, 91, 124, 125, 207, 224
Saul (in the New Testament, see Paul)
Scroll..7
Sennecherib...17, 92
Serpents and snakes.....................................190, 203

Seven sons of Sceva... 49
Shadrach, Meshach, and Abednego... 181
Sheep... 159, 202
Silas... 48, 188
Sisera... 24
Sodom and Gomorrah.. 22, 133
Solomon.. 102, 208, 209, 227

T

Tower of Babel... 132
Transfiguration of Jesus... 184

U

Uzzah.. 26
Uzziah... 58

V

Valley of Ben-Hinnom... 134

W

Wise men... 116
Witches and witchcraft.. 45, 46

X

Xerxes.. 72

Z

Zechariah (the prophet)... 35
Zechariah (John the Baptist's father)... 94
Zedekiah... 17
Ziklag... 16
Zimri... 210